Extradition law

a practitioner's guide

Edward Grange and Rebecca Niblock

LAG Legal Action Group
2013

This edition published in Great Britain 2013
by LAG Education and Service Trust Limited
242 Pentonville Road, London N1 9UN
www.lag.org.uk

© Edward Grange and Rebecca Niblock 2013

While every effort has been made to ensure that the details in this text are correct, readers must be aware that the law changes and that the accuracy of the material cannot be guaranteed and the author and the publisher accept no responsibility for any loss or damage sustained.

The rights of the authors to be identified as authors of this work have been asserted by them in accordance with the Copyright, Designs and Patents Act 1988.

All rights reserved. No part of this publication may be reproduced, stored in a retrieval system or transmitted in any form or by any means, without permission from the publisher.

British Library Cataloguing in Publication Data
a CIP catalogue record for this book is available from the British Library.

Crown copyright material is produced with the permission of the Controller of HMSO and the Queen's Printer for Scotland.

This book has been produced using Forest Stewardship Council (FSC) certified paper. The wood used to produce FSC certified products with a 'Mixed Sources' label comes from FSC certified well-managed forests, controlled sources and/or recycled material.

Print ISBN   978 1 908407 33 7
ebook ISBN   978 1 908407 34 4

Typeset by Regent Typesetting, London
Printed in Great Britain by Hobbs the Printers, Totton, Hampshire

Foreword

A person arrested on an extradition warrant needs help. Extradition is stressful, usually more stressful than domestic criminal proceedings. The law is complicated, and constantly developing. It can all happen rather suddenly: one day you are at work, and the next day you are at Westminster Magistrates' Court being asked whether you consent to extradition.

Important decisions need to be made at that first hearing. The lawyer giving advice needs to be well-informed and up to date. Often it is unhelpful to adjourn for a few days to consider the position. Apart from anything else, this may be the only occasion when the defendant has access to free legal advice. So the lawyer needs to get it right.

That is where this book comes in. It provides an excellent introduction to the law of extradition in England and Wales (and indeed to other jurisdictions within the United Kingdom). The lawyer who practises in this area, or who intends to practise in this area, will find the book very readable. It gives valuable practical advice on how the court works and what the judges expect. It covers the main arguments that can be raised against extradition. Even experienced lawyers will find they have something to learn, because the law is constantly developing.

Before the Extradition Act 2003 came into force in January 2004 there were fewer than 100 new cases a year at Bow Street Magistrates' Court (the only court at that time dealing with new extradition cases). Now there are over 1700 cases per year at Westminster Magistrates' Court, where all first instance extradition decisions in England and Wales are taken today. Moreover, we are still receiving advice through decisions of the Divisional Court and the Supreme Court. It is clear that the potential for litigating a new point is far from exhausted. If and when a new forum bar is introduced, no doubt many more novel questions will need to be explored. As a result, this is an area where the workload of the judges is increasing. As Grange and Niblock explain, there are now four extradition courts working every day, plus the court on Saturday.

Defendants, and frankly the extradition judges, rely heavily on the specialist lawyers. We recognise that we have the advantage of many excellent extradition lawyers, instructed by the CPS and by the defence. They already have access to specialist practitioners' books and to a significant volume of jurisprudence. Nevertheless this book fills a gap and will be a very significant addition to the literature in the field.

Howard Riddle
Senior District Judge (Chief Magistrate)
Westminster Magistrates' Court

March 2013

Preface

Extradition is a complex and rapidly developing area of law. Although those with a background in criminal law will be familiar with some of the concepts and procedure, there are a number of conventions which differ in extradition proceedings and which are not apparent from the legislation. This book, written by practising solicitors, aims to provide a practical guide to extradition law for those representing requested persons. It is written with the duty solicitor in mind, but should also be of assistance to solicitors and barristers acting for requested persons, from the magistrates' courts to the Supreme Court. The book is one that will fit handsomely into the busy lawyer's bag and prove invaluable as a tool to tackle the minefield of extradition law and procedure.

The following chapters will provide a solid foundation for the extradition duty solicitor to competently represent those facing extradition and to provide the necessary advice. The book begins by looking at practical considerations in chapter 2. Chapter 3 goes on to examine the European Arrest Warrant in detail. Chapter 4 deals with requests from outside the European Union. A guide to the areas which should be covered when meeting the client for the first time is provided in chapter 5. The book then gives an overview of ways in which extradition can be challenged, looking first at the bars to extradition and then at human rights considerations in chapters 6 and 7. The initial hearing is covered in chapter 8, with the preparation required for the contested hearing being covered in chapter 9. An explanation of the steps which will be taken in the full contested hearing (known as the extradition hearing) is dealt with in chapter 10. The book then goes on to provide a guide to appeals in chapter 11. The final chapter looks at various ancillary matters, such as compromising a warrant, funding and transfer of sentenced prisoners.

Edward Grange
Rebecca Niblock
March 2013

Acknowledgements

We are very grateful to all of those that have provided help and advice in writing this book. In particular, we must thank Myles Grandison, Sandra Cacchioli, Natalie Smith, Tim Niblock and Jeffrey Smele, all of whom have given a significant amount of time and energy in reading and commenting on the book.

Others have also helped us by taking a second look at the manuscript when our eyes have become tired, among whom we must mention Irene McMillan, James Tyler, Raoul Lumb, Julia Hicks, Claire Hegarty, Charlotte Wright and Olivia Stiles.

These are the hardest of times for legal aid lawyers. We hope this book goes some small way to making the life of the Westminster duty solicitor a little easier.

Contents

Foreword   v
Preface   vii
Acknowledgements   ix
Table of cases   xv
Table of statutes   xxi
Table of statutory instruments   xxv
Table of European and international legislation   xxvii
Abbreviations   xxix

1 Introduction   1
Extradition controversy   2
What is extradition?   3
The Extradition Act 2003   4
Framework Decision on the European Arrest Warrant   5
Extradition proceedings – participants   5

2 Practical considerations   9
Introduction   10
Arrest   10
The duty solicitor's day   11
Essential materials   14

3 Looking at a European Arrest Warrant   15
Introduction   16
The European Arrest Warrant   16
Challenging the validity of a European Arrest Warrant   28
Extradition offences   35

4 Extradition requests from outside the European Union   39
Introduction   41
Part 2 countries   41
Dealing with Part 2 extradition requests   42
Issuing a provisional warrant   42
Issuing a full request   44
Production at Westminster Magistrates' Court   46

xi

First hearing – provisional arrest 46
First hearing – full request 49
Initial stages of the extradition hearing 51
Challenges to extradition 51
Extradition offences 52
Prima facie case 54
The role of the Secretary of State 57

5 Attending the client 63
Introduction 64
Seeing the client 64

6 Bars to extradition 71
Introduction 72
Statutory bars to extradition 72

7 Human rights 93
Introduction 94
Human rights in Part 1 cases 94
Human rights in Part 2 cases 96
Article 2 (the right to life) and article 3 (the prohibition of torture) 96
Article 5 (the right to liberty and security) and article 6 (the right to a fair trial) 98
Article 8 (right to respect for private and family life) 101

8 The initial hearing in EAW cases 103
Introduction 104
Provisional or certified EAW request? 104
The initial hearing 105
Issues to be raised at the extradition hearing to resist extradition 111
Bail 113
The uncontested extradition hearing 114
Competing EAW requests 115
Removal where no appeal lodged 115

9 Preparing for the contested hearing 117
Introduction 119
Visiting the client in custody 119
Use of interpreters 119
Case management and court directions 120
Taking instructions 121
Statement of issues 124
Drafting a proof of evidence 124
Witness statements 125

Obtaining expert evidence   125
Objective evidence   127
Further information from the issuing state   128
Drafting a skeleton argument   129
Preparation of the bundle   129
Certificate for counsel   130

10 The contested extradition hearing   131
Introduction   132
Receivable and admissible documents   132
Burden and standard of proof   132
Requests for further information   133
Applications to adjourn   133
Housekeeping   134
Who goes first?   134
Calling your client – evidence in chief   135
Expert evidence   136
Adducing other evidence   136
Submissions   137
Judgment   137

11 Appeals   139
Introduction   141
Legal aid   141
Appeals under Part 1 of the Act   142
Appeals under Part 2 of the Act   145
Appeals in cases where risk of suicide is in issue   146
Appeals against the decision of the appropriate judge   146
Appeals against the decision of the SSHD   147
Out-of-time appeals   147
Case management conference – Part 2 cases only   148
Compliance with directions made by the High Court   149
Applications to adjourn   150
Bundles for the appeal hearing   150
Withdrawing the appeal   150
Withdrawing representation   152
Applying to extend the representation order   153
Introduction of new evidence   154
Court's powers on appeal in Part 1 cases   156
Appeal against discharge at the extradition hearing   156
Court's powers on appeal in Part 2 cases   157
Appeal against discharge at the extradition hearing   157
Appeal against the decision of the SSHD to order extradition   158
Appeals to the Supreme Court   159

Making the application to certify a point of law   160
   Supervening events   160
   Removal following dismissal of appeal   161
   Application to the European Court of Human Rights for rule 39 interim measures   161

12 Ancillary matters   163
   Introduction   164
   Compromising the extradition request   164
   'Iron letters'   165
   Transfer of prisoners   165
   Funding and billing   166

APPENDICES

A Framework Decision on the European Arrest Warrant   171

B Extradition Act 2003 ss1–25, 64, 65, 70–75, 137–138   191

C EAW validity checklist   215

D EAW first appearance checklist   217

E Bail checklist   219

F Case management form   221

G Application notice – Form N161   223

Index   231

Table of cases

Adedeji v Public Prosecutor's Office, Germany [2012] EWHC 3237 (Admin)	8.31
Agius v Court of Magistrates, Malta [2011] EWHC 759 (Admin)	7.7
Ahmad and Aswat v The Government of the United States of America [2006] EWHC 2927 (Admin), [2007] HRLR 8, [2007] UKHRR 525, [2006] Extradition LR 276, [2007] ACD 54, (2006) 156 NLJ 1882, (2006) *Times*, 5 December	6.71, 7.8
Assange v Swedish Prosecution Authority [2011] EWHC 2849 (Admin), (2011) 108(44) LSG 17	3.26, 3.42
Assange v Swedish Prosecution Authority [2012] UKSC 22, [2012] 2 AC 471, [2012] 2 WLR 1275, [2012] 4 All ER 1249, [2013] 1 CMLR 4, (2012) 109(24) LSG 22, (2012) *Times*, 19 June	3.2
Asztaslos v Szekszard City Court, Hungary [2010] EWHC 237 (Admin), [2011] 1 WLR 252, [2011] 1 All ER 1027	3.25
Baksys v Ministry of Justice of the Republic of Lithuania [2007] EWHC 2838 (Admin), [2008] Extradition LR 1	9.35
Balint v Municipal Court in Prague, Czech Republic [2011] EWHC 498 (Admin), [2012] 1 WLR 244	3.33
Banasinski v District Court in Sanok, Poland [2008] EWHC 3626 (Admin)	3.11
Bartkowiak v Judicial Authority of Poland [2012] EWHC 333 (Admin)	3.38
Benko v Hungary [2009] EWHC 3530 (Admin)	6.60
Bohm v Romania [2011] EWHC 2671 (Admin)	6.63
Brown v Government of Rwanda [2009] EWHC 770 (Admin), [2009] Extradition LR 197	7.18
Bulkowski (Kamil) v Regional Court of Elblag, Poland [2012] EWHC 281 (Admin)	3.37
Connelly v DPP [1964] AC 1254, [1964] 2 WLR 1145, [1964] 2 All ER 401, (1964) 48 Cr App R 183, (1964) 128 JP 418, (1964) 108 SJ 356	6.6
Dabas v High Court of Justice in Madrid, Spain [2007] UKHL 6, [2007] 2 AC 31, [2007] 2 WLR 254, [2007] 2 All ER 641, [2007] 2 CMLR 39, [2007] Extradition LR 69, (2007) 104(11) LSG 33, (2007) 151 SJLB 333, (2007) *Times*, 5 March	7.4

xvi *Extradition law / Table of cases*

Dabas v High Court of Justice, Madrid [2006] EWHC 971 (Admin), [2007] 1 WLR 145, [2006] Extradition LR 123, [2006] ACD 90, (2006) *Times*, 2 June	3.22
Dabkowski v Poland [2010] EWHC 1712 (Admin)	7.5
Dehwari v Netherlands (2000) 29 EHRR CD 74	7.10
District Court in Ostroleka, Second Criminal Division (A Polish Judicial Authority) v Dytlow [2009] EWHC 1009 (Admin), [2009] Extradition LR 238	6.76
Dudko v The Government of the Russian Federation [2010] EWHC 1125 (Admin)	4.49
Ektor v National Public Prosecutor of Holland [2007] EWHC 3106 (Admin), [2008] Extradition LR 28	3.32
EM (Lebanon) v Secretary of State for the Home Department [2008] UKHL 64, [2009] 1 AC 1198, [2008] 3 WLR 931, [2009] 1 All ER 559, [2008] 2 FLR 2067, [2009] 1 FCR 441, [2009] HRLR 6, [2009] UKHRR 22, [2009] Imm AR 189, [2009] INLR 123, [2008] Fam Law 1190, (2008) 105(42) LSG 21, (2008) 158 NLJ 1531, (2008) 152(41) SJLB 30, (2008) *Times*, 24 October	7.18
Fernandez v Government of Singapore [1971] 1 WLR 987, [1971] 2 All ER 691, (1971) 115 SJ 469	6.15
Fofana v Deputy Prosecutor Thubin Tribunal de Grande Instance de Meaux, France [2006] EWHC 744 (Admin), [2006] Extradition LR 102	3.29, 6.6
G v District Court of Czestochowa, Poland [2011] EWHC 1597 (Admin)	7.11
Gomes and Goodyer v Trinidad & Tobago [2009] UKHL 2, [2009] 1 WLR 276, [2009] 3 All ER 1035, [2009] Extradition LR 122, (2009) 153(4) SJLB 28, (2009) *Times*, 27 January	6.26, 6.31, 7.8
Hamburg Public Prosecutor's Office v Altun [2011] EWHC 397 (Admin)	6.6
Harkins and Edwards v United Kingdom Application No 9146/07, 17 January 2012	7.9
Haynes v Malta [2009] EWHC 880 (Admin), [2009] Extradition LR 189	6.72
HH v Deputy Prosecutor of the Italian Republic, Genoa [2012] UKSC 25, [2012] 3 WLR 90, [2012] 4 All ER 539, [2012] HRLR 25, (2012) 156(25) SJLB 31, (2012) *Times*, 2 July	7.23, 7.24, 7.25, 7.26
Hilali v National Court of Madrid [2006] EWHC 1239 (Admin), [2007] 1 WLR 768, [2006] 4 All ER 435, [2006] Extradition LR 154, [2006] ACD 92	6.51, 8.22
Hoholm v Government of Norway [2009] EWHC 1513 (Admin)	11.72
Huczko v Governor of HMP Wandsworth [2012] EWHC 4134 (Admin)	8.17
Hunt v The Court at First Instance, Antwerp, Belgium [2006] EWHC 165 (Admin), [2006] 2 All ER 735, [2006] Extradition LR 16	3.31

Italy v Merico [2011] EWHC 1857 (Admin)	6.40
Janovic v Prosecutor General's Office, Lithuania [2011] EWHC 710 (Admin)	6.74
Jansons v Latvian Judicial Authority [2009] EWHC 1845 (Admin)	6.66
JP v District Court at Ústí Nad Labem, Czech Republic [2012] EWHC 2603 (Admin), [2012] ACD 115	7.27
Kakis v Government of the Republic of Cyprus [1978] 1 WLR 779, [1978] 2 All ER 634, [1978] Crim LR 489, (1978) 122 SJ 400	6.25, 6.30, 6.33
King's Prosecutor, Brussels v Cando Armas [2005] UKHL 67, [2006] 2 AC 1, [2005] 3 WLR 1079, [2006] 1 All ER 647, [2005] Extradition LR 139, (2005) 155 NLJ 1809, (2005) *Times*, 18 November, (2005) Independent, 22 November	3.45
Kis (Emil) v District Court In Sokolov, Czech Republic [2012] EWHC 938 (Admin)	3.12, 6.60
Klimas v Prosecutor General's Office of Lithuania [2010] EWHC 2076 (Admin)	7.5
Klimeto v Westminster Magistrates' Court [2012] EWHC 2051 (Admin), [2013] 1 WLR 420	8.32
Knowles Jr v United States of America and another [2006] UKPC 38, [2007] 1 WLR 47, [2007] Extradition LR 230	6.31, 9.36
Konuksever v Government of Turkey [2012] EWHC 2166 (Admin)	7.9, 7.19
Kovac v Regional Court in Prague [2010] EWHC 1959 (Admin)	6.39
Kozlowski v District Court of Torun Poland Kozlowski v District Court of Torun, Poland [2012] EWHC 1706 (Admin)	6.75
Krolik v Several Judicial Authorities of Poland [2012] EWHC 2357 (Admin), [2013] 1 WLR 490, (2012) 162 NLJ 1125	7.9
La Torre v Italy [2007] EWHC 1370 (Admin), [2007] Extradition LR 185	6.37
Louca v A German Judicial Authority [2009] UKSC 4, [2009] 1 WLR 2550, [2010] 1 All ER 402, (2009) 159 NLJ 1667, (2009) *Times*, 24 November	3.35
Louca v Public Prosecutor in Bielefel, Germany [2008] EWHC 2907 (Admin), [2009] 2 All ER 719, [2009] Extradition LR 57, (2008) *Times*, 10 December	3.35
Lukaszewski v The District Court in Torun, Poland [2012] UKSC 20, [2012] 1 WLR 1604, [2012] 4 All ER 667, [2012] HRLR 22, [2013] Crim LR 147, (2012) 162 NLJ 749, (2012) *Times*, 7 June	7.16, 11.12, 11.13, 11.14, 11.35
Mamatkulov and Askarov v Turkey (2005) 41 EHRR 25	7.18
McLean v High Court of Dublin, Ireland[2008] EWHC 547 (Admin), [2008] Extradition LR 182	7.9
Mihai Sonea v Mehedinti District Court [2009] EWHC 89 (Admin), [2009] 2 All ER 821, [2009] Extradition LR 136	6.1

xviii   *Extradition law / Table of cases*

Ministry of Justice, Lithuania v Bucnys [2012] EWHC 2771 (Admin), [2013] 1 All ER 1220	3.2
Mitchell v High Court of Boulogne sur mer [2007] EWHC 2006 (Admin), [2007] Extradition LR 222	6.6
Mitoi v Romania [2006] EWHC 1977 (Admin), [2006] Extradition LR 168	6.60
MSS v Belgium, Application No 30696/09, 21 January 2011	7.6
MT (Algeria) v Secretary of State for Home Department [2009] UKHL 10, [2010] 2 AC 110, [2009] 2 WLR 512, [2009] 4 All ER 1045, [2009] HRLR 17, [2009] UKHRR 892, 26 BHRC 90, (2009) 159 NLJ 349, (2009) 153(7) SJLB 32, (2009) *Times*, 19 February	7.16
Mucelli v The Government of Albania [2009] UKHL 2, [2009] 1 WLR 276, [2009] 3 All ER 1035, [2009] Extradition LR 122, (2009) 153(4) SJLB 28, (2009) *Times*, 27 January	11.11, 11.12
Murtati v Albania [2008] EWHC 2856	6.60
Naczmanski v Regional Court in Wloclawek [2010] EWHC 2023 (Admin)	3.32
Nastase v Office of the State Prosecutor, Italy [2012] EWHC 3671 (Admin)	6.63
Nikonovs v Governor of Brixton Prison [2005] EWHC 2405 (Admin)	8.15, 8.16, 8.33
Office of the Prosecutor General of Turin v Barone [2010] EWHC 3004	7.19
Oncel v Governor of Brixton Prison, Government of the Republic of Turkey [2001] EWHC 1142 (Admin)	6.6
Osunta v The Public Prosecutor's Office in Dusseldorf [2007] EWHC 1562 (Admin), [2008] QB 785, [2008] 3 WLR 26, [2007] 4 All ER 1038, [2007] Extradition LR 200	3.45, 3.46, 4.60
Othman (Abu Qatada) v United Kingdom 8139/09 [2012] ECHR 56	7.19
Pilecki v Circuit Court of Legnica, Poland [2008] UKHL 7, [2008] 1 WLR 325	3.38
Poland v Wolkowicz, Poland v Biskup & Lithuania v Rizleriene [2013] EWHC 102 (Admin)	11.32
R on the application of Bagdanavicius v Secretary of State for the Home Department [2005] UKHL 38, [2005] 2 AC 668, [2005] 2 WLR 1359, [2005] 4 All ER 263, [2005] HRLR 24, [2005] UKHRR 907, [2005] Imm AR 430, [2005] INLR 422, (2005) *Times*, 30 May, (2005) Independent, 15 June	7.10
R on the application of Bermingham v Director of the Serious Fraud Office [2006] EWHC 200 (Admin), [2007] QB 727, [2007] 2 WLR 635, [2006] 3 All ER 239, [2006] UKHRR 450, [2006] Extradition LR 52, [2006] ACD 55, (2006) *Times*, 24 February	6.71
R on the application of Cepkauskas v District Court of Marijampole, Lithuania [2011] EWHC 757 (Admin)	6.43
R on the application of Chichvarkin v Secretary of State for the Home Department [2010] EWHC 1858 (Admin)	6.75

Table of cases xix

R on the application of Governor of Wandsworth Prison v Kinderis [2007] EWHC 998 (Admin), [2008] QB 347, [2008] 2 WLR 217, [2008] 1 All ER 499, [2007] Extradition LR 136, (2007) *Times*, 26 June	8.36
R on the application of Griffin v City of London Magistrates Court[2011] EWHC 943 (Admin), [2012] 1 WLR 270	6.66
R on the application of Kashamu v Governor of Brixton Prison [2001] EWHC Admin 980, [2002] QB 887, [2002] 2 WLR 907, [2002] ACD 36, (2002) 99(5) LSG 29, (2001) 145 SJLB 277, (2001) *Times*, 12 December	7.16
R on the application of Philip Harkins v SSHD [2007] EWHC 639 (Admin), [2007] Extradition LR 41	4.64
R on the application of Prosser v Secretary of State for the Home Department [2010] EWHC 845 (Admin), [2010] ACD 57	6.66
R on the application of Raissi v Secretary of State for the Home Department [2008] EWCA Civ 72, [2008] QB 836, [2008] 3 WLR 375, [2008] 2 All ER 1023, [2008] Extradition LR 109, [2008] ACD 49, (2008) 152(8) SJLB 33, (2008) *Times*, 22 February	10.6
R on the application of Tajik v City of Westminster Magistrates' Court [2012] EWHC 3347 (Admin)	4.76
R on the application of Ullah v Special Adjudicator [2004] UKHL 26, [2004] 2 AC 323, [2004] 3 WLR 23, [2004] 3 All ER 785, [2004] HRLR 33, [2004] UKHRR 995, [2004] Imm AR 419, [2004] INLR 381, (2004) 101(28) LSG 33, (2004) 154 NLJ 985, (2004) 148 SJLB 762, (2004) *Times*, 18 June, (2004) Independent, 22 June	7.10, 7.17
Rexha v Officer of the Prosecutor, Court of Rome [2012] EWHC 3397 (Admin)	6.63
Richards v The Queen [1993] AC 217, [1992] 3 WLR 928, [1992] 4 All ER 807, (1993) 96 Cr App R 268, (1992) 142 NLJ 1576, (1992) 136 SJLB 304, (1992) *Times*, 5 November	6.7
Richen Turner v Government of the USA [2012] EWHC 2426 (Admin)	6.66
Rimas v Lithuania [2011] EWHC 2084 (Admin)	3.3
Rot v District Court of Lublin, Poland [2010] EWHC 1820 (Admin)	6.66, 7.5
Sandi v Craiova Court, Romania [2009] EWHC 3079 (Admin)	3.27, 3.28
Sapstead v Governor of HMP Belmarsh [2004] EWHC 2352 (Admin)	6.34
Serbeh v Governor of HMP Brixton [2002] EWHC 2356 (Admin)	7.8
Skrzypczak v The Circuit Court in Poznan [2011] EWHC 1194 (Admin)	3.30
Soering v UK (1989) 11 EHRR 439	7.10
Sondy v Crown Prosecution Service [2010] EWHC 108 (Admin)	11.74
South Africa v Dewani [2010] EWHC 3398 (Admin)	7.9

South Africa v Dewani [2012] EWHC 842 (Admin), [2013] 1 WLR 82, (2012) 109(15) LSG 13(Admin)	6.64, 6.65, 9.33
Stopyra v District Court of Lublin, Poland [2012] EWHC 1787 (Admin), [2013] 1 All ER 187, [2012] ACD 94	5.19
Sullivan (Shawn) v USA [2012] EWHC 1680 (Admin), (2012) 156(25) SJLB 31	7.19
Symeou v Public Prosecutor's Officer, Patras, Greece [2009] EWHC 897 (Admin), [2009] 1 WLR 2384, [2009] Extradition LR 251, (2009) *Times*, 13 May	6.74
Szombathely City Court v Fenyvesi [2009] EWHC 231 (Admin), [2009] 4 All ER 324, [2009] Extradition LR 143	11.68, 11.70, 11.73
Tamarevichute v Russian Federation [1971] 1 WLR 987, [1971] 2 All ER 691, (1971) 115 SJ 469	6.18
Taylor v Public Prosecutor's Office, Berlin [2012] EWHC 475	3.38
United States v Tollman [2008] EWHC 184 (Admin), [2008] 3 All ER 150, [2008] Extradition LR 85, [2008] ACD 34	6.72
Von der Pahlen v The Government of Austria [2006] EWHC 1672 (Admin), [2006] Extradition LR 197, (2006) *Times*, 10 July	3.29, 3.32
Wenting v High Court of Valenciennes [2009] EWHC 3528 (Admin)	6.38
Wolkowicz v Polish Judicial Authority [2013] EWHC 102 (Admin)	6.67, 6.68
Wrobel v Poland [2011] EWHC 374 (Admin)	6.66
Wysocki v Polish Judicial Authority [2010] EWHC 3430 (Admin)	7.23
Zak v Regional Court of Bydgoszcz, Poland[2008] EWHC 470 (Admin), [2008] Extradition LR 134	3.42
Zakrzewski v Regional Court in Lodz, Poland [2013] UKSC 2, [2013] 1 WLR 324, [2013] 2 All ER 93, (2013) *Times*, 31January	3.22, 3.24
Zaporozhchenko v Westminster Magistrates' Court [2011] EWHC 34 (Admin), [2011] 1 WLR 994	4.67, 11.28
Zdinjak v Croatia [2012] EWHC 1554 (Admin), [2012] ACD 95	6.6

Table of statutes

Criminal Justice Act 1967		Extradition Act 2003 *continued*	
	9.25, 10.33, 10.35	s6	8.32, 8.33, 8.38
		s7	5.3, 5.5, 8.32, 8.33, 8.38
Criminal Justice Act 1988			
s32	9.33	s8	8.30, 8.32, 8.33
Criminal Justice Act 2003		s8A	8.34, 8.36
s5	19.33	s8B	8.35, 8.36
Extradition Act 2003	1.2, 1.5, 1.12, 1.13, 1.16, 1.21, 1.27, 1.31, 2.6, 2.17, 4.3, 4.15, 4.24, 6.70, 6.71, 6.76, 7.8, 8.2, 8.32, 10.17, 11.4, 11.102	s9	10.33
		s10	3.13, 3.22, 8.42, 8.46, 10.35
		s11	6.1, 6.3, 8.42
		s12	6.3, 6.5, 8.42
		s13	6.3, 6.10, 8.42
		s14	5.14, 6.3, 6.23, 8.42
Pt 1	1.13, 1.14, 2.17, 8.1, 8.3	s15	6.3, 6.45, 8.42
		s16	6.3, 6.47, 8.42
s2	1.22, 3.3, 3.13, 3.19, 3.21, 3.23, 3.24, 3.25, 3.43, 8.42, 8.58	s17	6.3, 6.49, 6.50, 8.42
		s18	6.3, 6.53, 8.42
		s19	6.3, 6.53, 8.42
s2(2)	3.22	s19A	6.3
s2(3)	3.5, 3.25	s19B	6.3, 6.55
s2(3)(a)	3.25	s19C	6.56
s2(3)(b)	3.25	s20	5.14, 6.4, 6.59, 6.60, 6.63, 8.42
s2(4)	3.3		
s2(4)(c)	3.27, 3.29, 3.32, 4.49	s20(8)	6.61
		s21	6.4, 7.1, 7.7, 7.19, 8.42
s2(5)	3.5		
s2(6)(b)	3.27, 3.32	s21(1)	7.7
s2(7)	3.2	s21(3)	8.60
s4	5.3, 8.32, 8.33, 8.38	s25(3)(a)	6.64
		s25(3)(b)	6.64
s4(2)	8.10, 8.11	s26	8.32, 11.75
s4(3)	2.5, 8.10, 8.14	s27(3)	11.75, 11.76
s4(4)	8.11, 8.13, 8.14	s27(4)	11.75, 11.76, 11.78
s4(5)	8.14		
s5	8.3, 8.32, 8.33, 8.38	s27(5)	11.77
		s28	8.32, 11.78

Extradition Act 2003 continued

s29(3)	11.78
s29(4)	11.69
s29(5)(a)	11.79
s29(5)(b)	11.79
s29(5)(c)	11.79
s31	11.19
s35	5.18
s35(3)	8.65
s35(5)	8.61
s36(8)	11.107
s39	5.15
s44(3)	8.63
s44(7)	8.64
s45	5.9
s54	5.10
s64	3.36, 3.39, 3.44, 3.46, 8.59
s64(2)	3.40
s64(3)	3.45
s65	3.36, 3.39, 3.44, 3.46, 8.59
s65(2)	3.40
s65(3)	3.45
Pt 2	1.13, 1.16, 2.5, 2.17, 3.10, 3.41, 4.1, 4.2, 4.3, 4.25, 11.28, 11.31, 11.39
s70	4.17
s70(4)	4.17
s70(4A)	4.17
s70(9)	4.19, 4.32, 4.34, 4.36, 4.50
s72(2)	4.20
s72(3)	4.20
s72(4)(a)	2.5, 4.21
s73(1)	4.8
s73(2)	4.7
s73(3)	4.9
s74(11)(b)	4.33
s74(2)	4.14
s74(3)	4.15
s74(4)(a)	2.5
s74(7)(a)	4.27
s74(7)(b)	4.28
s75(2)	4.40
s76(3)	4.38
s76A	4.28, 4.30
s76B	4.29, 4.30

Extradition Act 2003 continued

s78(2)(b)	4.37
s78(2)(c)	4.37
s78(2)(d)	4.37
s78(2)(e)	4.37
s78(4)(a)	4.44
s78(4)(b)	4.44
s78(4)(c)	4.44, 4.49
s78(5)	4.45
s78(6)	4.46
s79	4.47, 6.3
s80	4.48, 6.3, 6.6
s81	4.48, 6.3, 6.11, 9.28
s81(a)	6.21
s81(b)	6.21
s82	4.48, 6.3, 6.23
s83	4.48, 6.3, 6.47
s83A	4.48, 6.3, 6.55
s84	4.48, 4.63, 4.65
s85	4.51, 6.59, 6.60
s86	4.48, 4.63, 4.65
s87	4.52, 7.1, 7.8
s91	4.48
s92(3)	4.69
s93(5)	4.71
s94	6.3, 6.58
s95	6.3, 6.49
s96	6.3, 6.53
s96A	6.3
s97(2)	4.68
s98(2)	4.70
s101	4.73
s103	11.80
s103(9)	4.75
s104(1)(a)	11.80
s104(1)(b)	11.80
s104(1)(c)	11.80
s104(3)	11.81
s104(4)	11.81
s104(5)	11.82
s105	11.83
s105(4)	11.83
s105(5)	11.83
s106(1)(a)	11.83
s106(1)(b)	11.83
s106(1)(c)	11.83
s109(3)	11.88
s109(4)	11.88
s109(5)	11.89

Table of statutes xxiii

Extradition Act 2003 continued		Extradition Act 2003 continued	
s110	11.90	s179(3)(d)	4.79
s111(5)	11.90	s193	4.4
s114(4)	11.91	s194	4.4
s114(5)	11.92	s202(1)	10.2
s114(6)	11.93	s202(2)	10.3
s114(7)	11.97	s202(3)	10.3
s117(3)	4.76	s202(4)	10.3
s118(7)	11.107	s206	10.5
s121	5.15	s214	5.6, 6.64, 8.42, 9.28
s126	4.21, 4.77		
s126(2)(a)	4.77	Human Rights Act 1998	7.1, 8.58
s126(2)(b)	4.77		
s127	5.9	Legal Aid, Sentencing and Punishment of Offenders Act 2012	
s129	5.10		
s137	3.41, 4.60		
s137(2)	4.53, 4.54	Sch 7	12.12
s137(3)	4.57	Magistrates' Courts Act 1980	
s137(4)	4.58	s142	8.32
s137(6)	4.59	Police and Criminal Evidence Act 1984	
s138	3.41, 4.53, 4.56, 4.60	s58	2.4
s138(2)	4.53	Prosecution of Offences Act 1985	
s138(3)	4.57	s3(2A)	1.21
s138(4)	4.58	s3(2)(ea)	1.20
s138(6)	4.59	Public Order Act 1986	
s139(1)(a)	1.26	s5	4.55
Pt 3	1.13	Repatriation of Prisoners Act 1984	12.7, 12.11
Pt 4	1.13, 2.2		
s171(3)(d)	2.4	s1(1)	12.9
Pt 5	1.13	s1(1)(a)	12.10
s179	4.79	s1(1)(b)	12.11
s179(3)(a)	4.79	Taking of Hostages Act 1982	
s179(3)(b)	4.79	s1	6.47
s179(3)(c)	4.79		

Table of statutory instruments

Civil Procedure Rules 1998 SI No 3132	11.5
Pt 52.17(1)	11.104
Practice Direction 52A	
para 6.1	11.52
Practice Direction 52D	11.5
para 3.4(1)	11.26
para 21.1	11.5
para 21(1)(3)(b)	11.19
para 21.1(3)(c)	11.19
Costs in Criminal Cases (General) Regulations 1986 SI No 1335	9.33
Criminal Legal Aid (Remuneration) Regulations 2013 SI No 435	9.6, 9.29
Criminal Defence Service (General) (No 2) Regulations 2001 SI No 1437	9.40
reg 12	9.40
Criminal Procedure Rules 2011 SI No 1709 Pt 33	9.31
r33.3	9.31
Extradition Act 2003 (Designation of Part 2 Territories) Order 2003 SI No 3334	4.33

Table of European and international legislation

Council Framework Decision 2002/584/JHA of 13 June 2002	1.18, 3.1, 3.25, 3.39, 6.51, 7.3
art 4(6)	12.8
art 5(2)	3.17
art 8	3.1
art 26	5.11
Council Framework Decision 2008/909/JHA of 27 November 2008	12.10, 12.11
art 4(1)	12.11
Council Framework Decision 2009/299/JHA of 26 February 2009	3.12
European Convention on Extradition 1957	6.51
European Convention on Human Rights and Fundamental Freedoms 1950	7.1, 7.3, 7.6
art 2	5.16, 7.9, 9.19
art 3	5.16, 7.9, 9.3, 9.13, 9.19
art 5	5.16, 7.14, 7.16, 7.19, 7.20, 9.19
art 6	5.16, 6.62, 7.15, 7.17, 7.20, 9.19
art 8	3.11, 5.16, 6.57, 7.21, 7.23, 7.24, 9.19
art 51(e)	7.19
European Court of Human Rights Rules of Court 2009 r39	11.104, 11.112, 11.113

International conventions

International Convention against the Taking of Hostages 1979	6.47
United Nations Convention Relating to the Status of Refugees 1954	6.76

Abbreviations

ACO	Administrative Court Office
CLAS	Criminal Law Accreditation Scheme
CPS	Crown Prosecution Service
DPP	Director of Public Prosecutions
EA 2003	Extradition Act 2003
EAW	European Arrest Warrant
ECtHR	European Court of Human Rights
EU	European Union
IJO	International Jurisdiction Office
LAA	Legal Aid Agency
SCCO	Senior Courts Cost Office
SOCA	Serious Organised Crime Agency
SSHD	Secretary of State for the Home Department
WMC	Westminster Magistrates' Court

CHAPTER 1

Introduction

1.5	Extradition controversy
1.11	What is extradition?
1.12	**The Extradition Act 2003**
1.14	Part 1 and Part 2 requests for extradition
1.18	**Framework Decision on the European Arrest Warrant**
1.19	**Extradition proceedings – participants**
1.20	The Crown Prosecution Service
1.22	The Serious Organised Crime Agency
1.23	Home Office for Part 2 cases
1.24	Metropolitan Police Extradition Squad
1.25	Westminster Magistrates' Court
1.27	The Administrative Court
1.29	The Supreme Court
1.31	Extradition defence lawyers

2 Extradition law / chapter 1

1.1   The year 2012 saw several high-profile cases raise the prominence of extradition law in the public eye. The Supreme Court held that a public prosecutor is a judicial authority in the case of Julian Assange; Shrien Dewani was found to be too unwell to be extradited to South Africa to stand trial for the murder of his wife; and Gary McKinnon won his ten-year battle against extradition to the United States. After many years of litigation, Abu Hamza was extradited to the United States after he lost his battle against extradition in the European Court of Human Rights.

1.2   Since coming into force in 2004, the Extradition Act (EA) 2003 has created a plethora of litigation. The number of extradition cases that have reached the House of Lords/Supreme Court is in double figures.

1.3   For the period 1997–2003, 781 requests for extradition were made to the United Kingdom. In 2012, there were in excess of 1,000 arrests for extradition from EU member states under the European Arrest Warrant (EAW) system. Poland made the majority of these requests.

1.4   In October 2012 the Legal Services Commission (now the Legal Aid Agency) created a separate extradition rota for Westminster Magistrates' Court. The extradition duty solicitor is expected to represent those produced at court following arrest. The extradition courts currently span across four courtrooms with the majority of work being heard on the first floor in Courts 1, 2 and 3. A fourth court room was recently set aside to conduct extradition work due to the increased number of those subject to extradition requests appearing before the court. Although there is no formal requirement[1] for the extradition duty solicitor to have had any extradition training, the courts will expect the duty solicitor to be competent to undertake the work.

Extradition controversy

1.5   The EA 2003 has not been without its controversies. In particular, the EAW scheme has been criticised for overuse. It is said to have been abused with instances of EAWs being issued for 'trivial' offences, such as theft of a chicken, stealing a garage gate and riding a bicycle while drunk.

1.6   The US/UK extradition arrangements have also come under attack from opponents who maintain that they are one-sided and do not afford British citizens sufficient protection.

---

1 The Criminal Law Accreditation Scheme (CLAS) does not contain any assessment of extradition law.

1.7 On 8 September 2010, the new coalition government announced plans to review the UK's extradition arrangements. On 14 October 2010, Sir Scott Baker, David Perry QC and Anand Doobay were tasked with the challenge of conducting a review. On 18 October 2011, the review panel's report was published.[2] The report concluded that 'apart from the problem of proportionality, we believe that the European arrest warrant scheme has worked reasonably well'.

1.8 Despite the review panel concluding that a forum bar was not necessary, in October 2012 the Secretary of State for the Home Department (SSHD) announced that she would proceed to introduce a forum bar into the EA 2003. A forum bar would allow a UK court to determine where a person should be tried. The SSHD also announced that her duty to consider human rights issues arising after a person's appeal rights have been exhausted should be transferred to the High Court rather than remain with her.

1.9 At the Second Reading of the Crime and Courts Bill, in January 2013, the Home Secretary stated:

> Members will recall that on 16 October, when I made a statement on our extradition arrangements, I indicated that I would present legislation as soon as parliamentary time allowed to make two key changes to the Extradition Act 2003. The first would introduce a new forum bar to extradition, and the second would transfer to the High Court the Home Secretary's responsibilities for considering representations on human rights grounds. I have decided that we should seize the opportunity provided by the Bill so that we can give effect to the changes as soon as possible.

1.10 At the time of writing it is anticipated that these amendments will be introduced at the Committee Stage of the Crime and Courts Bill.

What is extradition?

1.11 Extradition is the formal process whereby the *requesting state* asks the *requested state* to return an individual that is in the requested state in order to stand trial or to serve a custodial sentence imposed in the requesting state. The EA 2003 governs extradition proceedings in the United Kingdom.

---

2 *A Review of the United Kingdom's Extradition Arrangements* available from www.gov.uk.

The Extradition Act 2003

1.12 The EA 2003 came into force on 1 January 2004. Extradition requests received after this date are dealt with under the EA 2003. Requests received on or before 31 December 2003 are dealt with under the Extradition Act 1989.

1.13 The EA 2003 is split into five parts:

Part 1 – Extradition to category 1 territories (known as EAW cases);
Part 2 – Extradition to category 2 territories (known as Part 2 cases);
Part 3 – Extradition to the United Kingdom;
Part 4 – Police powers;
Part 5 – Miscellaneous and general provisions.

Part 1 and Part 2 requests for extradition

1.14 The UK has extradition arrangements with over 100 territories. Part 1 warrants (referred to as EAW cases) are the most common types of request.

1.15 The following territories have been designated category 1 territories and all issue EAWs:

- Austria, Belgium, Bulgaria, Cyprus, Czech Republic, Denmark, Estonia, Finland, France, Germany, Gibraltar, Greece, Hungary, Ireland, Italy, Latvia, Lithuania, Luxembourg, Malta, the Netherlands, Poland, Portugal, Romania, Slovakia, Slovenia, Spain and Sweden.

1.16 Category 2 territories include the following:[3]

- Albania, Algeria, Andorra, Antigua and Barbuda, Argentina, Armenia, Australia, Azerbaijan, The Bahamas, Bangladesh, Barbados, Belize, Bolivia, Bosnia and Herzegovina, Botswana, Brazil, Brunei, Canada, Chile, Colombia, Cook Islands, Croatia,[4] Cuba, Dominica, Ecuador, El Salvador, Fiji, The Gambia, Georgia, Ghana, Grenada, Guatemala, Guyana, Hong Kong Special Administrative Region, Haiti, Iceland, India, Iraq, Israel, Jamaica, Kenya, Kiribati, Lesotho, Liberia, Libya, Liechtenstein, Macedonia (FYR), Malawi, Malaysia, Maldives, Mauritius, Mexico, Moldova,

---

3 At the time of writing, an amendment to the EA 2003 has been laid before parliament that, when in force, will add the Republic of Korea to the list of territories designated for the purposes of Part 2 of the EA 2003. This is a result of the Republic of Korea acceding to the European Convention on Extradition.
4 On 1 July 2013 Croatia will accede to the European Union and become a Category 1 territory for the purposes of the EA 2003.

Monaco, Montenegro, Nauru, New Zealand, Nicaragua, Nigeria, Norway, Panama, Papua New Guinea, Paraguay, Peru, Russian Federation, Saint Christopher and Nevis, Saint Lucia, Saint Vincent and the Grenadines, San Marino, Serbia, Seychelles, Sierra Leone, Singapore, Solomon Islands, South Africa, Sri Lanka, Swaziland, Switzerland, Tanzania, Thailand, Tonga, Trinidad and Tobago, Turkey, Tuvalu, Uganda, Ukraine, United Arab Emirates, United States, Uruguay, Vanuatu, Western Samoa, Zambia, Zimbabwe.

1.17   If a country does not appear above it does not mean that there cannot be an extradition request. Those countries that are not extradition treaty partners with the United Kingdom can still make extradition requests and be treated as if they were a category 2 territory. These arrangements are known as ad hoc arrangements.

Framework Decision on the European Arrest Warrant

1.18   The EAW came into effect as a result of the Council Framework Decision 2002/584/JHA of 13 June 2002 (see appendix A). EAWs are valid throughout the European Union. They are intended to allow an issuing judicial authority to secure the return of a requested person quickly and easily. The aim of the Framework Decision was to replace the complex system of extradition with a system of *surrender* between member states.

Extradition proceedings – participants

1.19   There are many organisations that all play a part in extradition proceedings in the United Kingdom. They are:
- CPS Extradition Unit;
- Serious Organised Crime Agency (SOCA);
- Home Office for Part 2 cases;
- Metropolitan Police Extradition and International Assistance Unit (Extradition Squad);
- Westminster Magistrates' Court (WMC);
- Administrative Court, Royal Courts of Justice;
- Supreme Court; and
- extradition defence lawyers.

The Crown Prosecution Service

1.20 The Director of Public Prosecutions (DPP) has a duty to have conduct of any extradition proceedings.[5] The Crown Prosecution Service (CPS) is appointed and acts as the representative for the requesting state. The Extradition Unit is part of the Special Crime Division based at Rose Court, London. Unlike its domestic role, the Extradition Unit does not have to apply the Code for Crown Prosecutors to proceedings. The role of the CPS can include providing advice to foreign states on the preparation of an extradition request; advising foreign states on the content and validity of an extradition request received from SOCA/Home Office; representing judicial authorities/requesting states in proceedings before WMC, the High Court and the Supreme Court and advising foreign states on the merits of an appeal.

1.21 It is possible for the requesting state to instruct a private firm of solicitors to act on its behalf under section 3(2A) of the Prosecution of Offences Act 1985. At the time of writing, this has only happened once since the EA 2003 came into force.

The Serious Organised Crime Agency

1.22 SOCA is the designated central authority to receive EAWs. SOCA certifies the EAWs in accordance with EA 2003 s2 and facilitates communication between the CPS and the issuing judicial authority. SOCA will also arrange for the surrender of those whose extradition has been ordered by the courts in EAW cases.

Home Office for Part 2 cases

1.23 The SSHD is responsible for certifying extradition requests from category 2 territories and all extradition requests are received at the Home Office for processing. The Home Office is also responsible for arranging removal in Part 2 cases. The SSHD plays an important role in Part 2 cases.

Metropolitan Police Extradition Squad

1.24 The extradition squad carries out arrests of those sought under extradition warrants who are located within the Metropolitan Police area.

---

5 Prosecution of Offences Act 1985 s3(2)(ea).

Outside this area, it offers support and assistance where required to local officers. The extradition squad is based at New Scotland Yard.

Westminster Magistrates' Court

1.25 WMC is the only court of first instance in England and Wales where extradition proceedings are conducted. The International Jurisdiction Office (IJO) at WMC deals with the administration of extradition cases.

1.26 Extradition hearings will always be heard before specially trained district judges (known as appropriate judges). A district judge is designated an appropriate judge by the Lord Chief Justice of England and Wales after consulting the Lord Chancellor (EA 2003 s139(1)(a)). There are currently 13 appropriate judges. The Senior District Judge (Chief Magistrate) is Howard Riddle and the Deputy Senior District Judge is Emma Arbuthnot.

The Administrative Court

1.27 Appeals under the EA 2003 are heard in the Administrative Court, Royal Courts of Justice, London. Appeals are either heard by a single judge or by a Divisional Court made up of two judges, one of whom will be a Lord/Lady Justice. The current President of the Queen's Bench Division is Sir John Thomas.

1.28 Each appeal case is allocated to a lawyer at the Administrative Court who will be the initial contact for enquiries regarding the case. The Administrative Court also hears appeals against the refusal/granting of bail by WMC.

The Supreme Court

1.29 In October 2009, the Supreme Court superseded the Appellate Committee of the House of Lords as the highest court in the United Kingdom. An appeal can only be brought to the Supreme Court if the High Court has certified that there is a point of law of general public importance and where the High Court or the Supreme Court has granted leave to appeal.

1.30 The Supreme Court has 12 justices and the President of the Supreme Court is Lord Neuberger.

Extradition defence lawyers

1.31 Those arrested under the EA 2003 are very often represented at the first court appearance by the duty solicitor. It is therefore imperative that they receive competent advice and representation from a solicitor who is knowledgeable in extradition law.

1.32 The following chapters will go some way to providing practitioners with the foundations needed to adequately represent 'requested persons' in extradition proceedings.

CHAPTER 2

Practical considerations

2.1 Introduction
2.2 Arrest
2.6 The duty solicitor's day
2.17 Essential materials

Introduction

2.1 This chapter looks at practical matters for lawyers acting on behalf of those making their first appearance at the magistrates' court in extradition cases and, in particular, duty solicitors. It looks first at police powers and the arrest of a requested person, and goes on to describe a typical day of the duty solicitor in the extradition courts.

Arrest

2.2 A solicitor will often have minimal involvement when a requested person is first arrested. Police powers[1] allow for the arrest and search of a requested person for extradition and that person's treatment will be governed by the special code of practice that applies to extradition.[2] Police have the power to search both the person and the premises and to seize and retain material, but only if that material shows evidence of the requested person's identity, or relates to the extradition offence for which the person is sought.

2.3 Police will generally ask the requested person to identify themselves and seek to obtain evidence of their identity. Upon arrest, the police will caution the requested person in the usual way. Anything that the requested person says (for example, 'Oh yes, I know all about this, it's the burglary that I committed in Krakow in 2007') will be noted and may be used in subsequent proceedings.

2.4 The right of access to legal advice at the police station under section 58 of the Police and Criminal Evidence Act 1984 applies to those arrested in extradition cases.[3] However, for the vast majority of those requested persons who are unable to pay for legal advice, this will be limited to telephone advice. Given that the police do not interview requested persons, it is unlikely that physical attendance at the police station would pass the 'sufficient benefit' test as set out in the 2010 Standard Crime Contract provisions. The requested person will also have the right to have someone informed of their arrest, and, if necessary, will have access to an interpreter; very often by way of Language Line.

---

1 See EA 2003 Pt 4.
2 www.homeoffice.gov.uk/publications/police/operational-policing/extradition-codes-of-practice?view=Binary.
3 EA 2003 s171(3)(d).

2.5 A person may not be granted bail by the police when arrested on an EAW. A person arrested under Part 2 of the Act may be granted bail (EA 2003 s72(4)(a) and s74(4)(a)). Where a person is held in custody following arrest, he or she must be brought before a court as soon as practicable.[4]

The duty solicitor's day

2.6 Unlike general criminal matters, it is unusual for those making their first appearance after an arrest under the EA 2003 to have their own solicitor. Many arrested will, moreover, require the assistance of an interpreter.

2.7 The duty solicitor's day in the extradition courts can be a busy one. It is not unusual for the duty solicitor to be fully occupied throughout the day and until after 6 pm. There are three full-time extradition court rooms at WMC and each one has a different function. The court's work is generally separated as follows:

- Court 1 – full extradition hearings;
- Court 2 – remand hearings (custody and bail) and short extradition hearings;
- Court 3 – video-link remand hearings, short hearings and initial hearings.

2.8 A fourth court room has also been set aside to deal with extradition matters.

2.9 The magistrates' court at Westminster sits at 10 am. Duty solicitors should arrive at 9 am and sign in at the first floor enquiries counter. Although the first hour or so may be quiet, requested persons arrive throughout the day, and any preparation that has been done before the court begins to sit will be useful later on in the day when it is likely to be very busy. It is important that duty solicitors make themselves known to the list caller and to the CPS so that all the extradition work is handed to them. While those arrested on an EAW or extradition request will occasionally have their own solicitor, the majority will not. It is therefore advisable to obtain the EAWs/ extradition requests from the CPS early on in the day, in order to allow time to properly consider them (see chapter 3). The CPS should also provide a statement from the arresting officer and the requested person's record of previous convictions. The prosecution may be

4 EA 2003 s4(3).

found in the extradition courts, or outside the courtrooms just before they open. They are easily identifiable by the red and yellow files they carry. They also have an unmarked office on the third floor, which is attended between 9 am and 10 am and during the lunch adjournment.

2.10 It is good practice for the duty solicitor to make him or herself known to the gaolers. By attending the cells, one can garner a considerable amount of information from the whiteboard that shows who is in custody there and who is expected to be brought in to custody. The whiteboard displays information that can help in this regard. In particular, it will show the police station or prison that the person is coming from. If a person is coming from a police station or prison that is not in London, it is very likely that the person will be an extradition client. The gaolers should be able to give an indication of when the person is expected to arrive. Once the person has arrived, the gaolers will ask him or her whether an interpreter is required, and will note that information on the board. The cells are open throughout the lunch break but interpreters tend to use this time for lunch. If the interpreter cannot be persuaded to stay, this is time that can usefully be used either reading EAWs, speaking to family members about bail arrangements or submitting any legal aid forms.

2.11 Because requested persons are arrested all over the country, they will arrive throughout the day until the 'referral time',[5] which is 12.30 pm. Any persons arriving after that time will be referred to the judge, who will decide whether or not they will be accepted by the gaolers, or whether they will be detained in a local police station overnight to appear at court the following day. It is possible, therefore, to have a very quiet morning as duty solicitor but to have a number of clients in the afternoon. Generally, if there are more than four extradition clients that require a duty solicitor, the court will ask another duty solicitor to assist. If it is apparent that there are a large number of cases to deal with, it is wise to seek assistance at an early stage. In every case, there is a significant amount of important information to convey to, and obtain from, the requested person and, particularly where an interpreter is required, this can take some time. In addition, it will often take time to obtain information from third parties required for a bail application, such as a bail surety or security, a suitable address, location of identity documents, or the nearest police station for a reporting condition. Duty solicitors should allow for a

---

5 While sometimes called the 'cut-off time', 'referral time' is a more accurate description – not all those arriving after 12.30 pm will be turned away.

minimum of 45 minutes for every client, allowing time for completion of legal aid and case management forms. Although there is sometimes pressure from the court, it is important that the necessary time is spent looking at the warrant and advising the client. A failure to explain something at this stage, or to ask a particular question, can mean that a person is extradited when they ought not to have been.

2.12 If it is apparent that a client requires an interpreter for a language other than Polish or Romanian, it is important that this is made known to the list caller as soon as possible. In theory, the court should be notified by the police officers who carried out the arrest that an interpreter is needed, but this frequently fails to happen and, for a more unusual language, it can take hours for an interpreter to arrive. If no interpreter has been booked, the legal adviser should make arrangements to book one by notifying the IJO. At the time of writing, all interpreters are provided to the court by one company under contract. The quality of interpreters varies greatly, and solicitors should be alive to the possibility that the interpreter that has been provided may be inexperienced or unfamiliar with the terminology used on extradition.

2.13 New cases are likely to be heard in Court 3 after the video-link remand hearings have concluded. Any overflow will go to any other available extradition court room.

2.14 Legal aid forms should be submitted at the first floor counter on the day of the requested person's first appearance to ensure that any work done thereafter is covered. A requested person in custody should not have to provide evidence of income and, as long as the form is fully completed and he or she is financially eligible, legal aid will be granted in the interests of justice for all extradition cases.

2.15 Ideally, following the hearing the client should be seen and the outcome explained. This is often impracticable when dealing with several clients in succession in court. One may find at the end of the day that the client has been taken to prison before it has been possible to see him or her again. For this reason it is important to ensure that all matters, including appeal procedure, are covered before the court appearance.

2.16 At the time of writing, the Criminal Procedure Rules Committee is consulting on rules relating to extradition.

Essential materials

2.17 Duty solicitors in the extradition court should take with them:
- a sufficient number of forms CRM14 and CRM15;
- an updated copy of the EA 2003 (an electronic copy can be stored, for example on a mobile phone or tablet device);
- this book;
- checklists.

CHAPTER 3

Looking at a European Arrest Warrant

3.1	Introduction
3.2	**The European Arrest Warrant**
3.2	Certification by the Serious Organised Crime Agency
3.4	Statement of purpose and box A
3.7	Box B
3.9	Box C
3.12	Box D
3.12	Box D as amended by Framework Decision of 2009
3.13	Box E
3.15	Box F
3.16	Box G
3.17	Box H
3.18	Box I
3.19	**Challenging the validity of a European Arrest Warrant**
3.19	EA 2003 s2
3.23	Key principles for challenges under section 2
	Lack of clarity as to the purpose of the warrant • Deficient particulars of accusation/conviction • Deficient particulars of other warrants • Deficient particulars of sentence
3.39	**Extradition offences**
3.42	Dual criminality
3.44	Location of conduct

15

Introduction

3.1 The purpose of the Framework Decision of 2002 (see appendix A), which created the EAW scheme, was to simplify and facilitate extradition procedures across EU countries. To this end, the extradition scheme became a form-filling exercise. The model EAW form is annexed to the Framework Decision; its purpose is to ensure that all of the relevant information required by Article 8 of the Framework Decision is included by the judicial authority.[1] It should, however, be noted that if the form is incorrectly filled out, for example if there are boxes that are not filled in, this does not in itself invalidate the warrant.[2] This chapter will go on to look at the warrant and at each box of the form as set out in the appendix. It will look in some detail at challenges to the validity of the warrant, along with extradition offences.

The European Arrest Warrant

Certification by the Serious Organised Crime Agency

3.2 EAWs in the United Kingdom must be certified by SOCA, and the certificate will be attached at the front of the warrant. To qualify for certification, the EAW must have been issued by a judicial authority (being an authority that SOCA believes has the function of issuing arrest warrants in the territory concerned: EA 2003 s2(7)).[3]

---

1 The European Judicial Network website contains an 'EAW wizard', which provides an online form for judicial authorities to complete to create an EAW: www.ejn-crimjust.europa.eu.
2 See paragraph 3.19 and following below for the circumstances in which a warrant may be held to be invalid.
3 The case of *Assange v Swedish Prosecution Authority* [2012] UKSC 22 looked at whether a public prosecutor could be properly classified as a judicial authority or not, and concluded that, in that particular case, it could be. This issue was revisited in relation to EAWs issued by ministries of justice in the case of *Ministry of Justice, Lithuania v Bucnys* [2012] EWHC 2771 (Admin), which held that while the warrant had been issued by the Lithuanian Ministry of Justice, this could be classified as a judicial authority because the request for the EAW was based on an enforceable judgment of conviction and sentence. It also, however, looked at an EAW that had been issued by the Ministry of Justice in Estonia and found that it had not been issued by a judicial authority because the decision to issue that warrant could not be regarded as a 'judicial decision'. This is a rapidly changing area of law, currently being appealed to the Supreme Court and any warrant issued by a body other than a court should be carefully checked against the case-law to determine whether it can be argued that the warrant was not issued by a judicial authority.

3.3 The EAW must also contain a statement of purpose and specified information (EA 2003 s2(4) and (6)). The certificate will give the date that the requesting state issued the EAW and the date on which it was certified by SOCA. It should also be signed. If it is not signed and dated, this may mean that the arrest and subsequent detention of the person named in the warrant are unlawful.[4] Once the warrant has been certified, it may be executed by a police officer or a customs officer in any part of the United Kingdom.

Statement of purpose and box A

3.4 The first page of the EAW will usually contain the statement of purpose along with information required to identify the requested person, which is set out in box A.

(a) Information regarding the identity of the requested person:

Name:

Forename(s):

Maiden name, where applicable:

Aliases, where applicable:

Sex:

Nationality:

Date of birth:

Place of birth:

Residence and/or known address:

Language(s) which the requested person understands (if known):

Distinctive marks/description of the requested person:

Photo and fingerprints of the requested person, if they are available and can be transmitted, or contact details of the person to be contacted in order to obtain such information or a DNA profile (where this evidence can be supplied but has not been included)

---

4 *Rimas v Lithuania* [2011] EWHC 2084 (Admin).

3.5 In theory, the statement of purpose will be different for accused or convicted persons (see EA 2003 s2(3) and (5)), but in practice most warrants will contain the standard statement set out in the proforma, which states:

> This warrant has been issued by a competent judicial authority. I request that the person mentioned below be arrested and surrendered for the purposes of conducting a criminal prosecution or executing a custodial sentence or detention order.

In order to determine whether the EAW has been issued for an accusation or following conviction, it will, therefore, be necessary to look at boxes B and C of the EAW.

3.6 Box A sets out information that enables the authorities to identify the requested person. Frequently some fields in this box will be left blank – this will not invalidate the warrant, but the name of the requested person and the date of birth will clearly be essential in order to ensure that the right person is arrested.

Box B

(b) Decision on which the warrant is based:
1. Arrest warrant or judicial decision having the same effect:
Type: ....
2. Enforceable judgement: ....
Reference: ....

3.7 Box B requires the judicial authority to state the decision on which the warrant is based, and will either be:
- an 'arrest warrant or judicial decision having the same effect' (in the case of an accusation warrant); or
- an 'enforceable judgment' (in the case of a conviction warrant).

3.8 It is from this box, therefore, that it will usually be possible to determine whether the requested person wanted by the judicial authority is being accused or has been convicted. In some cases, the requested person will be wanted for both accusation and conviction offences and the judicial authority will, therefore, have to provide both sets of information. These EAWs are known as hybrid warrants. The judicial authority should provide the type of decision along with its date and the case reference.

Box C

> (c) Indications on the length of the sentence:
>
> 1. Maximum length of the custodial sentence or detention order which may be imposed for the offence(s): ....
> ....
>
> 2. Length of the custodial sentence or detention order imposed:
> ....
> ....
>
> Remaining sentence to be served: ....
> ....

3.9 This section will contain the information regarding either (in the case of (1) above) the maximum custodial sentence or, in the case of (2) above, the length of the sentence imposed and the remaining sentence to be served. As with box B, it is divided into two sections, which should correspond with those in the box above (ie if (1) is completed in box B, it should also be (1) that is filled in for box C).

3.10 The function of this box is to ensure that the offences for which the warrant has been issued meet the minimum requirements for the punishment threshold for which EAWs can be issued, that is, for those yet to be sentenced, an offence that carries imprisonment of 12 months or more, or, in the case of requested persons who have been sentenced, an offence for which the person has been sentenced to a term of four months' imprisonment or more. It is the sentence that will be imposed in the requesting state that is determinative, and not the sentence in the requested state. This means that, unlike in Part 2 cases, a person can be extradited for an offence that does not carry a sentence of imprisonment in this country, as long as the minimum sentence in the requesting state is 12 months (for those yet to be sentenced) and four months (for sentenced persons). Different minimum sentence periods apply to those offences in the Framework list (see paragraph 3.14 below).

3.11 Box C also allows the judicial authority to state the remaining sentence to be served. A failure to complete this part of box C or an error as to the amount of time left to serve will not invalidate the warrant.[5] The idea of an outstanding sentence to be served may be unfamiliar to many UK criminal practitioners who see their clients

---

5 *Banasinski v District Court in Sanok, Poland* [2008] EWHC 3626 (Admin).

serving sentences immediately and then being released at the half-way point without returning to prison (apart from in very specific circumstances, such as breach of licence, or bail granted pending an appeal). Many European countries, however, allow those sentenced for offences to be released part way through their sentence, with a requirement to return to prison at a date in the future. Some countries do not imprison people immediately following a sentence, but require them to surrender themselves to serve a sentence when notified. A very large proportion of Polish EAWs are issued in respect of those who have breached the Polish equivalent of a suspended sentence or licence, and are therefore required to serve a sentence of imprisonment. While the minimum period of imprisonment required for a warrant to be issued for sentenced prisoners is four months, there is no requirement that there be a minimum period remaining of a sentence to be served in order for an EAW to be issued. It is, therefore, theoretically possible for a person's extradition to be sought in order to serve a remaining sentence of, for example, one month as long as the original sentence was longer than four months. Such a case, however, would be open to challenge on the grounds that it would amount to a disproportionate interference with the requested person's rights under article 8 of the European Convention on Human Rights. See paragraph 3.36 below regarding the requirement to state particulars of sentence.

Box D

> (d) Decision rendered in absentia and:
>
> The person concerned has been summoned in person or otherwise informed of the date and place of the hearing which led to the decision rendered in absentia
>
> or
>
> The person concerned has not been summoned in person or otherwise informed of the date and place of the hearing which led to the decision rendered in absentia but has the following legal guarantees after surrender (such guarantees can be given in advance)
>
> Specify the legal guarantees ....

3.12 Box D is used in conviction cases only to give details of the requested person's right to a retrial where he or she has been convicted in absentia (see paragraph 6.60). This box has been amended by Council Framework Decision 2009/299/JHA of 26 February 2009 to require more detail in the case of those convicted in absentia, although the provisions of EA 2003 s20 are such that the amendment makes no practical difference in the United Kingdom[6] (see the amended box D below). Whether or not the issuing state has used the old or the new proforma for box D, it will still be necessary for the court to be satisfied to the criminal standard that a requested person not deliberately absent but convicted in his or her absence will have a right to a retrial. Where a requesting state had filled in the original box D (above) with 'not applicable', this was taken by the court to be 'the clearest possible assertion on behalf of the judicial authority that the decision was not rendered in absentia but rather that he was present'.[7]

---

[6] Italy has deferred the implementation of the Framework Decision to 1 January 2014.
[7] *Kis (Emil) v District Court In Sokolov, Czech Republic* [2012] EWHC 938 (Admin).

Box D as amended by Framework Decision of 2009

(d) Indicate if the person appeared in person at the trial resulting in the decision:

1. ☐ Yes, the person appeared in person at the trial resulting in the decision.

2. ☐ No, the person did not appear in person at the trial resulting in the decision.

3. If you answered 'no' to question 2 above, please indicate if:

☐ 3.1a the person was summoned in person and thereby informed of the scheduled date and place of the trial which resulted in the decision and was informed that a decision may be handed down if he or she does not appear for the trial;

Date at which the person was summoned in person:

.... (day/month/year)

Place where the person was summoned in person:

....

OR

☐ 3.1b the person was not summoned in person but by other means actually received official information of the scheduled date and place of the trial which resulted in the decision, in such a manner that it was unequivocally established that he or she was aware of the scheduled trial, and was informed that a decision may be handed down if he or she does not appear for the trial;

Describe how it is established that the person concerned was aware of the trial:

....

OR

☐ 3.2 being aware of the scheduled trial the person had given a mandate to a legal counsellor, who was either appointed by the person concerned or by the State, to defend him or her at the trial, and was indeed defended by that counsellor at the trial;

Provide information on how this condition has been met:

....

OR

☐ 3.3 the person, after being served with the decision, expressly stated that he or she does not contest this decision.

Describe when and how the person expressly stated that he or she does not contest the decision:

....

OR

☐ 3.4 the person was entitled to a retrial or appeal under the following conditions:

☐ 3.4.1 the person was personally served with the decision on .... (day/month/year); and

– the person was expressly informed of the right to a retrial or appeal and to be present at that trial; and

– after being informed of this right, the person did not request a retrial or appeal within the applicable timeframe.

OR

☐ 3.4.2 the person was not personally served with the decision, but

– the person will be personally served with this decision without delay after the surrender; and

– when served with the decision, the person will be expressly informed of his/her right to a retrial or appeal and to be present at that trial; and

– after being served with the decision, the person will have the right to request a retrial or appeal within ..... days.

If you ticked this box 3.4.2, please confirm

☐ that if the person sought, when being informed in the executing State about the content of the European arrest warrant, requests to receive a copy of the judgment before being surrendered, that person shall immediately after such request via the executing authority be provided with a copy of the judgment;

and

☐ that if the person has requested a retrial or appeal, the detention of the person awaiting such retrial or appeal shall, until the proceedings are finalised, be reviewed in accordance with the law of the issuing State, either on a regular basis or upon request of the person concerned; such a review shall in particular include the possibility of suspension or interruption of the detention;

and

☐ that if the person has requested a retrial or appeal, such retrial or appeal shall begin within due time after the surrender.

Box E

(e) Offences:

This warrant relates to in total: .... offences.

Description of the circumstances in which the offence(s) was (were) committed, including the time, place and degree of participation in the offence(s) by the requested person:

....

Nature and legal classification of the offence(s) and the applicable statutory provision/code:

....

I. If applicable, tick one or more of the following offences punishable in the issuing Member State by a custodial sentence or detention order of a maximum of at least 3 years as defined by the laws of the issuing Member State:

☐ participation in a criminal organisation;

☐ terrorism;

☐ trafficking in human beings;

☐ sexual exploitation of children and child pornography;

☐ illicit trafficking in narcotic drugs and psychotropic substances

☐ illicit trafficking in weapons, munitions and explosives;

☐ corruption;

☐ fraud, including that affecting the financial interests of the European Communities within the meaning of the Convention of 26 July 1995 on the protection of European Communities' financial interests;

- ☐ laundering of the proceeds of crime;
- ☐ counterfeiting of currency, including the Euro;
- ☐ computer-related crime;
- ☐ environmental crime, including illicit trafficking in endangered animal species and in endangered plant species and varieties;
- ☐ facilitation of unauthorised entry and residence;
- ☐ murder, grievous bodily injury;
- ☐ illicit trade in human organs and tissue;
- ☐ kidnapping, illegal restraint and hostage-taking;
- ☐ racism and xenophobia;
- ☐ organised or armed robbery;
- ☐ illicit trafficking in cultural goods, including antiques and works of art;
- ☐ swindling;
- ☐ racketeering and extortion;
- ☐ counterfeiting and piracy of products;
- ☐ forgery of administrative documents and trafficking therein;
- ☐ forgery of means of payment;
- ☐ illicit trafficking in hormonal substances and other growth promoters;
- ☐ illicit trafficking in nuclear or radioactive materials;
- ☐ trafficking in stolen vehicles;
- ☐ rape;
- ☐ arson;
- ☐ crimes within the jurisdiction of the International Criminal Court;
- ☐ unlawful seizure of aircraft/ships;
- ☐ sabotage.

II. Full description of offence(s) not covered by section I above:

....

....

3.13 Box E is a particularly important part of the EAW. It is essential to examine it carefully to ensure that the warrant complies with both EA 2003 s2 and s10. As shown above, it requires the requesting state to provide information regarding the circumstances of the offence. Failure to provide sufficient detail here will invalidate the warrant (see paragraph 3.19 below).

3.14 The list set out in Box E shows the 32 'Framework offences'. If the requesting state has ticked one of these boxes, and the offence is punishable in the member state by at least three years' imprisonment in the case of accusation warrants, or 12 months' imprisonment in the case of conviction warrants, it is not necessary to satisfy the dual criminality test (see paragraph 3.42 regarding dual criminality). The description of the offence must contain sufficient detail to establish that the conduct in question amounts to an offence in the United Kingdom (see paragraph 3.39 below for more information on extradition offences).

Box F

(f) Other circumstances relevant to the case (optional information):

....

3.15 Box F is used where the requesting state has identified potential problems with the execution of the warrant. It can be used, for example, where temporary surrender (see paragraph 8.37) is anticipated, or to give detail about limitation periods or extraterritoriality. It often also provides details of attempts made to locate the requested person and statements about his or her knowledge of the proceedings.

Box G

(g) This warrant pertains also to the seizure and handing over of property which may be required as evidence:

This warrant pertains also to the seizure and handing over of property acquired by the requested person as a result of the offence:

Description of the property (and location) (if known):

....

3.16 This box allows for the seizure and return of evidence to the requesting state in pre-trial cases, or, post-conviction, for property which is the subject of a confiscation order. It is at present unusual for this box to be completed.

Box H

> (h) The offence(s) on the basis of which this warrant has been issued is(are) punishable by / has(have) led to a custodial life sentence or lifetime detention order:
>
> the legal system of the issuing Member State allows for a review of the penalty or measure imposed – on request or at least after 20 years – aiming at a non-execution of such penalty or measure,
>
> and/or
>
> the legal system of the issuing Member State allows for the application of measures of clemency to which the person is entitled under the law or practice of the issuing Member State, aiming at non-execution of such penalty or measure.

3.17 Article 5(2) of the Framework Decision allows countries to refuse to execute an EAW if the warrant is issued for an offence punishable by a life sentence where there is no provision for a review. This provision was not transposed into UK law and this box is, therefore, irrelevant where the United Kingdom is the executing state.

Box I

> (i) The judicial authority which issued the warrant:
>
> Official name: ....
>
> Name of its representative: ....
>
> Post held (title/grade): ....
>
> File reference: ....
>
> Address: ....
>
> Tel. No.: (country code) (area/city code) (...) ....

28 Extradition law / chapter 3

> Fax No.: (country code) (area/city code) (...) ....
>
> E-mail: ....
>
> Contact details of the person to contact to make necessary practical arrangements for the surrender: ....
>
> Where a central authority has been made responsible for the transmission and administrative reception of European arrest warrants:
>
> Name of the central authority: ....
>
> Contact person, if applicable (title/grade and name): ....
>
> Tel. No.: (country code) (area/city code) (...) ....
>
> Fax No.: (country code) (area/city code) (...) ....
>
> E-mail: ....
>
> Signature of the issuing judicial authority and/or its representative:
>
> ....
>
> Name: ....
>
> Post held (title/grade): ....
>
> Date: ....
>
> Official stamp (if available)

3.18 The final boxes in the EAW, as set out above, are self-explanatory. It is necessary for this information to be provided so that practical arrangements can be made where extradition has been ordered. In order to determine whether the warrant has been issued by a 'judicial authority' it will be necessary to refer to these boxes.

Challenging the validity of a European Arrest Warrant

EA 2003 s2

3.19 When an EAW is received by SOCA the latter must, according to EA 2003 s2, check that the warrant has been issued by a judicial authority of the requesting state and that it contains the following information:

- a statement that the person in respect of whom the warrant is issued is accused/convicted of an offence specified in the warrant and that it has been issued with a view to his arrest and extradition for the purpose of conducting a prosecution or executing a custodial sentence;
- particulars of the person's identity;
- (in the case of a conviction warrant) particulars of the conviction;
- particulars of any other warrant issued in the category 1 territory for the person's arrest in respect of the offence;
- (in the case of an accusation warrant) particulars of the circumstances in which the person is alleged to have committed the offence, including the conduct alleged to constitute the offence, the time and place at which he or she is alleged to have committed the offence and any provision of the law of the category 1 territory under which the conduct is alleged to constitute an offence;
- particulars of the sentence that may be imposed under the law of the category 1 territory in respect of the offence if the person is convicted of it/has not been sentenced; and
- (in the case of a sentenced person) particulars of the sentence that has been imposed.

3.20 If the warrant contains this information and SOCA believes that the authority which issued the Part 1 warrant has the function of issuing arrest warrants in the category 1 territory, SOCA may issue a certificate (see paragraph 3.3 above).

3.21 While SOCA is initially responsible for checking that the information required by section 2 is included, EAWs that do not contain this information are frequently certified.[8] It is vital, therefore, that the warrant is carefully checked for compliance with section 2. Failure to comply with section 2 may mean that the warrant is invalid, and it may be possible for the requested person to be discharged.

3.22 In the case of *Dabas v High Court of Justice, Madrid*[9] Lord Hope stated that a judge conducting an extradition hearing:

> must first be satisfied that the warrant with which he is dealing is a Part 1 warrant within the meaning of section 2(2). A warrant which does not contain the statements referred to in that subsection cannot be eked out by extraneous information. The requirements of section

---

8 Practitioners will clearly never come across an EAW that has not been certified, and it is, therefore, impossible to know how many warrants SOCA do not certify, but given the number of warrants that are certified that do not comply with the requirements of section 2, it would appear that the process of checking the warrant is fairly rudimentary.
9 [2006] EWHC 971 (Admin).

2(2) are mandatory. If they are not met, the warrant is not a Part 1 warrant and the remaining provisions of that Part of the Act will not apply to it.

It should be noted that this does not apply to section 10; further information can be provided to show that an offence satisfies the dual criminality test (see paragraph 3.42 below). It would, however, appear from the recent case of *Zakrzewski v Regional Court in Lodz, Poland*[10] that if the statements made in a warrant cease to be true (for example, where a sentence is subsequently altered), this can be cured by the provision of further information from the requesting state.[11]

Key principles for challenges under section 2

3.23 The main grounds of challenge under section 2 are as follows:
- lack of clarity as to the purpose of the warrant;
- deficient particulars of accusation or conviction;
- deficient particulars of other warrants; and
- deficient particulars of sentence.

3.24 This chapter will go on to look at each of these headings in turn. It is, however, important to bear in mind that the courts will generally take a 'cosmopolitan' approach and favour a purposive construction when looking at whether the requirements of section 2 are satisfied, in order to accommodate differences in legal systems across member states. The court will take the statements and information in the warrant at face value. Where the EAW contains information that is demonstrably incorrect, but is nevertheless valid at face value, it should be challenged as an abuse of process rather than under section 2, following the principles set out by Lord Sumption in the case of *Zakrzewski v Regional Court in Lodz, Poland*.[12]

Lack of clarity as to the purpose of the warrant

3.25 By virtue of section 2(3), the warrant must contain a statement that it has been issued in respect of an accused or convicted person (see paragraph 3.5 above regarding the statement of purpose). To seek a person's extradition in order to conduct an investigation with a view to possible prosecution is not a legitimate purpose. Where it is unclear from the warrant, when read as a whole, whether a person

---

10 [2013] UKSC 2.
11 At para 10.
12 At para 13.

is wanted as an accused or a convicted person, or where it appears that the person is wanted as a suspect and not for prosecution, there may be grounds to challenge the validity of the warrant under section 2. It may, in some circumstances, be necessary to obtain expert evidence addressing the stage the proceedings have reached and the classification of the requested person under the law of the requesting state (although see point 7 in the list below). A helpful summary of the principles deriving from the case-law is set out by Aikens LJ in *Asztaslos v Szekszard City Court, Hungary*:[13]

> (1) The court will look at the warrant as a whole to see whether it is an 'accusation case' warrant or a 'conviction case' warrant. It will not confine itself to the wording on the first page of the warrant, which may well be equivocal.
>
> (2) In the case of an 'accusation case' warrant, issued under Part 1 of the Act, the court has to be satisfied, looking at the warrant as a whole, that the requested person is an 'accused' within *section 2(3)(a)* of the Act.
>
> (3) Similarly, the court will look at the wording of the warrant as a whole to decide whether the warrant indicates, unequivocally, that the purpose of the warrant is for the purpose of the requested person being prosecuted for the offences identified.
>
> (4) The court must construe the words in *section 2(3)(a)* and *(b)* in a 'cosmopolitan' sense and not just in terms of the stages of English criminal procedure.
>
> (5) If the warrant uses the phrases that are used in the English language version of the EAW annexed to the Framework Decision, there should be no (or very little scope) for argument on the purpose of the warrant.
>
> (6) Only if the wording of the warrant is equivocal should the court consider examining extrinsic evidence to decide on the purpose of the warrant. But it should not look at extrinsic material to introduce a possible doubt as to the purpose where it is clear on the face of the warrant itself.
>
> (7) Consideration of extrinsic factual or expert evidence to ascertain the purpose of the warrant should be a last resort and it is to be discouraged. The introduction of such evidence is clean contrary to the aspiration of the Framework Decision, which is to introduce clarity and simplicity into the surrender procedure between member states of the European Union. Therefore the introduction of extrinsic factual and expert evidence must be discouraged, except in exceptional cases.

---

13 [2010] EWHC 237 (Admin) at para 38.

3.26 In the case of *Assange*,[14] the High Court examined the question of whether a person who had not been charged could properly be said to be an accused person. In such cases, it was said, the court must 'ask whether the case against him has moved from where he can be seen only as a suspect where proof may be lacking or whether there is an accusation against him supported by proof'[15] and found that, on the particular facts of that case (a detailed investigation and clear evidence of two complainants), he was plainly accused.

Deficient particulars of accusation/conviction

3.27 The courts have recognised the differing requirements set out in the legislation for accusation and conviction warrants. While an accusation warrant must contain particulars of the circumstances of the offence (according to EA 2003 s2(4)(c)), a conviction warrant simply requires 'particulars of the conviction' (EA 2003 s2(6)(b)) – greater particularisation is therefore needed in accusation cases than in conviction cases.[16]

3.28 Each case will depend on its own particular facts. A useful guide to the necessary detail to be provided in a conviction warrant is provided in the case of *Sandi v Craiova Court, Romania*:[17]

> it will almost always be necessary for a conviction warrant to contain the number of offences for which the requested person has been convicted – and some information about when and where the offences were committed, and the requested person's participation in them, although not necessarily in the same level of detail as would be required in an accusation warrant. Furthermore, common sense dictates that it is likely that more particulars will be appropriate in more complex crimes such as fraud than in crimes such as simple theft. However, there is no formula for appropriate particularisation.[18]

3.29 In accusation cases, section 2(4)(c) requires that the circumstances of the alleged offence, including the conduct, time, place and the relevant provision of law are set out. The language of this section is 'not obscure and [...] should be given its plain and ordinary meaning'.[19] Successful challenges have been made to warrants that do not

---

14 *Assange v Swedish Prosecution Authority* [2011] EWHC 2849 (Admin).
15 At para 152.
16 *Sandi v Craiova Court, Romania* [2009] EWHC 3079 (Admin) at para 32.
17 [2009] EWHC 3079 (Admin).
18 At para 32.
19 *Von Der Pahlen v Government of Austria* [2006] EWHC 1672 (Admin) at para 21.

contain sufficient particulars of time or place. In general, however, the courts do not require precision as to these particulars:[20]

> Providing that the description in a warrant of the facts relied upon as constituting an extradition offence identifies such an offence and when and where it is alleged to have been committed, it is not, in my view, necessary or appropriate to subject it to requirements of specificity accorded to particulars of, or sometimes required of, a count in an indictment or an allegation in a civil pleading in this country.

3.30 In one case, for example, offences were said to have been committed on unknown dates over four 12-month periods and one two-year period. It was held that this was sufficiently particularised – the use of the word 'time' does not mean that the exact date need be specified.[21]

3.31 An obvious typographical error will not invalidate the warrant.[22] While there is no requirement to cite the text of the provision of law under which the alleged conduct constitutes an offence, the relevant provision of law must be identified somewhere in the warrant – failure to do so will invalidate the warrant.[23]

3.32 By far the greatest number of challenges under EA 2003 s2(4)(c) are made on the grounds that the conduct has not been sufficiently particularised. As with section 2(6)(b), each case will depend on its own facts. However, it is clear from the case-law that the particulars of the offence must provide a person with 'a clear understanding of why his extradition is being sought'.[24] Thus, 'a broad omnibus description of the alleged criminal conduct, "obtaining property by deception", to take an English example, will not suffice'.[25] The conduct must be fairly, accurately and properly set out in the warrant. Guidance was given by Cranston J in *Ektor v National Public Prosecutor of Holland*,[26] who said:

> the person sought by the warrant needs to know what offence he is said to have committed and to have an idea of the nature and extent of

---

20 *Fofana v Deputy Prosecutor Thubin Tribunal de Grande Instance de Meaux, France* [2006] EWHC 744 (Admin).
21 *Crean v Ireland* [2007] EWHC 814 (Admin) at para 17.
22 *Skrzypczak v The Circuit Court in Poznan* [2011] EWHC 1194 (Admin).
23 *Hunt v The Court at First Instance, Antwerp, Belgium* [2006] EWHC 165 (Admin).
24 *Naczmanski v Regional Court in Wloclawek* [2010] EWHC 2023 (Admin) at para 17.
25 *Von der Pahlen v The Government of Austria* [2006] EWHC 1672 (Admin) at para 21.
26 [2007] EWHC 3106 (Admin).

the allegations against him in relation to that offence. The amount of detail may turn on the nature of the offence. Where dual criminality is involved the detail must also be sufficient to enable the transposition exercise to take place.[27]

3.33 In the case of *Balint v Municipal Court in Prague, Czech Republic*[28] Jackson LJ stressed the importance of the cosmopolitan approach, saying:

> In examining the conduct alleged in the warrant and any further information the court must not be pedantic or overly technical. Instead, the court must make reasonable allowance for (a) the fact that methods of particularising criminal offences differ from one jurisdiction to another and (b) the fact (if it be the case) that the warrant has been translated from a foreign language into English.[29]

3.34 In many cases where there is doubt as to the sufficiency of the particulars of conduct set out, there may be a parallel challenge as to whether the conduct amounts to an extradition offence (see paragraph 3.39 below).

Deficient particulars of other warrants

3.35 The requirement to provide particulars of 'any other warrant' does not amount to a requirement to include details of previous EAWs that have been withdrawn. Rather, it requires the requesting state to provide particulars of the domestic warrant on the basis of which the EAW was issued, for example a warrant of arrest or an order for surrender to custody.[30] The rationale for this is that it enables the court 'to ascertain that there are criminal proceedings in the requesting state'.[31]

Deficient particulars of sentence

3.36 The EAW must set out either the sentence that may be imposed (where a person is yet to be sentenced), or the sentence that has been imposed (where a person has been sentenced). It is necessary to state the particulars of sentence to enable the court to determine whether

---

27 [2007] EWHC 3106 (Admin) at para 7.
28 [2011] EWHC 498 (Admin).
29 At para 28.
30 *Louca v A German Judicial Authority* [2009] UKSC 4.
31 *Louca v Public Prosecutor in Bielefel, Germany* [2008] EWHC 2907 (Admin) at para 26.

3.37 Failure to state that a sentence has been suspended will not invalidate the warrant.[32] Indeed, practitioners will find that a large number of Polish clients are subject to a suspended sentence that has been activated, although this will not be clear from the warrant.

3.38 Complications arise in relation to this requirement where a person's extradition is sought for multiple offences. In a conviction case, if there are several offences that are dealt with by way of an aggregate penalty, it is enough for the warrant to state the aggregate sentence.[33] Conversely, while it is necessary to state the sentence that has been imposed, if there is more than one offence, there is no requirement to state the aggregate penalty.[34] Indeed, a warrant will still be valid even if it can be shown that the sentence has been aggregated after the warrant has been issued (meaning that there is a different sentence to serve than that set out in the warrant). In an accusation case, the maximum sentence for each offence must be stated.[35]

Extradition offences

3.39 EA 2003 ss64 and 65 define extradition offences for accusation and conviction cases respectively, with different minimum periods of sentence applying in both cases. These sections are complicated and are by no means a direct transposition of the relevant provisions of the Framework Decision.[36] Where an offence is listed in the Framework list contained within box E, it will not be necessary to look into whether the conduct alleged would amount to an offence if it had taken place in this country. It will, however, be necessary to check the sentence applicable to the offence against the minimum periods set out in the Act and that the conduct occurred in the category 1 territory. If the offence does not appear in the Framework list, the conduct alleged should be carefully analysed to determine whether it satisfies the dual criminality requirement. This is the primary area of challenge under these sections. This chapter will go on to look at the

---

32 *Bulkowski (Kamil) v Regional Court of Elblag, Poland* [2012] EWHC 281 (Admin).
33 *Pilecki v Circuit Court of Legnica, Poland* [2008] UKHL 7, [2008] 1 WLR 325, HL.
34 *Bartkowiak v Judicial Authority of Poland* [2012] EWHC 333 (Admin).
35 *Taylor v Public Prosecutor's Office, Berlin* [2012] EWHC 475 (Admin).
36 See JR Spencer 'Implementing the European Arrest Warrant: A Tale of How Not to Do It' (2009) 30(3) *Statute Law Review* 184 at pp191–192.

minimum periods of sentence, and will then cover dual criminality and the relevance of the location of the offence.

3.40 If one of the boxes in the list of Framework offences set out in box E is ticked, it will be an extradition offence if it is punishable by at least three years' imprisonment (in accusation cases) or a sentence of 12 months' imprisonment was imposed (in conviction cases) – see EA 2003 s64(2) and s65(2).[37]

3.41 If the offence is not on the Framework list, but would have constituted an offence had it taken place in the United Kingdom, it will be an extradition offence if it is punishable by at least 12 months' imprisonment (in accusation cases) or a sentence of four months' imprisonment was imposed (in conviction cases). This can be contrasted with Part 2 cases, where the offence must be punishable in the United Kingdom with a minimum of 12 months' imprisonment.[38]

Dual criminality

3.42 In order to determine whether an offence satisfies the dual criminality requirement, it is necessary to look at the conduct complained of in the warrant and, if the judicial authority has provided it, any further information. It would be wrong to look at whether the elements of the offence have a precise equivalent in this country.[39] If the *mens rea* is not specifically set out in the description of the conduct, it can be inferred, but only where the facts are such that the inference is the only reasonable one to draw.[40] If the conduct set out in the warrant would not amount to an offence in this country, the offence is not an extradition offence and the requested person should be discharged.

3.43 In looking at dual criminality, the courts will follow the same principles that apply to EA 2003 s2, that is, a cosmopolitan approach will be taken in order to give effect to the principle of mutual recognition.

---

37 Although the legislation states that the conduct will constitute an extradition offence if (*inter alia*) 'a certificate issued by an appropriate authority of the category 1 territory shows that the conduct falls within the European Framework list', there is no need for a 'certificate' to be attached to the warrant: the warrant itself has been held to be the certificate: see *Dabas v High Court of Justice, Madrid* [2006] EWHC 971 (Admin) at para 26.
38 EA 2003 ss137 and 138.
39 *Zak v Regional Court of Bydgoszcz, Poland* [2008] EWHC 470 (Admin) at para 5.
40 *Assange v Swedish Prosecution Authority* [2011] EWHC 2849 (Admin) at para 55.

Location of conduct

3.44 In most cases, the location of the conduct will not be an issue – the conduct will take place in the jurisdiction of the requesting state. There are, however, a number of offences that take place across borders and in such cases the location of the conduct may be crucial. In some cases, if the offence took place outside the requesting state, it may be possible to argue that it is not an extradition offence. The relevant provisions of the Act are sections 64 and 65.

3.45 The provisions that cover cases in which conduct took place outside the requesting state are complicated. There are ten different ways that conduct which took place abroad may be an extradition offence. These provisions have been simplified by the case-law, which has held that if conduct takes place outside the requesting state but has an intended effect within it, the court will consider that the conduct took place in that state.[41] Furthermore, while it may appear from reading EA 2003 ss64(3) and 65(3) that a Framework offence that occurs partially in the United Kingdom will not be an extradition offence, this is not the case: if the Framework offence also satisfies the dual criminality test, these sections will also apply.[42] If some of the conduct took place within the United Kingdom, the relevant conduct can be excised from the warrant.[43]

3.46 The flow charts following at figure 3.1 and figure 3.2 illustrate the various ways in which conduct may be an extradition offence under sections 64 and 65 respectively. These flowcharts should be used in conjunction with the legislation, bearing in mind the provisions of sections 64(8) and 65(8) for tax or customs offences, and the rule in *Osunta v The Public Prosecutor's Office in Dusseldorf*,[44] which allows for excision from the warrant of conduct which would not amount to an extradition offence.

---

41 *King's Prosecutor, Brussels v Cando Armas* [2005] UKHL 67 at para 35.
42 At para 17.
43 *Osunta v The Public Prosecutor's Office in Dusseldorf* [2007] EWHC 1562 (Admin).
44 [2007] EWHC 1562 (Admin).

Figure 3.1: Part 1 extradition offence (accusation)

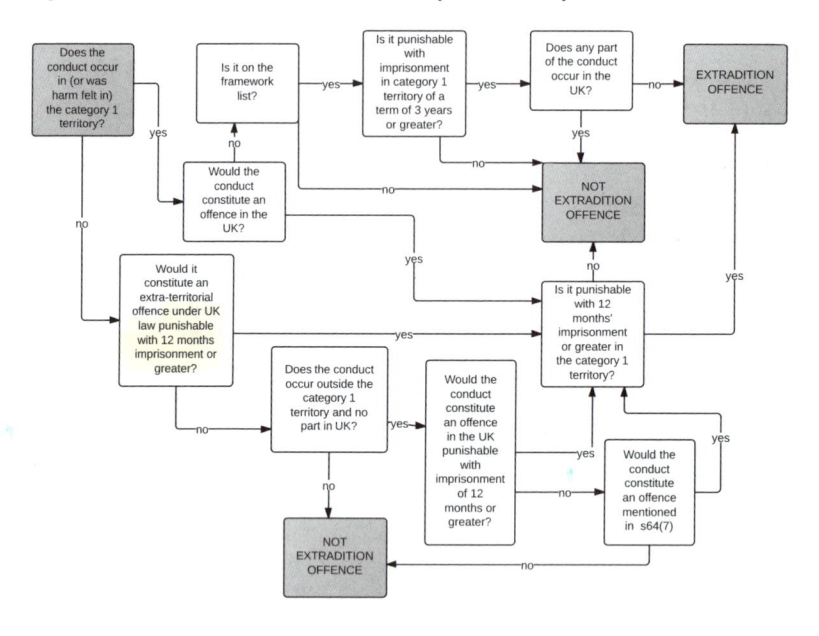

Figure 3.2: Part 2 extradition offence (conviction)

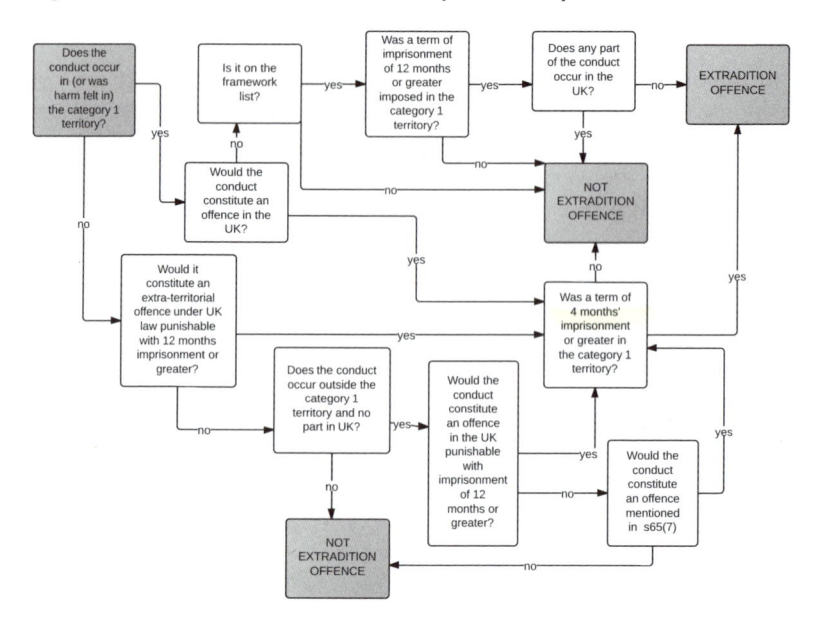

CHAPTER 4

Extradition requests from outside the European Union

4.1	Introduction
4.3	**Part 2 countries**
4.4	Ad hoc arrangements
4.5	**Dealing with Part 2 extradition requests**
4.7	**Issuing a provisional warrant**
4.12	Arrest following the issuing of a provisional warrant
4.17	**Issuing a full request**
4.20	Arrest on a full request
4.22	**Production at Westminster Magistrates' Court**
4.26	**First hearing – provisional arrest**
4.28	Person charged with an offence in the UK or serving a sentence of imprisonment
4.32	Date for service of the full extradition request
4.36	Service of the full extradition request
4.39	**First hearing – full request**
4.43	**Initial stages of the extradition hearing**
4.48	**Challenges to extradition**

continued

4.53	**Extradition offences**
4.61	**Prima facie case**
4.66	**The role of the Secretary of State**
4.68	Person charged with an offence in the United Kingdom/ sentenced to imprisonment
4.71	Representations to the SSHD
4.77	Competing extradition requests
4.79	Competing EAW and Part 2 requests for extradition

Introduction

4.1 This chapter looks at extradition requests from outside the European Union. Such requests are governed by Part 2 of the EA 2003 and are often referred to as 'Part 2 requests'. The procedure for dealing with Part 2 requests is very different from the procedure for dealing with EAW requests.

4.2 Part 2 requests can either be 'provisional' or 'full requests'. The procedure following arrest is different depending on whether it is a 'provisional' or 'full request' for extradition. This chapter will cover the following areas: the validity of Part 2 requests, the issue and execution of a Part 2 request, the initial hearing for provisional arrests and full requests, challenges at the extradition hearing, extradition offences, the requirement to show a prima facie case and the role of the SSHD.

Part 2 countries

4.3 The following countries all have extradition treaties with the United Kingdom and requests for extradition are made in accordance with Part 2 of the Act:[1]

- Albania, Algeria, Andorra, Antigua and Barbuda, Argentina, Armenia, Australia, Azerbaijan, The Bahamas, Bangladesh, Barbados, Belize, Bolivia, Bosnia and Herzegovina, Botswana, Brazil, Brunei, Canada, Chile, Colombia, Cook Islands, Croatia,[2] Cuba, Dominica, Ecuador, El Salvador, Fiji, The Gambia, Georgia, Ghana, Grenada, Guatemala, Guyana, Hong Kong Special Administrative Region, Haiti, Iceland, India, Iraq, Israel, Jamaica, Kenya, Kiribati, Lesotho, Liberia, Libya, Liechtenstein, Macedonia (FYR), Malawi, Malaysia, Maldives, Mauritius, Mexico, Moldova, Monaco, Montenegro, Nauru, New Zealand, Nicaragua, Nigeria, Norway, Panama, Papua New Guinea, Paraguay, Peru, Russian Federation, Saint Christopher and Nevis, Saint Lucia, Saint Vincent and the Grenadines, San Marino, Serbia, Seychelles, Sierra Leone, Singapore, Solomon Islands, South Africa, Sri Lanka, Swaziland, Switzerland, Tanzania, Thailand, Tonga, Trinidad

---

1 At the time of writing, an amendment to the EA 2003 has been laid before parliament that, when in force, will add the Republic of Korea to the list of territories designated for the purposes of Part 2 of the EA 2003. This is a result of the Republic of Korea acceding to the European Convention on Extradition.

2 On 1 July 2013 Croatia will accede to the European Union and become a Category 1 territory for the purposes of the EA 2003.

and Tobago, Turkey, Tuvalu, Uganda, Ukraine, the United Arab Emirates, the United States, Uruguay, Vanuatu, Western Samoa, Zambia and Zimbabwe.

Ad hoc arrangements

4.4 A country that has not been designated a category 2 territory but is a party to an international convention to which the United Kingdom is a party can request the extradition of a person under EA 2003 s193. A country that is not an extradition treaty partner with the United Kingdom can also make extradition requests and be treated as if they were a category 2 territory. This can be achieved by the government of the United Kingdom and the government of the requesting state entering into an arrangement for the person's extradition and by the SSHD recognising that the two countries have entered into a 'special extradition arrangement'. Once this is done, the SSHD will issue a certificate under EA 2003 s194 and the extradition proceedings will be as for those of a category 2 request under Part 2 of the Act.

Dealing with Part 2 extradition requests

4.5 The duty solicitor at WMC will from time to time have to deal with Part 2 requests. They are far less common than Part 1 (EAW) requests.

4.6 On notification from the CPS extradition prosecutor or the court that a Part 2 extradition request is expected, the first question to ask will be 'is it a provisional or full request?' The answer to this question will determine how the case will proceed that day and how much time is likely to be spent with the client. If it is a full request, then it will be necessary to consider possible bars to extradition and human rights considerations. This is because the court will ask the representative to identify the likely issues in the case and will proceed to fix a date for the extradition hearing to take place. If it is a provisional warrant, only bail instructions will be required as, until the full request is received, it is likely to be premature to identify the possible challenges to extradition.

Issuing a provisional warrant

4.7 A provisional warrant of arrest can be issued if an appropriate judge is satisfied on information in writing or on oath that a person is accused of an offence in a Category 2 country or is alleged to be unlawfully at large after conviction[3] and that the person is either in the UK or is believed to be in the UK or the person is on their way to the UK or is believed to be on their way to the UK.[4]

4.8 The appropriate judge may issue a warrant for a person's arrest if he has reasonable grounds for believing that:[5]

- The offence for which the person is accused of/convicted of is an extradition offence and;
- There is written evidence/information[6] about this.

4.9 The evidence/information is evidence/information that would justify the issue of a warrant for the arrest of a person accused of the offence within the judge's jurisdiction (if accused of an offence) or evidence/information that would justify the issue of a warrant for the arrest of a person unlawfully at large after conviction.

4.10 Neither the duty solicitor nor the defence is involved in the issuing of a provisional warrant of arrest. Applications are often made in camera and the first a person will know about the issue of a Part 2 arrest warrant is when it is executed.

4.11 An example of where a provisional warrant may be used is where a person is in transit in the United Kingdom en route to another country and the person has been identified as being wanted in another country. In those circumstances a full request may not have been sent to the Home Office because the requesting state is not aware of the presence of the requested person in the United Kingdom.

Arrest following the issuing of a provisional warrant

4.12 Once a provisional warrant of arrest has been issued it will be circulated. Any police officer or customs officer can execute it even if neither the warrant nor a copy of it is in the possession of the person executing it.[7]

4.13 If the offence is very serious or the subject of the warrant is high profile, the extradition squad at New Scotland Yard may actively pursue the person. A provisional warrant is very often issued at short notice because the person is believed to be en route to the United Kingdom.

3 EA 2003 s73(2).
4 EA 2003 s73(1).
5 EA 2003 s73(3).
6 Evidence is required for those countries required to demonstrate a prima facie case, otherwise it is information.
7 EA 2003 s73(b).

4.14 A person arrested under a provisional warrant must be given a copy of it as soon as practicable after arrest.[8] The person will be cautioned in the following terms: 'You do not have to say anything. Anything you do say may be given in evidence.' This is the pre-1995 caution and does not contain the reference to failing to mention facts that are later relied upon.

4.15 Following arrest the requested person will be taken to the local police station where he or she will be booked into custody and have their detention authorised. Like all of those arrested and taken to a police station, those arrested under a provisional warrant will be entitled to speak to a solicitor. This will very often be the duty solicitor although it appears recently that those arrested under the EA 2003 are being referred straight to Criminal Defence Direct. There will be no interview and the sole purpose of the detention is to secure the requested person's attendance at WMC as soon as practicable.[9] Production as soon as practicable is not required if the person is granted bail by a constable following his arrest or the SSHD decides that the request for the person's extradition is not to be proceeded with because there is a competing extradition request in existence.

4.16 The IJO at WMC will be notified of the person's arrest and arrangements will be made for production at the court. If the arrest is after the court 'referral time' for accepting prisoners (currently 12.30 pm) then the person will be kept at the police station for production the following day unless the judge agrees to accept the person into the cells after 12.30 pm.

Issuing a full request

4.17 If the SSHD receives a valid request for extradition she must issue a certificate pursuant to EA 2003 s70.[10] A valid request for extradition from a category 2 territory must be made in the approved way and also contain the statement referred to in section 70(4) or (4A).

- In relation to section 70(4) the statement is one that:
    - the person is accused in the category 2 territory of the commission of an offence specified in the request, and

---

8 EA 2003 s74(2).
9 EA 2003 s74(3).
10 This is subject to section 70(2), which contains circumstances in which the SSHD may refuse to issue a certificate.

Extradition requests from outside the European Union

- the request is made with a view to his arrest and extradition to the category 2 territory for the purpose of being prosecuted for the offence.
- In relation to section 70(4A) the statement is one that:
  - the person has been convicted of an offence specified in the request by a court in the category 2 territory, and
  - the request is made with a view to his arrest and extradition to the category 2 territory for the purpose of being sentenced for the offence or of serving a sentence of imprisonment or another form of detention imposed in respect of the offence.

4.18 A request for extradition is made in the approved way if it is made by an authority of the territory that the SSHD believes has the function of making requests for extradition in that territory, or by a person recognised by the SSHD as a diplomatic or consular representative of the territory.

4.19 Once a full request for extradition has been certified the request and the certificate must be sent to the appropriate judge[11] at WMC for an arrest warrant to be issued.

Arrest on a full request

4.20 A person arrested under a 'full request' must be given a copy of the extradition request as soon as practicable after his or her arrest[12] and must be brought as soon as practicable before the appropriate judge.[13] If the warrant is not provided to the requested person as soon as practicable and he or she applies to the judge to be discharged, the judge *may* order his discharge. If the person is not brought to court as soon as practicable after arrest and an application for discharge is made, the judge *must* order his or her discharge.

4.21 The person need not be brought before the appropriate judge if he or she is granted bail by a constable following his arrest[14] or the SSHD decides that the request for the person's extradition is not to be proceeded with because there is a competing extradition request in existence (see EA 2003 s126 and paragraph 4.77 below).

---

11 EA 2003 s70(9).
12 EA 2003 s72(2).
13 EA 2003 s72(3).
14 EA 2003 s72(4)(a) – in reality it is rare for a requested person to be granted bail after arrest to appear at court.

Production at Westminster Magistrates' Court

4.22 WMC is the only court in England and Wales that deals with extradition cases at first instance. Requested persons must therefore be transported to that court following arrest.

4.23 There are often difficulties in getting a person to WMC as soon as practicable after arrest and practitioners must consider the reasons for any delay very carefully: it can sometimes result in the proceedings quickly coming to an end if the authorities have not managed to secure the attendance of the person at court as soon as practicable.

4.24 An arrest can take place anywhere in England and Wales. Unless it is a planned arrest, this can itself cause difficulties, as it may be the first time an officer has made an arrest under EA 2003. The officer may not be familiar with EA 2003 and may overlook the need to get the person to WMC as soon as practicable. The arrest may have taken place over 300 miles from London and transport will need to be arranged.

4.25 Further complications can arise when a person has been arrested and charged with an offence in England and Wales and is then arrested under EA 2003 on a Part 2 request. If the person is denied bail on the domestic matter and taken to the local magistrates' court before being taken to WMC to be dealt with under EA 2003, it may not be deemed to be 'as soon as practicable'. A more detailed assessment of what is deemed to be 'as soon as practicable' can be found at paragraph 8.15.

First hearing – provisional arrest

4.26 At the first hearing the requested person will be produced from custody and, as in all court hearings, will be asked for his or her name and date of birth. Note that identity is not to be determined at the initial hearing although the person will be identified in the dock.

4.27 The appropriate judge must inform the person that he or she is either accused of the commission of an offence in a category 2 territory or that he or she is alleged to be unlawfully at large after conviction.[15] The required information about consent must then be given[16] unless the appropriate judge is informed that the person is charged with an offence in the United Kingdom or serving a sentence of

---

15 EA 2003 s74(7)(a).
16 EA 2003 s74(7)(b).

imprisonment. The consent procedure is the same as that discussed in Part 1 cases (see paragraph 5.7).

Person charged with an offence in the UK or serving a sentence of imprisonment

4.28 If the person before the court is subject to a charge in the United Kingdom then the extradition hearing must be adjourned at this point pursuant to EA 2003 s76A until the charge is either disposed of, withdrawn, proceedings are discontinued or an order is made for the charge to lie on file. Consent will not be taken and the court will proceed to deal with bail.

4.29 If the person before the court is subject to a sentence of imprisonment in the United Kingdom then the judge may adjourn the extradition hearing until the sentence of imprisonment has been served. A judge can adjourn the hearing for up to six months before the matter has to be brought back before the court. Again, under section 76B consent will not be taken.

4.30 Sections 76A and 76B were introduced into legislation in order to prevent a requested person escaping prosecution or having to serve a sentence in the United Kingdom by consenting to extradition and being removed from the United Kingdom before domestic proceedings are concluded.

4.31 If a requested person is subject to a lengthy sentence of imprisonment, the CPS will obtain instructions from the requesting state as to whether it wishes to seek the requested person's temporary extradition – this is known as 'temporary surrender'. The requesting state will be required to provide an undertaking stating that the requested person will be kept in custody pending their trial and returned to the United Kingdom after proceedings have concluded in that state. If the court agrees to temporary surrender, the requested person will be returned to the United Kingdom to serve the remainder of the sentence.

Date for service of the full extradition request

4.32 On a provisional arrest, neither the requested person nor the court will have the papers referred to in section 70(9) (certificate issued by the SSHD and the extradition request). The judge must therefore set a date by which he or she must have received the documents referred to in section 70(9).

4.33 The required period for service of the papers is 45 days, starting with the date of arrest. Certain countries are designated by the SSHD[17] for the purposes of section 74(11)(b) with a longer period for service of papers. Those countries and relevant periods are:[18]

- Bolivia – 65 days
- Bosnia and Herzegovina – 65 days
- Chile – 90 days
- Cuba – 65 days
- Haiti – 65 days
- Iraq – 65 days
- Liberia – 95 days
- Monaco – 65 days
- Nicaragua – 65 days
- Panama – 65 days
- Paraguay – 65 days
- Peru – 95 days
- San Marino – 65 days
- Thailand – 65 days
- United States – 65 days.

4.34 The court will fix a date for the service of the papers and list the case for a review hearing a few days before the papers are due to be served. If the papers referred to in section 70(9) are not received by the judge by the date for service, the requested person must be discharged from the request upon his or her application.

4.35 The final matter for the court to determine at the first hearing after a person has been arrested under a provisional arrest warrant is the issue of bail.

Service of the full extradition request

4.36 A request for extradition is only valid if it contains a certificate issued by the SSHD and the documents referred to in section 70(9).

4.37 The documents are:

- particulars of the person whose extradition is requested;[19]

---

17 Extradition Act 2003 (Designation of Part 2 Territories) Order 2003 SI No 3334.
18 At the time of writing a statutory instrument has been laid before parliament that will amend the Extradition Act 2003 (Designation of Part 2 Territories) Order 2003 SI No 3334 to allow India 65 days from the date of arrest under a provisional warrant for the service of the extradition papers.
19 EA 2003 s78(2)(b).

- particulars of the offence specified in the request;[20]
- in an accusation case, a warrant for the person's arrest that has been issued in the category 2 territory;[21]
- in a conviction case, a certificate of the conviction issued in the category 2 territory and (if the person has been sentenced) of the sentence imposed.[22]

4.38 Once the papers have been received the judge must then proceed to fix a date within which the extradition hearing must begin. This period is two months starting from the date the papers are received.[23] In reality, the court will fix a date beyond the two-month deadline. In order to do this, the extradition hearing will be 'formally opened' and then adjourned with no decisions made. Opening or starting the extradition hearing and adjourning it in this way means that the two-month period set down in the Act has been complied with. There is no timeframe within which the extradition hearing must be concluded.

First hearing – full request

4.39 As with the first hearing under a provisional arrest, the judge must inform the person that he or she is either accused of the commission of an offence in a category 2 territory or that he or she is alleged to be unlawfully at large after conviction. The consent procedure must then be given (unless the requested person is subject to a charge in the United Kingdom or is serving a sentence of imprisonment) and then the judge must either remand the person in custody or on bail.

4.40 The judge must fix the date on which the extradition hearing is to begin. This must be within two months, starting from the date on which the person first appears before the court.[24] If the extradition hearing does not begin on or before the date fixed, the judge must order the discharge of that person if such an application is made.

4.41 The judge can fix a later date for the extradition hearing if he or she believes it is in the interests of justice to do so. This is predicated on the extradition hearing having been formally opened and adjourned with no substantive decisions having been made.

20 EA 2003 s78(2)(c).
21 EA 2003 s78(2)(d).
22 EA 2003 s78(2)(e).
23 EA 2003 s76(3).
24 EA 2003 s75(2).

Case management forms

4.42 The case management forms discussed in chapter 7 do not need to be completed in Part 2 provisional warrant cases. However, the court will still expect the advocate to identify the issues at the initial hearing on a full request for extradition or when full papers have been served following arrest on a provisional warrant.

Figure 4.1: Process following arrest under EA 2003 Part 2

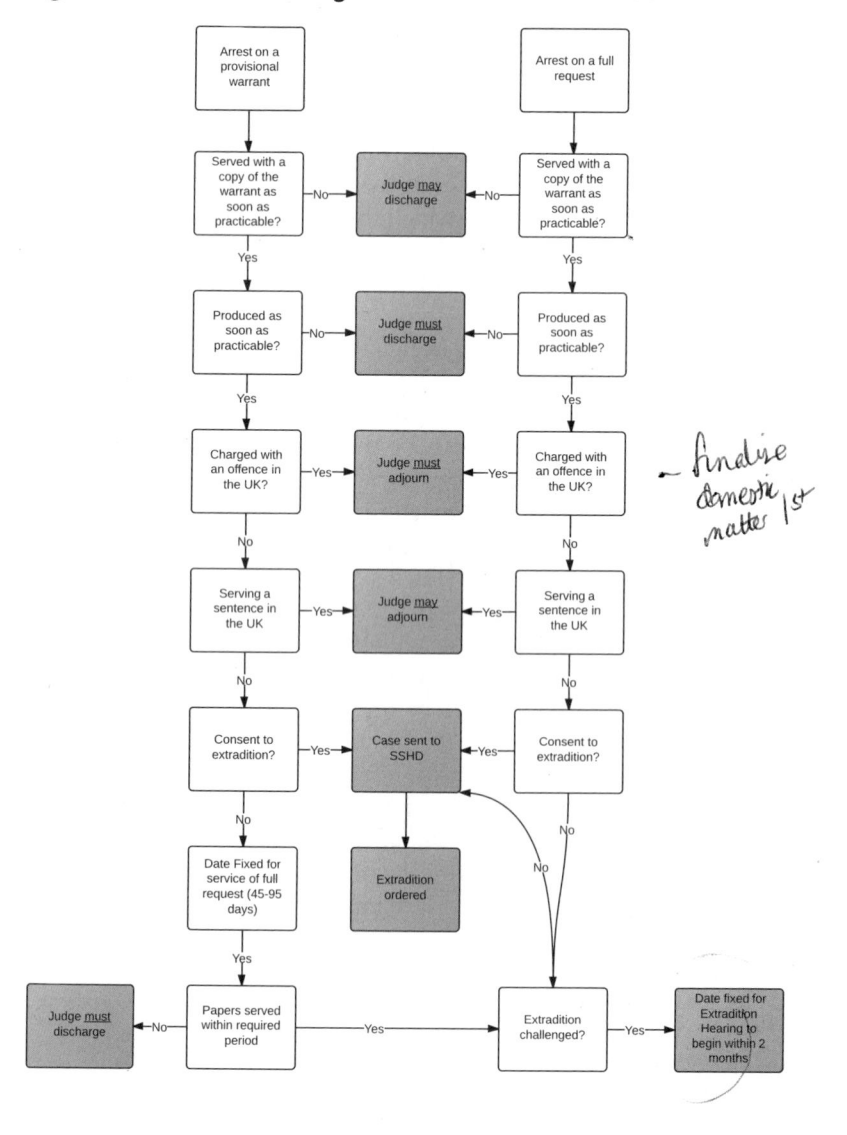

```
                    Arrest on a                              Arrest on a full
                    provisional                              request
                    warrant
                         │                                        │
                         ▼                                        ▼
                  Served with a        Judge may          Served with a
                  copy of the     ──No── discharge ──No── copy of the
                  warrant as                               warrant as
                  soon as                                  soon as
                  practicable?                             practicable?
                         │Yes                                   │Yes
                         ▼                                        ▼
                  Produced as         Judge must          Produced as
                  soon as        ──No── discharge ──No── soon as
                  practicable?                            practicable?
                         │Yes                                   │Yes
                         ▼                                        ▼
                  Charged with        Judge must          Charged with
                  an offence in  ──Yes── adjourn ──Yes── an offence in
                  the UK?                                  the UK?
                         │No                                    │No
                         ▼                                        ▼
                  Serving a           Judge may           Serving a
                  sentence in    ──Yes── adjourn ──Yes── sentence in
                  the UK                                   the UK
                         │No                                    │No
                         ▼                                        ▼
                  Consent to          Case sent to        Consent to
                  extradition?   ──Yes── SSHD    ──Yes── extradition?
                         │No              │                    │No
                         ▼                ▼                      
                  Date Fixed for     Extradition
                  service of full    ordered
                  request (45-95
                  days)
                         │Yes
                         ▼
   Judge must      Papers served                Extradition          Date fixed for
   discharge ──No── within required ──Yes──     challenged? ──Yes── Extradition
                   period                                             Hearing to
                                                                      begin within 2
                                                                      months
```

— Analyse domestic matter 1st

Initial stages of the extradition hearing

4.43 At the outset of the extradition hearing the appropriate judge must decide whether the documents sent by the SSHD consist of (or include) the information that is set out in paragraph 4.37 above.

4.44 If any of the documents referred to above are not before the appropriate judge he or she *must* order the person's discharge. If they are all present the appropriate judge must then consider whether:

- the person appearing or brought before him is the person whose extradition is requested;[25]
- the offence specified in the request is an extradition offence;[26]
- copies of the documents sent to the appropriate judge by the SSHD have been served upon the person whose extradition is sought.[27]

4.45 Identity – as in EAW cases – is to be determined by the appropriate judge on the balance of probabilities.[28]

4.46 If the judge decides any of the questions in paragraph 4.44 in the negative he or she must order the person's discharge.[29]

4.47 Once the preliminary stages of the extradition hearing have been conducted and the questions answered in the affirmative, the appropriate judge must then proceed under section 79 and consider whether the person's extradition is barred.

Challenges to extradition

4.48 Challenges to extradition are dealt with in chapter 6. In short, the following bars can be raised to resist extradition:

- section 80 – the rule against double jeopardy;
- section 81 – extraneous considerations;
- section 82 – passage of time;
- section 83 – hostage-taking considerations;
- section 83A – forum (not yet in force);
- sections 84 and 86 – prima facie case;
- section 91 – physical or mental condition.

---

25 EA 2003 s78(4)(a).
26 EA 2003 s78(4)(b).
27 EA 2003 s78(4)(c).
28 EA 2003 s78(5).
29 EA 2003 s78(6).

4.49 A challenge can also be brought on the basis that the warrant does not contain sufficient particulars of the offence. Although the wording in section 78(4)(c) is narrower than than in section 2(4)(c) (for Part 1 cases) it was held in the case of *Dudko v The Government of the Russian Federation*[30] by Thomas LJ that: '[...] the provision in s.78(4)(c) should be interpreted to the same effect as that in s.2(4)(c) using solely, as Dyson LJ suggested, the plain and ordinary meaning of that section without any gloss'.

4.50 The requested person could also seek to resist extradition on the basis that the conduct alleged would not amount to an extradition offence had the conduct occurred in England and Wales and that the request for extradition is not valid because it does not contain the papers referred to in section 70(9).

4.51 As with Part 1 requests, in a conviction case, the court must consider whether the person was convicted in his absence (EA 2003 s85). If he or she was, the court must consider whether the person deliberately absented him or herself from his trial. If he or she was not deliberately absent from his or her trial, the court must consider whether he or she would be entitled to a retrial or (on appeal) to a review amounting to a retrial.

4.52 The requested person also has the protection of the Human Rights Act 1998 and the appropriate judge must consider whether the person's extradition would be compatible with ECHR rights (EA 2003 s87): see chapter 7. Finally, the court has the inherent power to stay proceedings as an abuse of process (see paragraph 6.72).

Extradition offences

4.53 If the conduct alleged in the extradition request does not meet the requirements of 'dual criminality' then the judge must order the person's discharge. Section 137 of the Act deals with accusation cases and section 138 with conviction cases. The most common conduct that constitutes an extradition offence can be found in sections 137(2) and 138(2), although the representative should also be aware of the other subsections in sections 137 and 138.

4.54 Section 137(2) states that:

> The conduct constitutes an extradition offence in relation to the category 2 territory if these conditions are satisfied –
> (a) the conduct occurs in the category 2 territory;

---

30 [2010] EWHC 1125 (Admin) at para 16.

(b) the conduct would constitute an offence under the law of the relevant part of the United Kingdom punishable with imprisonment or another form of detention for a term of 12 months or a greater punishment if it occurred in that part of the United Kingdom;
(c) the conduct is so punishable under the law of the category 2 territory (however it is described in that law).

4.55 The requirement in (b) is different from that which is required under Part 1. The conduct not only has to be an offence in the relevant part of the United Kingdom had it occurred there, it must also carry a sentence of at least 12 months' imprisonment. This means that conduct that would be extraditable under Part 1 of the Act – such as section 5 of the Public Order Act 1986 or assaulting a police constable in the execution of his duty – would not amount to an extradition offence under Part 2 because it would not satisfy the requirement that it is punishable with a form of detention of 12 months or greater in the UK.

4.56 The provisions for those convicted and sentenced also impose a similar requirement that the conduct carries a sentence of 12 months or greater in the United Kingdom. The difference for conviction extradition requests is that the sentence passed in the category 2 territory has to be for a term of four months or greater. Section 138 states that:

The conduct constitutes an extradition offence in relation to the category 2 territory if these conditions are satisfied –
(a) the conduct occurs in the category 2 territory;
(b) the conduct would constitute an offence under the law of the relevant part of the United Kingdom punishable with imprisonment or another form of detention for a term of 12 months or a greater punishment if it occurred in that part of the United Kingdom;
(c) a sentence of imprisonment or another form of detention for a term of 4 months or a greater punishment has been imposed in the category 2 territory in respect of the conduct.

4.57 Conduct that occurs outside of the category 2 territory can also be an extradition offence if it would constitute an extraterritorial offence under the relevant part of the United Kingdom. For accusation cases the offence would have to provide for a sentence of 12 months' imprisonment or greater in the category 2 territory and in the United Kingdom.[31] For conviction cases the sentence imposed in the category 2 territory has to be four months' imprisonment or greater and punishable in the United Kingdom with at least 12 months' imprisonment.

4.58 Conduct can be an extradition offence if it occurs outside the category 2 territory and no part of it in the United Kingdom; the conduct

---

31 EA 2003 ss137(3) and 138(3).

would be an offence in the United Kingdom punishable with at least 12 months' imprisonment and it is so punishable in the category 2 territory (in accusation cases) or a sentence of imprisonment of four months or greater has been imposed by the category 2 territory (in conviction cases).[32]

4.59 Finally, conduct can amount to an extradition offence if it occurred outside the category 2 territory and no part of it occurred in the United Kingdom, is punishable under the law of the category 2 territory with 12 months' imprisonment (in accusation cases) or four months' imprisonment has been imposed (in conviction cases) and the conduct constitutes or if committed in the United Kingdom would constitute an offence as set out in sections 137(6) and 138(6).

4.60 The flowcharts opposite at figure 4.2 and figure 4.3 illustrate the various ways described above in which conduct may be an extradition offence under sections 137 and 138 respectively. These flowcharts should be used in conjunction with the legislation, bearing in mind the provisions of sections 137(8) and (8) for tax or customs offences, and the rule in *Osunta v The Public Prosecutor's Office in Dusseldorf*,[33] which allows for excision from the warrant of conduct that would not amount to an extradition offence

Prima facie case

4.61 One of the main differences between extradition requests from Part 1 and Part 2 is the requirement for the requesting state to establish a prima face case. This is only applicable for the Part 2 countries that have *not* been designated by the SSHD. If a country has been designated, they need only provide 'information' about the accusation or conviction. This requirement is often satisfied in an affidavit from the investigating police officer or the prosecutor.

4.62 The following countries are *not* required to provide evidence in support of their extradition requests:
- Albania, Andorra, Armenia, Australia, Azerbaijan, Bosnia and Herzegovina, Canada, Croatia, Georgia, Iceland, Israel, Liechtenstein, Macedonia FYR, Moldova, Montenegro, New Zealand, Norway, Russian Federation, Serbia, South Africa, Switzerland, Turkey, Ukraine and the United States.

32 EA 2003 ss137(4) and 138(4).
33 [2007] EWHC 1562 (Admin).

Extradition requests from outside the European Union   55

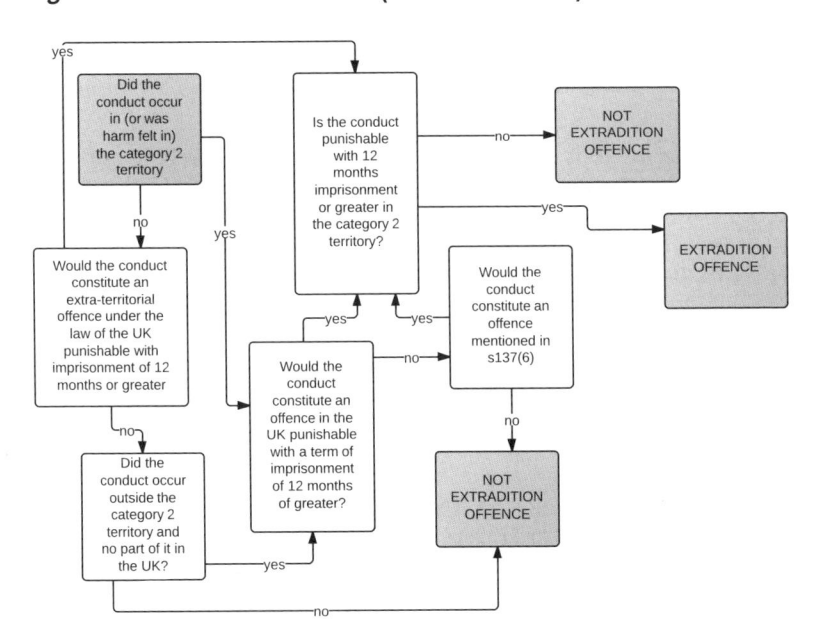

Figure 4.2: Extradition offences (accusation cases)

Figure 4.3: Extradition offences (conviction cases)

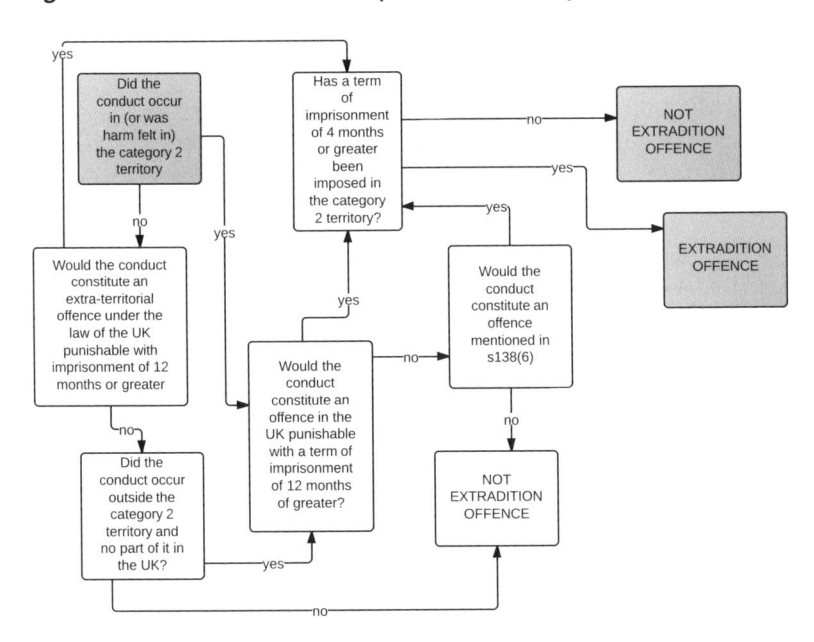

4.63 Where required to do so a court must consider whether the requesting state can establish a prima facie case. Section 84 deals with cases where the requested person has not been convicted and section 86 where a person has been convicted. Sections 84 and 86 are in identical terms:

> (1) If the judge is required to proceed under this section he must decide whether there is evidence which would be sufficient to make a case requiring an answer by the person if the proceedings were the summary trial of an information against him.
> (2) In deciding the question in subsection (1) the judge may treat a statement made by a person in a document as admissible evidence of a fact if –
>   (a) the statement is made by the person to a police officer or another person charged with the duty of investigating offences or charging offenders, and
>   (b) direct oral evidence by the person of the fact would be admissible.
> (3) In deciding whether to treat a statement made by a person in a document as admissible evidence of a fact, the judge must in particular have regard –
>   (a) to the nature and source of the document;
>   (b) to whether or not, having regard to the nature and source of the document and to any other circumstances that appear to the judge to be relevant, it is likely that the document is authentic;
>   (c) to the extent to which the statement appears to supply evidence which would not be readily available if the statement were not treated as being admissible evidence of the fact;
>   (d) to the relevance of the evidence that the statement appears to supply to any issue likely to have to be determined by the judge in deciding the question in subsection (1);
>   (e) to any risk that the admission or exclusion of the statement will result in unfairness to the person whose extradition is sought, having regard in particular to whether it is likely to be possible to controvert the statement if the person making it does not attend to give oral evidence in the proceedings.
> (4) A summary in a document of a statement made by a person must be treated as a statement made by the person in the document for the purposes of subsection (2).
> (5) If the judge decides the question in subsection (1) in the negative he must order the person's discharge.
> (6) If the judge decides that question in the affirmative he must proceed under section 87.
> (7) If the judge is required to proceed under this section and the category 2 territory to which extradition is requested is designated

for the purposes of this section by order made by the Secretary of State –
(a) the judge must not decide under subsection (1), and
(b) he must proceed under section 87.[34]

4.64 The test to be applied by the court in order to determine whether there is a case to answer is whether the prosecution evidence, taken at its highest, is such that no jury properly directed could convict upon it. In *R on the application of Philip Harkins v SSHD*,[35] Lloyd Jones J at paragraph 31 approved the test used by the judge in the magistrates' court. The test was expressed by Tubbs DJ in the following terms:

> The evidence produced would, according to the Law of England and Wales, make a case requiring an answer by the defence if the proceedings were for trial here on these charges so there is sufficient evidence to justify an order for committal.

4.65 It is generally accepted that if the court finds that there is a case to answer, the defence are entitled to call evidence in order to demonstrate that, in the light of all the evidence tendered by the requesting state, there is insufficient evidence to establish a case to answer. For this reason, if a challenge is made under EA 2003 s84 or s86 it will allow the defence to properly test the case.

The role of the Secretary of State

4.66 In Part 1 cases it is the appropriate judge that orders a person's extradition. In Part 2 cases the SSHD performs this function.

4.67 Once a case is sent by the appropriate judge to the SSHD she has two months to make an order for extradition. The two-month period starts on the day on which the case is sent to the SSHD. Thus, if a case is sent to the SSHD on, for example, 17 May, she must order extradition by midnight on 16 July. If she does not, the requested person *must* be discharged.[36] That time period can be extended on application to WMC.

---

34 Subsections (8)–(9) omitted.
35 [2007] EWHC 639 (Admin).
36 *Zaporozhchenkov Westminster Magistrates' Court* [2011] EWHC 34 (Admin).

Person charged with an offence in the United Kingdom/ sentenced to imprisonment

4.68 If a person is charged with an offence in the United Kingdom while the case is pending before the SSHD then the SSHD *must* not make a decision with regard to the person's extradition until the charge is disposed of; the charge is withdrawn; proceedings are discontinued or an order is made for the charge to lie on file.[37]

4.69 If a sentence of imprisonment has been imposed in respect of the offences charged then the SSHD *may* defer making a decision with regard to the person's extradition until the person is released from detention.[38]

4.70 If the case is sent to the SSHD by the appropriate judge and the person is serving a sentence of imprisonment, the SSHD may also defer in making a decision with regards to the person's extradition until the person is released from detention.[39]

Representations to the SSHD

4.71 During the first four weeks following the case being sent to the SSHD, the SSHD cannot make an order for extradition. This is to allow for representations to be made by the requested person. If representations are not received in the four weeks following the case being sent, then the SSHD need not consider them.[40] This four-week period may be extended on application to the SSHD. The SSHD need not delay the making of a decision during the first four weeks if the person consented to extradition.

4.72 The SSHD has a limited remit when considering representations. Representations can be made regarding:
- the death penalty;
- specialty;
- earlier extradition from a category 1 territory;
- earlier extradition from a category 2 territory.

4.73 The SSHD is required to consider the above issues whether or not representations are received. If no issues are found, she will order extradition. If representations are received and rejected by the SSHD

---

37 EA 2003 s97(2).
38 EA 2003 s92(3).
39 EA 2003 s98(2).
40 EA 2003 s93(5).

then an extradition order will be signed. An order for extradition (or discharge) must be made under the hand of one of the following[41]:
- the SSHD;
- a minister of state;
- a parliamentary under-secretary of state;
- a senior official.[42]

4.74 If the representations are rejected, the requested person and his legal representatives will receive a response from the SSHD to the representations together with the order for extradition. If the representations are accepted the SSHD will order the person's discharge from the extradition request.

4.75 Once the extradition order is received the requested person has 14 days in which to lodge an appeal from the date the SSHD informs the requested person (or his legal representatives) that an order for extradition has been made.[43] If no appeal is lodged the person must be extradited to the category 2 territory within 28 days of the decision of the SSHD. This period can be extended on an application to the court.

4.76 If the requested person is not removed within the relevant period an application should be made to the appropriate judge at WMC for discharge.[44] Discharge must follow unless reasonable cause can be shown for the delay in removal.[45]

Competing extradition requests

4.77 There may be very rare occasions where two different category 2 territories make extradition requests for the same person. Under EA 2003 s126 if the SSHD receives a valid request for extradition, the person is in the United Kingdom and before the person is extradited the SSHD receives another valid request for the person's extradition the SSHD may:

---

41 EA 2003 s101.
42 A senior official is defined as a member of the senior civil service (grade 7 or above) or a member of the senior management structure of Her Majesty's Diplomatic Service.
43 EA 2003 s103(9).
44 EA 2003 s117(3).
45 *R on the application of Tajik v City of Westminster Magistrates' Court* [2012] EWHC 3347 (Admin).

- order proceedings on one of the requests to be deferred until the other one has been disposed of, if neither of the requests has been disposed of;[46] or
- order the person's extradition to be deferred until the other request has been disposed of, if an order for extradition has already been made.[47]

4.78 The SSHD must take into account the following factors when applying section 126(2):
- the relative seriousness of the offences concerned;
- the place where each offence was committed (or alleged to have been committed);
- the date when each request was received;
- whether, in the case of each offence, the person is accused or unlawfully at large after conviction.

Competing EAW and Part 2 requests for extradition

4.79 In even rarer scenarios there may be a situation where there are in existence an EAW and a Part 2 extradition request for the same person. Where there is a valid EAW in existence and a valid Part 2 request, and the person has not been extradited on either, the SSHD may:[48]
- order proceedings on either the EAW or the Part 2 request to be deferred until the other one has been disposed of;
- order the person's extradition in pursuance of the EAW to be deferred until the Part 2 request has been disposed of, if an order for extradition has been made on the EAW;
- order the person's extradition on the Part 2 request to be deferred until the EAW has been disposed of, if an order for extradition on the Part 2 request has been made.

4.80 The factors to be taken into consideration by the SSHD are:[49]
- the relative seriousness of the offences concerned;
- the place where each offence was committed (or alleged to have been committed);
- the date when the EAW was issued and the date when the Part 2 request was received;

---

46 EA 2003 s126(2)(a).
47 EA 2003 s126(2)(b).
48 EA 2003 s179.
49 EA 2003 s179(3)(a)–(d).

- whether the person is accused or alleged to be unlawfully at large.

4.81 The SSHD is under no obligation to inform a requested person of a competing request and as a matter of policy the Home Office will not inform a requested person of the existence of a request until the person has been arrested.

CHAPTER 5

Attending the client

5.1	Introduction
5.2	**Seeing the client**
5.4	Sections 4 and 7 of the Extradition Act 2003
5.6	Persons facing charges in the United Kingdom
5.7	Specialty and consent
5.11	Time on remand
5.12	Personal circumstances
	General instructions
	Bail instructions
5.14	Awareness of proceedings
5.15	Immigration status
5.16	Issues to be taken
5.18	Procedure if extradition is ordered
5.19	Legal aid

Introduction

5.1 Often the first interaction a lawyer will have with the requested person will be in the cells at WMC. Time will often be limited, particularly for the duty solicitor, and it is therefore important to be able both to give and to obtain the necessary information as quickly as possible. This chapter looks at what should be covered in the first meeting with the client, in particular how to explain the law and procedure. It also looks at the information that should be obtained at the first meeting in order to be in a position properly to represent the requested person at the initial hearing.

Seeing the client

5.2 Requested persons are unlikely to be familiar with the extradition process. When acting for those arrested on EAWs, it will be necessary briefly to explain the nature of the fast-track extradition procedure within Europe, specifically that the court's primary concern is to ensure that the procedural requirements have been met, and that the purpose of the hearing in this country is not to decide whether and by whom the offence was committed – guilt and innocence are for the courts in the requesting state to determine. Given the limited amount of time that will often be available, this should be explained at the outset. It is important for clients to be given a realistic assessment of their prospects of success: they should be informed of the difficulties inherent in contesting extradition, and that most requested persons are eventually extradited.

5.3 Using the procedure that the court will follow as a way of structuring the interview, the preliminary points regarding the question of production, service of the warrant (EA 2003 s4) and identity (EA 2003 s7) should be covered with the requested person. The law in relation to these areas is set out in detail in chapter 8. In brief, however, the requested person must be given a copy of the EAW (in both languages) as soon as practicable after arrest; failure to comply means a judge *may* grant his or her discharge. In addition, the requested person must be produced before WMC as soon as practicable; failure to comply means a judge *must* discharge the requested person. In relation to section 7, the judge must decide, on a balance of probabilities, whether the person before him or her is the person in respect of whom the warrant was issued.

Sections 4 and 7 of the Extradition Act 2003

5.4 While it will often be clear from the arrest statement whether or not the warrant has been served and whether the requested person has been produced as soon as practicable, it is always worth checking these points briefly with the client. If it is apparent from the arrest statement that the warrant has not been served, or that the person has not been produced as soon as practicable, these points will need to be covered in more detail. In particular, should there have been any obvious delay, a full chronology of events should be taken from the client, along with his or her understanding of any cause for the delay.

5.5 The question of identity (section 7) will often have been resolved by the arresting officer asking the person to confirm their name and date of birth, and seizing any identity documents in his or her possession. If the requested person disputes that he or she is the person in respect of whom the warrant was issued, it will be necessary to take full instructions as to identity. Requested persons should, however, be warned that disputing identity could have an impact upon their credibility at the extradition hearing and their prospects of obtaining bail.

Persons facing charges in the United Kingdom

5.6 If the requested person has been produced from a prison, he or she is very likely to be a serving prisoner. The court will ask for confirmation of the early release date for any such requested persons, as the extradition hearing may be adjourned while the sentence is served. In the case of persons facing charges in England and Wales, the court must adjourn proceedings until the domestic case is disposed of.[1] Relevant dates should be established with the requested person. There is no equivalent provision for those on UK police bail. While requested persons in these circumstances may sometimes wish to return to the requesting state as quickly as possible, they will of course need to be warned about the consequences of failing to surrender in this jurisdiction.

---

1 EA 2003 s214 states that a charge is disposed of when a person is either acquitted of it, or, if convicted, when there is no further possibility of an appeal against conviction.

Specialty and consent

5.7 The rule of specialty prevents a person being prosecuted in the requesting state for conduct not detailed in the warrant; it is therefore an important protection for those whose extradition is sought. All requested persons should be made aware of their 'specialty' rights as they will be asked in court whether or not they consent to their extradition. If they do consent, they will waive their specialty rights. It will almost always be in the requested person's interest not to consent, so as to preserve specialty protection. Clients who do not wish to contest their extradition can sometimes believe that a refusal to consent will be seen as a failure to co-operate with the court process – it is worth emphasising that this is not the case.

5.8 The advantage of consenting to extradition is that it will result in an expedited process: a person who has consented cannot appeal, and he or she will not, therefore, have to wait for the seven-day appeal period following the making of the extradition order to pass.

5.9 Consent must be given in writing and is irrevocable.[2] The legal adviser will have a form that can be completed during the hearing for those who wish to consent. The requested person must have had the opportunity to receive legal advice before giving consent.

5.10 It is worth noting that, if the requesting state does wish to prosecute an extradited person for offences for which they have not been extradited, it is possible for that state to seek consent from the United Kingdom to deal with the person for the further offences.[3] Consent will be sought at a hearing where the person is unlikely to be represented. The grounds on which consent can be refused are limited.

Time on remand

5.11 Requested persons should be advised that any time spent on remand in the United Kingdom will count towards any sentence in the requesting state.[4] The requested state has the responsibility under the Framework Decision of transmitting information about the duration of detention to the requesting state at the time of surrender. To fulfil this requirement, SOCA should provide the requesting state with a notice setting out the days spent in detention on the day that he or she is returned to the requesting state. Note that this does not apply to

---

2 EA 2003 s45 or s127.
3 EA 2003 s54 and s129.
4 Article 26 Framework Decision 2002.

Part 2 countries – it will be necessary to look at the specific arrangements with a Part 2 country in order to determine whether time spent on remand will count towards any sentence. In some cases, time spent on a curfew will count towards a sentence in the requesting state, but this will vary according to the specific circumstances of the requested person and the jurisdiction. It will therefore be necessary, in appropriate cases, to check with a lawyer in the requesting state whether time spent on a curfew will count towards a sentence.

Personal circumstances

5.12 Details of the client's personal circumstances should be taken. If it is clear that extradition will be contested, completion of the legal aid form will provide a good deal of necessary background information.[5] An interview with a client will inevitably be determined by the facts of the case; however the following questions should assist in providing a starting point both in advising as to any grounds on which the requested person may challenge the extradition proceedings and in preparing for a bail application:

General instructions

- When did he or she come to the United Kingdom?
- Why did he or she come to the United Kingdom?
- Has he or she been back to the requesting state?
- Is the requested person aware of the criminal proceedings (see paragraph 5.14 below)?
- Was he or she present at the trial (conviction cases). If not, why not?
- Does he or she have family in the United Kingdom/ requesting state? Are they dependent? Full details should be taken;
- Is he or she employed? If so, what are the hours of work? Is it possible to contact the employer?
- What is his or her housing situation? How long has he or she been at the present address?
- Where was he or she arrested? At home/work?
- Has the requested person instructed lawyers in the requesting state?
- What is his or her immigration status (see paragraph 5.15 below)?

---

5 Time should, however, not be wasted on completion of the legal aid form if it is clear that an extradition order will be made that day.

- Does he or she have any health problems?
- Why does the requested person think that he or she should not be extradited?

Bail instructions

- Is any security or surety available? Contact numbers will need to be obtained.
- What is the nearest police station to the requested person's address? If possible, attempt to find out the opening hours prior to the hearing.
- Where are the identity documents of the requested person? Is it possible to obtain those that have not been seized by the police in order to surrender them?
- Does the requested person have any commitments that would make compliance with a curfew or a condition to report to the police station difficult?
- What are the circumstances of any offending on bail/failure to surrender that appears on the list of previous convictions.

5.13 See chapter 8 for further information on making a bail application and refer to the checklists at appendices D and E.

Awareness of proceedings

5.14 The question of whether the requested person had been aware of the allegation or conviction prior to arrest will be relevant for any passage of time point: his or her knowledge of any outstanding proceedings will go to the question of the requested person's status as a fugitive. In the case of a conviction warrant, it will be crucial to ascertain for the purpose of EA 2003 s20 whether or not he or she was present upon conviction (see paragraph 6.23 in relation to EA 2003 s14).

Immigration status

5.15 The large majority of those facing EAWs will be exercising their right of residence in the United Kingdom as EU citizens. Sections 39 and 121 of the EA Act 2003, however, prevent the extradition of a person who has claimed asylum after a warrant or request has been certified, until the determination of that claim. Similarly, refugees cannot be returned to their home country (see paragraph 6.78 for more detail).

Issues to be taken

5.16 It is worth briefly explaining to the client the most common bars and challenges to extradition. Not only will this assist the requested person's understanding of the extradition process (and the limited grounds on which it is possible to contest extradition), it will also ensure that no possible grounds of challenge are overlooked. The list below sets out those most commonly relied upon:

- rule against double jeopardy;
- extraneous considerations;
- passage of time;
- human rights considerations:
  - article 2 – right to life;
  - article 3 – prohibition of torture and ill-treatment;
  - article 5 – right to liberty and security;
  - article 6 – right to a fair trial;
  - article 8 – right to respect private and family life;
- conviction in absence; and
- physical or mental health.

5.17 In some jurisdictions, it will be possible to persuade the judicial authority to withdraw the warrant by negotiating a voluntary return to the issuing state. This is known as 'compromising the warrant'. Given that a negotiated return will be on bail, this will be preferable to a return under a warrant. Indeed, it is far more likely that an extradition request will be defeated in this way than if surrender is contested in the United Kingdom and for this reason it is important that clients who wish to contest their extradition are made aware of this possibility. In order to pursue this route, it will be necessary for the requested person to instruct (and pay for) lawyers in the requesting state, who may be able to secure the withdrawal of the warrant on condition that the requested person will, for example, pay a security and return voluntarily or enter a guilty plea.[6] This will of course be more difficult for those in custody who will need assistance from a friend or relative should they wish to pursue this. In general, the courts are reluctant to adjourn extradition proceedings to allow the requested person to attempt to compromise the warrant. See also chapter 12 on transfer of sentenced prisoners.

---

6 This is sometimes referred to as an 'iron letter'. See chapter 12.

Procedure if extradition is ordered

5.18 Requested persons should be advised of the timescales that apply if extradition is ordered. EA 2003 s35 provides that a requested person must be extradited before the end of a ten-day period, starting with either the day on which extradition is ordered (if the person has consented to be extradited) or on the eighth day after extradition has been ordered (ie after the period in which a person can lodge an appeal has passed, for those who have not consented to be extradited). Section 35 does, however, allow the judge and the issuing authority to agree a later date. In practice, extensions of time are frequently sought and requested persons are rarely returned within the time limits set out in section 35. Where a person has not been removed within the required period, it is possible to apply for discharge: see paragraph 8.66.

Legal aid

5.19 Forms CRM14 and 15 should be completed as with any other legal aid case and submitted to the court on the day of the first appearance for those cases where extradition is being contested. The majority of those arrested on EAWs will be in employment – if this is the case, they will need to provide supporting documentation unless they have been remanded in custody. Partners of applicants are also required to sign the form. Where a person has been remanded in custody, he or she can self-certify as to wages on form CRM15 and his or her partner need not sign the form (although note that the fact that the partner is unable to sign the form must be fully explained).[7] For those in custody, as long as the forms have been fully completed and they are eligible, the grant of legal aid should not, in theory, be problematic. Unfortunately this is not the case in practice, and even those who have fully completed the form, self-certified and are apparently eligible will (depending on how busy court staff are) be likely to face delays and adjournments while awaiting the outcome of legal aid applications.[8] For those granted bail, they should be advised to prioritise obtaining supporting documentation for the legal aid application in order to ensure that it is dealt with expeditiously.

---

7 Criminal Legal Aid Manual, April 2013, paras 4.4.3 and 19.8 and 4.4.7 (www.justice.gov.uk/downloads/legal-aid/eligibility/criminal-legal-aid-manual.pdf).

8 See the case of *Stopyra v District Court of Lublin, Poland* [2012] EWHC 1787 (Admin) 28 June 2012, in which there was an 11-week delay in the grant of legal aid: the Divisional Court pointed out the necessity of reform to prevent further breaches of the UK's treaty obligations.

CHAPTER 6

Bars to extradition

6.1	Introduction
6.3	**Statutory bars to extradition**
6.5	Double jeopardy – sections 12/80
6.10	Extraneous considerations – sections 13/81
	Test
6.23	Passage of time – sections 14/82
	Fugitives and passage of time • Injustice or oppression • Cases where passage of time has barred extradition
6.45	Person's age – section 15
6.47	Hostage taking considerations – sections 16/83
6.49	Specialty – sections 17/95
6.53	Earlier extradition – sections 18/19/19A/96/96A
6.55	Forum – sections 19B/83A
6.58	Death penalty – section 94
6.59	Conviction in absence – sections 20/85
6.64	Physical or mental health – sections 25/91
6.70	Abuse of process
6.75	Immigration status

Introduction

6.1 There are a limited number of grounds that can be relied upon to resist extradition. This chapter will look at the statutory bars to extradition, which are set out in EA 2003 s11. It will then go on to look at the other grounds for resisting extradition, namely conviction in absence, physical or mental condition, the forum bar (yet to be implemented), death penalty and finally abuse of process. The judge will follow these in the order set out in the statute in looking at each ground during the extradition hearing (if raised). The structure of the Act envisages a 'step-by-step' approach by the judge (see figure 6.1).[1]

6.2 These bars are common to both Part 1 and Part 2 cases, with the exception of age (which only applies in Part 1 cases) and death penalty (which only applies to Part 2 cases).

Statutory bars to extradition

6.3 Under section 11 (Part 1 cases) and section 79 (Part 2 cases) the judge must decide whether a person's extradition is barred by reason of:

- sections 12/80 – the rule against double jeopardy;
- sections 13/81 – extraneous considerations;
- sections 14/82 – passage of time;
- section 15 – the person's age;
- sections 16/83 – hostage-taking considerations;
- sections 17/95 – specialty;
- sections 18, 19 and 19A/96 and 96A – earlier extradition from territory or by the ICC;
- sections 19B/83A – forum; and
- section 94 – death penalty.

6.4 Having considered these, the judge will go on to look at conviction in absence (s20/85); human rights (s21/87) and whether a person's mental or physical condition should prevent extradition (s25/91). This chapter will follow the statutory numbering in looking at each of these in turn, and end by looking at abuse of process, which, although not a statutory bar, is within the court's inherent jurisdiction and has on occasion prevented a person's extradition. Human rights considerations are explored in chapter 7.

---

1 *Mihai Sonea v Mehedinti District Court* [2009] EWHC 89 (Admin) at para 16.

Bars to extradition 73

Figure 6.1: Extradition hearing

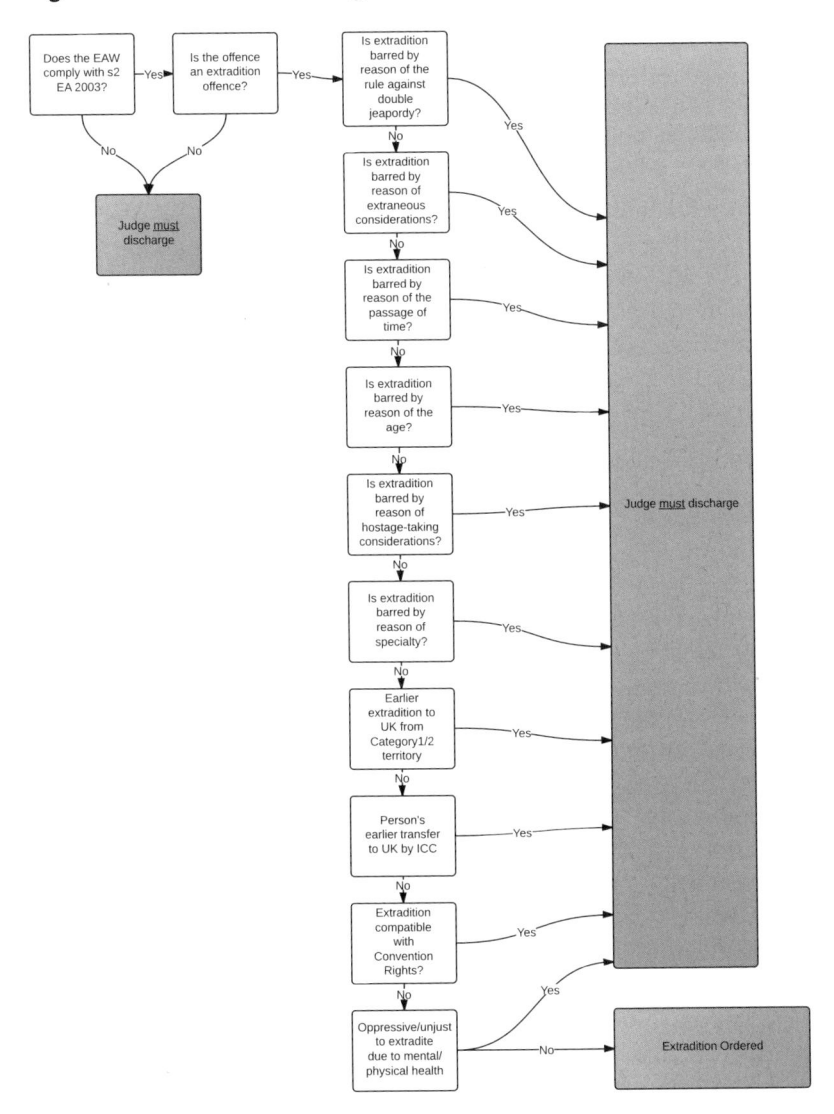

Double jeopardy – sections 12/80

6.5 Section 12 provides that:

> A person's extradition to a category 1 territory is barred by reason of the rule against double jeopardy if (and only if) it appears that he would be entitled to be discharged under any rule of law relating to previous acquittal or conviction.

6.6 In order for the bar to apply the requested person must previously have been put in peril of conviction for the offence for which he or she now faces extradition.[2] The court must therefore assess whether the requested person has been previously acquitted or convicted of the same offence, or an offence arising out of the same or substantially the same facts as those set out in the warrant.[3] Any conviction or acquittal must be final, and finality 'is to be judged by the process in the requesting state'.[4] The judge is then required to proceed on the basis of two statutory assumptions:[5]

- the English courts had jurisdiction to try him or her for those offences and
- he or she was facing trial for them in England.

The court has then to ask itself whether English rules of law on double jeopardy would apply.[6]

6.7 It is important to bear in mind that the doctrine of *autrefois convict* can only be relied upon once sentence has been passed,[7] although there is no requirement for the sentence to have been completed, nor indeed commenced.

6.8 This is a bar to extradition that is likely to become of increasing relevance, and can arise in cases where there is an element of cross-border activity, such that one country has already taken action against

---

2 *Connelly v DPP* [1964] AC 1254 (HL), *Mitchell v High Court of Boulogne sur mer* [2007] EWHC 2006 (Admin), *Zdinjak v Croatia* [2012] EWHC 1554.
3 *Fofana v Deputy Prosecutor Thubin Tribunal De Grande Instance De Meaux, France* [2006] EWHC 744 (Admin).
4 *Oncel v Governor of Brixton Prison, Government of the Republic of Turkey* [2001] EWHC 1142 (Admin) at para 32.
5 In relation to Part 1 cases, the judge is required to assume (a) that the conduct constituting the extradition offence constituted an offence in the part of the UK where the judge exercises jurisdiction and that (b) that the person were charged with the extradition offence in that part of the United Kingdom. In relation to Part 2 cases (under EA 2003 s80, the judge is not required to make these assumptions.
6 *Hamburg Public Prosecutor's Office v Altun* [2011] EWHC 397 (Admin) at para 19.
7 *Richards v The Queen* [1993] AC 217, PC.

the requested person. A person, for example, committing a customs fraud may commit an offence in two jurisdictions. It may be that a prosecution in jurisdiction A deals with one part of the conduct and that jurisdiction B then seeks to prosecute for another part of the conduct or indeed a larger conspiracy that subsumes the element that has already been prosecuted. Depending on the particular facts of the case, this may give rise to an argument that the requested person's extradition falls within the double jeopardy bar.

6.9 To establish this bar, evidence from both lay and expert witnesses will almost certainly be required.

Extraneous considerations – sections 13/81

6.10 Section 13 states:

> A person's extradition to a category 1 territory is barred by reason of extraneous considerations if (and only if) it appears that –
> (a) the Part 1 warrant issued in respect of him (though purporting to be issued on account of the extradition offence) is in fact issued for the purpose of prosecuting or punishing him on account of his race, religion, nationality, gender, sexual orientation or political opinions, or
> (b) if extradited he might be prejudiced at his trial or punished, detained or restricted in his personal liberty by reason of his race, religion, nationality, gender, sexual orientation or political opinions.

6.11 Section 81 uses precisely the same formulation in relation to Part 2 requests.

6.12 The 'extraneous considerations' are:

- race;
- religion;
- nationality;
- gender;
- sexual orientation; or
- political opinions.

6.13 There are two categories within the extraneous considerations bar that are set out as alternatives: it is enough to show one or the other. The bar prevents the extradition of a person if, broadly, the 'extraneous considerations' have resulted in the issue of the warrant or request, or will prejudice the person upon his return. The first category (subsection (a)) looks at the reasons behind the issue of the warrant or request: it prevents extradition where a country has ostensibly sought the return of a person for a particular offence, but where the real motive for seeking his or her return is to prosecute or punish that person because of the 'extraneous considerations.' The second category (subsection (b)) is directed at what might happen to the person if he or she is extradited. If he or she will suffer prejudice, punishment or detention by reason of the 'extraneous considerations' then extradition will be barred.

6.14 There is an obvious overlap between this bar and human rights considerations, in particular articles 3, 5 and 6 and in practice they are often argued in parallel (see chapter 7).

Test

6.15 The test is set out in the pre-2003 Act case of *Fernandez v Government of Singapore*,[8] which states that:[9]

> The burden is on the appellant to show a causal link between the issue of the warrant, his detention, prosecution, punishment or the prejudice which he asserts he will suffer and the fact of his race or his religion. He does not have to prove on the balance of probabilities that the events described in s13 (b) will take place, but he must show that there is a 'reasonable chance' or 'reasonable grounds for thinking' or a 'serious possibility' that such events will occur.

6.16 As such, while it may appear that the test is set at a low bar (less than the balance of probabilities), in reality it is difficult to succeed on this bar because of the problems one may face in adducing evidence to show the causal link between the issue of the warrant, the person's detention, prosecution, punishment or the prejudice that he or she asserts he or she will suffer and the extraneous considerations.

6.17 By way of example, it may be helpful to consider a case in which reliance was unsuccessfully placed on this bar alongside a case in which extraneous considerations did bar a person's extradition.

6.18 In the case of *Tamarevichute v Russian Federation*[10] the defence sought to argue that there was a 'reasonable chance' or a 'serious possibility' that, as a person of Roma origin, the appellant might be prejudiced at her trial in Kaliningrad on account of her race. The Administrative Court found[11] that the appellant had 'adduced powerful evidence of widespread discrimination against the Roma within the Russian Federation ... [which included] attacks on Roma

---

8 [1971] 1 WLR 987.
9 At 993–994.
10 [2008] EWHC 1239 (Admin) (DC).
11 At para 98.

people and their property, the voicing of anti-Roma sentiments in the media and in political speeches, and human rights abuses by the law enforcement authorities'.

6.19 This, however, was not enough to bar her extradition. The judge said:

> The fact that, if returned to the Russian Federation, the appellant would be at risk of suffering general prejudice as a result of her Roma origin is not, however, sufficient to constitute a bar to her extradition under the provisions of section 81(b) of the Act. She must demonstrate that there exists a 'reasonable chance' or a 'serious possibility' of her being prejudiced at her trial, or 'punished, detained or restricted in her personal liberty' by reason of her race.

6.20 In deciding that the causal link had not been demonstrated, the judge looked at whether the appellant had actually suffered prejudice when in Russia on account of her Roma origin, and found that she had not.

6.21 This can be contrasted with the case of *Government of the Republic of Serbia v Ejup Ganic*[12] in which the district judge found that extradition was barred under both subsection (a) and (b) of EA 2003 section 81. In that case, the return of the former acting president of Bosnia was sought for war crimes. The requested person had been subject to two international investigations, both of which had found that there was no case to answer. The defence called a number of witnesses who gave evidence to say that the prosecution was politically motivated, resulting in the discharge of the requested person under both section 81(a) and (as a result of evidence called to show that he or she would be prejudiced at trial on account of his race) section 81(b).

6.22 Again, as can be seen from the above examples, a requested person will need to obtain a significant body of evidence from experts and others to persuade a judge that extraneous considerations should bar his or her extradition.

Passage of time – sections 14/82

6.23 Passage of time is frequently raised by requested persons seeking to resist their extradition. Under section 14 of EA 2003 Part 1, or section 82 of Part 2, a person's extradition is barred if it appears that it would be *unjust or oppressive* to extradite him or her by reason of the passage of time since he or she is alleged to have committed the offence or since he or she is alleged to have become unlawfully at large.

12 [2010] EW Misc 11 (MC).

6.24 To rely on this bar, it is not enough to show a long delay. It is also necessary to show either injustice or oppression occasioned by the time that has passed. This bar replicates provisions in earlier Acts, and there is a significant body of pre-2003 case-law on passage of time that still applies.

Fugitives and passage of time

6.25 Perhaps the most important point that can be derived from the case-law is that delay brought about by the accused fleeing the country will prevent that person from relying on the passage of time in all but the most exceptional circumstances. In the case of *Kakis v Government of the Republic of Cyprus*[13] Lord Diplock said:

> Delay in the commencement or conduct of extradition proceedings which is brought about by the accused himself by fleeing the country, concealing his whereabouts or evading arrest cannot, in my view, be relied upon as a ground for holding it to be either unjust or oppressive to return him.

6.26 This principle was refined in the more recent case of *Gomes and Goodyer v Trinidad and Tobago*[14] in two important ways. First, the court decided that if a defendant deliberately flees, he or she cannot then rely on passage of time, even if the requesting state has contributed to the delay significantly.[15] Secondly, the burden is on the requesting state to prove beyond all reasonable doubt that the requested person has deliberately fled the jurisdiction.

6.27 It is therefore important to establish with requested persons the circumstances in which they came to leave the country. In accusation cases, lawyers will need to ask questions such as:

- whether they knew of the offence;
- whether they were arrested;
- what they had understood to have happened following arrest;
- whether any assertions were made by the authorities.

6.28 Similarly, in conviction cases, it will be necessary to carefully establish:

- whether they were present when convicted;
- if so, why they then left the country;
- what contact they had with the authorities and so on.

13 [1978] 1 WLR 779.
14 [2009] UKHL 21.
15 In the case of *Gomes*, the requesting state had lost the file.

Injustice or oppression

6.29 The burden of proof is on the requested person to establish on the balance of probabilities that it would be unjust or oppressive to extradite him or her.

6.30 In the case of *Kakis*, Lord Diplock set out a definition of injustice or oppression. He stated that:

> Unjust I regard as directed primarily to the risk of prejudice to the accused in the conduct of the trial itself, oppressive as directed to the hardship to the accused resulting from changes in his circumstances that have occurred during the period to be taken into consideration.[16]

6.31 The case of *Gomes and Goodyer* also looked again at injustice, approving a definition of injustice endorsed in a 2006 Privy Council case,[17] as follows:[18]

> First, the question is not whether it would be unjust or oppressive to try the accused but whether ... it would be unjust or oppressive to extradite him ... Secondly, if the court of the requesting state is bound to conclude that a fair trial is impossible, it would be unjust or oppressive for the requested state to return him ... But, thirdly, the court of the requested state must have regard to the safeguards which exist under the domestic law of the requesting state to protect a defendant against a trial rendered unjust or oppressive by the passage of time ... Fourthly, no rule of thumb can be applied to determine whether the passage of time has rendered a fair trial no longer possible: much will turn on the particular case ... Fifthly, there can be no cut-off point beyond which extradition must inevitably be regarded as unjust or oppressive.

6.32 The judgment emphasises the strong public interest in honouring extradition arrangements and means that it will be difficult for a requested person to establish that it would be unjust to extradite him or her by reason of passage of time.

6.33 The judgment did not, however, give significant further guidance on the meaning of oppression save to approve of what was said by Lord Diplock in *Kakis*:[19]

> the gravity of the offence is relevant to whether changes in the circumstances of the accused which have occurred during the relevant period are such as would render his return to stand his trial oppressive.

---

16 *Kakis v Government of the Republic of Cyprus* [1978] 1 WLR 779 at para 782.
17 *Knowles Jr v United States of America (The Bahamas)* [2006] UKPC 38.
18 [2009] UKHL 21 at para 32.
19 *Gomes and Goodyer v Trinidad and Tobago* [2009] UKHL 21 at para 31.

6.34 If a person therefore is sought for a minor offence and a lengthy period of time has passed, he or she will be more likely to be able to establish that their extradition will be oppressive than if the offence for which he or she is requested is grave.[20]

6.35 The gravity of the offence will be clear from the warrant. To show oppression, a detailed proof of evidence from the requested person will be required, alongside evidence from family members and, in some cases, expert witnesses such as social workers or psychologists who can comment on the impact that extradition will have on family members. There will often be an overlap between passage of time and article 8 and they are often relied on by requested persons in tandem.

Cases where passage of time has barred extradition

6.36 The passage of time bar will always be fact-specific, but practitioners may find it helpful to consider examples of cases where passage of time has been successfully raised by requested persons.

La Torre v Italy[21]

6.37 The requested person in this case was the subject of five extradition requests from Italy, both accusation and conviction covering serious offences. There had been delays of between 6 and 16 years. Mr La Torre had been in custody since 1999, and the Italian authorities had been aware of this. He was only partially successful, but the case is useful in that it emphasises an important point: specifically, that in a marginal case, culpable delay on the part of the state could tip the balance in the requested person's favour. The judgment says:[22]

> All the circumstances must be considered in order to judge whether the unjust/oppressive test is met. Culpable delay on the part of the State may certainly colour that judgment and may sometimes be decisive, not least in what is otherwise a marginal case ... And such delay will often be associated with other factors, such as the possibility of a false sense of security on the extraditee's part.

Wenting v High Court of Valenciennes[23]

6.38 Mr Wenting had been sentenced to five years' imprisonment imposed 20 years earlier for importation of 585 grams of cocaine. He had left

---

20 *Sapstead v Governor of HMP Belmarsh* [2004] EWHC 2352 (Admin) at para 34.
21 [2007] EWHC 1370 (Admin).
22 At para 37.
23 [2009] EWHC 3528 (Admin).

France with the express permission of the French authorities, having been granted bail to live in the Netherlands. He had been living a law-abiding life; he had built up two successful businesses over the years and he had a partner who was seriously ill. Although he had been aware that he had been convicted after a trial had taken place in his absence, he had been informed by the Dutch probation service that he should wait for a summons. He was never notified that he was required to return to France to serve the sentence. The court found that it would be oppressive to extradite him.

Kovac v Regional Court in Prague[24]

6.39　In this case, the requested person had been convicted on six occasions for 18 offences of coercion of a young girl into prostitution and had been sentenced to nine years' imprisonment. There was, however, a 16-year unexplained delay between the conviction and the issue of the warrant, and the court found that this inactivity on the part of the authorities had lulled Mr Kovac into a false sense of security. In the intervening period, he had married and was the father of three children and two adopted children. He had also been working until his remand in custody as a night shift cleaner. The judge concluded that this was a borderline case and that the Czech authorities' failure to offer any explanation meant that it was a case of oppression.

Italy v Merico[25]

6.40　This case illustrates the principle that the court must take all factors into account cumulatively, in considering the passage of time bar. Ms Merico had been convicted of drug-trafficking offences in 1997 and sentenced to six years' imprisonment. She was released from prison having served two years of that sentence.

6.41　In 2005 the Italian authorities were notified that she was living in the United Kingdom. Since she had left, however, her circumstances had altered drastically. The court took into account the following factors in deciding that it would be oppressive to extradite her by reason of the passage of time:

- First, the offences were committed a very long time ago.
- Second, she had been released from prison 12 years before, after she had served nearly two years' imprisonment.
- Third, she had travelled on a valid passport to the United Kingdom, where she had lived openly.

24　[2010] EWHC 1959 (Admin).
25　[2011] EWHC 1857 (Admin).

- Fourth, she had not been convicted of any further offences.
- Fifth, she had been bringing up her children and looking after her mother who was suffering from a terminal illness.

6.42 Those were factors which, taken together, were relevant to the decision that it would be oppressive to order her extradition. The court stated that each reason individually would not suffice but, taken together, they were capable of amounting to oppression.

R on the application of Cepkauskas v District Court of Marijampole, Lithuania[26]

6.43 The requested person was wanted on an accusation warrant for four offences of theft of cars, and one offence of theft, from 1997 to 1998. He had numerous convictions in the United Kingdom, including one that had resulted in an 18-month period of imprisonment. This sentence had led to a deportation order being made, although it was subsequently appealed successfully. The court found that it would be oppressive to extradite him for the following reasons: he had lived in the United Kingdom since 2003 and had no remaining family ties in Lithuania; it was an accusation rather than a conviction warrant; there had been no explanation for the delay in issuing the warrant and he had had no knowledge that there were matters outstanding against him in Lithuania; he had one child and four stepchildren who were dependent on him.

Summary of the case-law

6.44 In summary, some of the factors considered relevant to a finding of oppression in the cases above were:
- culpable delay on the part of the requesting state (in a marginal case);
- length of delay;
- whether a false sense of security has been engendered;
- whether the person's circumstances have changed significantly;
- the circumstances in which the person left the requesting state;
- the effect on those reliant on the requested person.

Person's age – section 15

6.45 Section 15 provides that a person's extradition is barred by reason of his age if it would be conclusively presumed because of his age that

26 [2011] EWHC 757 (Admin).

he or she could not be guilty of the extradition offence. The judge will be required to assess whether extradition is barred on the assumptions that the conduct would amount to an offence in the United Kingdom, had it taken place in the United Kingdom and that the person had carried out the conduct.

6.46 In short, given that the age of criminal responsibility in this country is ten, if a person is said to have committed an offence when he or she was younger than ten, extradition will be barred. This bar only applies in Part 1 cases. Practitioners may have difficulty imagining circumstances in which a warrant for a child younger than ten would be issued, particularly given that there is now no EU country with a lower age of criminal responsibility than England and Wales.

Hostage taking considerations – sections 16/83

6.47 Section 16 (or, in Part 2, section 83) sets out another highly unusual bar to extradition. It only applies where:
- the conduct set out in the warrant would constitute an offence under section 1 of the Taking of Hostages Act 1982 or an attempt to commit such an offence;[27] and
- the requesting country is a party to the Hostage Taking Convention.

6.48 If both of these conditions apply, the court will have to examine whether the requested person might be prejudiced at trial because communications between him or her and the appropriate authorities (ie consular authorities) would not be possible.[28]

---

27 Section 1 of the Taking of Hostages Act 1982 states that:
A person, whatever his nationality, who, in the United Kingdom or elsewhere, –
(a) detains any other person ('the hostage'), and
(b) in order to compel a State, international governmental organisation or person to do or abstain from doing any act, threatens to kill, injure or continue to detain the hostage,
commits an offence.
The Taking of Hostages Act 1982 was enacted to implement the International Convention against the Taking of Hostages.
28 The Convention carries a clause which modifies extradition arrangements between state signatories and indeed allows extensive extradition which goes beyond that provided for in EA 2003.

Specialty – sections 17/95

6.49 The principle of specialty[29] provides that, where a person is extradited, he or she will be prosecuted or proceeded against only for the offences in respect of which he or she is extradited, that is, those set out in the warrant or request.

6.50 In respect of Part 1 cases, section 17 is a bar to extradition to be considered by the judge at the extradition hearing. For Part 2 cases, it falls to be considered by the Secretary of State after the extradition hearing.

6.51 To rely on the specialty bar, a requested person must show that there are no specialty arrangements with the requesting state. This will be difficult to show in Part 1 cases, given that all EU countries are signatories to the 1957 European Convention on Extradition, which includes a provision preventing an extraditee from being dealt with for offences other than those for which he or she has been extradited.[30] The specialty rule also features in the Framework Decision.

6.52 A person consenting to extradition cannot rely on specialty protection.

Earlier extradition – sections 18/19/19A/96/96A

6.53 Sections 18, 19 and 96 offer some (limited) protection to a person who has been extradited *to* the United Kingdom and subsequently faces a new warrant or request to be extradited from the United Kingdom.[31]

6.54 If the country that originally extradited the requested person to the United Kingdom is required to give consent to onward extradition and does not do so, that will act as a bar to extradition. As with the specialty bar, this is considered by the judge at the extradition hearing for Part 1 cases and by the Secretary of State where the requesting state is a Part 2 territory.

---

29 Specialty is also sometimes referred to as 'speciality'.
30 For an example of a case where the requested person sought to rely on this bar in respect of a Part 1 state, see the case of *Hilali v National Court of Madrid* [2006] EWHC 1239 (Admin). Although the court did not rule out reliance on this bar in Part 1 cases, they gave the argument short shrift, saying (at para 52): 'It seems to us a surprising submission that Spain is likely to act in breach of the international obligations to which it has signed up. There is no evidence before us that it has done so in the past and in these circumstances we would need compelling evidence that it is likely to do so in the future'.
31 There is a similar provision in s19A which applies when a person has been transferred to a country by the International Criminal Court.

Forum – sections 19B/83A

6.55 The Crime and Courts Bill introduces amendments at sections 19B and 83A of the EA 2003 to prevent extradition 'by reason of forum' if the extradition would not be in the interests of justice. While still to be enacted, it does appear likely that this forum amendment will eventually be implemented.

6.56 The proposed amendment sets out the factors the judge should take into account in deciding the question of forum. Section 19C of the Act, however, heavily curtails the discretion of the judge by providing that he or she 'must decide that the extradition is not barred by reason of forum if (at a time when the judge has not yet decided the proceedings) the judge receives a prosecutor's certificate relating to the extradition'. Given this prosecutorial veto, it appears unlikely that the enactment of these sections in their current form will in fact enable defence practitioners to argue that the forum bar should prevent a requested person's extradition.

6.57 Where forum cannot be raised as a bar, it may nevertheless be appropriate to consider the question of forum in the context of any article 8 argument.

Death penalty – section 94

6.58 The death penalty bar prevents the Secretary of State from ordering a person's extradition to a Part 2 country if he or she could be, will be or has been sentenced to death. If, however, the Secretary of State receives a written assurance that the death penalty will not apply to the requested person or will not be carried out (and he considers that assurance adequate), the requested person will not be able to rely on this bar.

Conviction in absence – sections 20/85

6.59 This bar prevents the extradition of persons convicted in their absence where they will not have a right to a retrial. There is, however, an important caveat: if the requested person deliberately fled the jurisdiction, he or she will not be able to rely on sections 20/85 to prevent extradition.

6.60 The steps that the judge must follow in deciding this question are prescribed by EA 2003 ss20/85. In the extradition hearing, the judge must decide whether the person was convicted in absence, and if so, whether he or she deliberately absented himself. It is the judicial authority that bears the burden of proving, to the criminal standard, that a person was deliberately absent.[32] In any conviction case, it is imperative for the duty solicitor to ask whether the person was present when convicted, and if not, whether that person was deliberately absent from the trial.[33]

6.61 If the judge finds that the person was convicted in absence without having deliberately absented himself, the judge must then go on to look at whether the person would be entitled to a retrial, or (on appeal) a review amounting to a retrial. Section 20(8) provides that the judge must not decide that a person would be entitled to a retrial unless:

> in any proceedings that it is alleged would constitute a retrial or a review amounting to a retrial, the person would have these rights –
> (a) the right to defend himself in person or through legal assistance of his own choosing or, if he had not sufficient means to pay for legal assistance, to be given it free when the interests of justice so required;
> (b) the right to examine or have examined witnesses against him and to obtain the attendance and examination of witnesses on his behalf under the same conditions as witnesses against him.

6.62 A warrant or request may sometimes address the right to a retrial, or it may be information that the requesting authority provides by way of further information. Nevertheless, in cases where there is doubt it may be necessary to instruct a defence expert (such as a legal academic or an experienced lawyer practising in the requesting state) to address this point. EAWs from Italy and Romania in particular should be carefully scrutinised to check whether the requested person will be entitled to a retrial, and that any retrial will conform to article 6 standards.

6.63 A number of cases have examined the meaning of 'entitled', looking at whether a person can be said to be entitled where the entitlement to a retrial is subject to a court's discretion. In the single judge decision of *Bohm v Romania*,[34] it was said that 'the right has to be automatic, and cannot be automatic if it is subject to the exercise of discretion, since the discretion might be exercised against retrial'.

---

32 *Murtati v Albania* [2008] EWHC 2856 (Admin); *Benko v Hungary* [2009] EWHC 3530 (Admin); *Mitoi v Romania* [2006] EWHC 1977 (Admin).
33 *Emil Kis v District Court In Sokolov, Czech Republic* [2012] EWHC 938 (Admin).
34 [2011] EWHC 2671 (Admin).

Contrast this however with the judgment of Rafferty LJ in *Nastase v Office of the State Prosecutor, Italy*:[35]

> The existence of procedural steps does not remove the entitlement to a retrial. Rather, the Italian authorities must be premitted [sic] to regulate their own proceedings by imposition of their own rules. Section 20 may create entitlements, but procedural rules set parameters within which such rights are exercisable.

While *Nastase* is a Divisional Court judgment, this is an unsettled area in extradition law and it will be necessary to check the developing case-law if relying on section 20.

Physical or mental health – sections 25/91

6.64 Under section 25, if, during the extradition hearing, it appears to the judge that it would be unjust or oppressive to extradite the person by virtue of his physical or mental condition, the judge must either order his discharge,[36] or adjourn the hearing[37] until it appears to the judge that the person's physical or mental condition is such that it would no longer be unjust or oppressive to extradite him.[38] It is important to note that the mere fact that a person suffers from an illness is not enough to prevent extradition. It must be shown that, because of the illness or complaint, it will be unjust or oppressive to extradite the requested person.

6.65 In order to satisfy a finding of 'oppression' a high threshold must be reached. The Administrative Court has said that: 'The term "unjust or oppressive" requires regard to be had to all the relevant circumstances, including the fact that extradition is ordinarily likely to cause stress and hardship; neither of those is sufficient.'[39]

---

35 [2012] EWHC 3671 (Admin) at para 45. See also *Rexha v Officer of the Prosecutor, Court of Rome* [2012] EWHC 3397 (Admin) in which extradition was ordered where the judicial authority stated that whilst an absolute assurance of that the requested person would be entitled to a retrial, it was 'highly probable' (para 43).
36 EA 2003 s25(3)(a).
37 EA 2003 s25(3)(b).
38 See paras 6.29–6.34 for more detail on injustice or oppression: the Administrative Court in *Government of the Republic of South Africa v Shrien Dewani* [2012] EWHC 842 (Admin) confirmed that the words are 'to be read in the sense used in cases such as *Kakis*.'
39 *Government of the Republic of South Africa v Shrien Dewani* [2012] EWHC 842 (Admin) at para 73.

6.66 There is a significant body of case-law that looks, in particular, at those requested persons who are at risk of suicide.[40] In *Richen Turner v Government of the USA*,[41] Aikens LJ summarised the following propositions from the case-law:

> (1) The court has to form an overall judgment on the facts of the particular case.
>
> (2) A high threshold has to be reached in order to satisfy the court that a requested person's physical or mental condition is such that it would be unjust or oppressive to extradite him.
>
> (3) The court must assess the mental condition of the person threatened with extradition and determine if it is linked to a risk of a suicide attempt if the extradition order were to be made. There has to be a 'substantial risk that [the appellant] will commit suicide'. The question is whether, on the evidence the risk of the appellant succeeding in committing suicide, whatever steps are taken is sufficiently great to result in a finding of oppression.
>
> (4) The mental condition of the person must be such that it removes his capacity to resist the impulse to commit suicide, otherwise it will not be his mental condition but his own voluntary act which puts him at risk of dying and if that is the case there is no oppression in ordering extradition.
>
> (5) On the evidence, is the risk that the person will succeed in committing suicide, whatever steps are taken, sufficiently great to result in a finding of oppression?
>
> (6) Are there appropriate arrangements in place in the prison system of the country to which extradition is sought so that those authorities can cope properly with the person's mental condition and the risk of suicide?
>
> (7) There is a public interest in giving effect to treaty obligations and this is an important factor to have in mind.

6.67 Approving the above propositions in the case of *Wolkowicz v Polish Judicial Authority*[42] the President of the Queen's Bench Division stated that the key issue in almost every case will 'be the measures that are in place to prevent any attempt at suicide by a requested person with a mental illness being successful'. These should be examined in three stages:

---

40 See, for example: *Jansons v Latvian Judicial Authority* [2009] EWHC 1845 (Admin), *Rot v District Court of Lublin, Poland* [2010] EWHC 1820 (Admin), *R on the application of Prosser v Secretary of State for the Home Department* [2010] EWHC 845 (Admin), *Wrobel v Poland* [2011] EWHC 374 (Admin), *R on the application of Griffin v City of London Magistrates Court* [2011] EWHC 943 (Admin).
41 [2012] EWHC 2426 (Admin) at para 28.
42 [2013] EWHC 102 (Admin) at para 10.

- The position while the requested person is being held in custody in the United Kingdom.
- Arrangements that will be in place when the person is being transferred to ensure there are proper arrangements in place to prevent suicide. Medical records should be sent to those who will have custody during transfer.
- It is to be presumed that the receiving state within the EU will discharge its responsibilities to prevent the person committing suicide. It should not be necessary to require any assurances from requesting states within the EU.

6.68 In *Wolkowicz* the court emphasised that, following these principles, it is 'only in a very rare case that a requested person will be likely to establish that measures to prevent a substantial risk of suicide will not be effective'.

6.69 The solicitor representing any requested persons with physical or mental health problems will need to obtain medical evidence which will show the court why their complaint will lead to injustice or oppression. The legal representative should also carefully consider whether there are any other facts that lend support to a finding of oppression, for example: family circumstances; delay or a significant change in circumstance. It may be helpful to consider the examples given above of cases where oppression caused by the passage of time has led to discharge.

Abuse of process

6.70 Although EA 2003 does not state that an abuse of the court's process will bar extradition, the courts have found that in certain circumstances it will.

6.71 The jurisdiction of the court to consider abuse of process in the context of extradition proceedings was decided in relation to the 2003 Act in the case of *R on the application of Bermingham v Director of the Serious Fraud Office*.[43] The court will start from the assumption that a requesting state is acting in good faith, which may be displaced by evidence.[44] A person requested by a Part 1 territory will also face the difficulty of overcoming the principle of mutual trust and recognition inherent in the operation of the system of EAWs.

---

43 *R on the application of Bermingham v Director of the Serious Fraud Office* [2006] EWHC 200 (Admin).
44 *Ahmad and Aswat v The Government of the United States of America* [2006] EWHC 2927 (Admin), [2007] UKHRR 525 at para 101.

6.72 Procedural guidance from the case of *United States v Tollman*[45] is succinctly set out in *Haynes v Malta*:[46]

> To sustain an allegation of abuse of process in relation to proceedings under the Act, it is necessary, first to identify with specificity what is alleged to constitute the abuse; secondly to satisfy the court that the matter complained of is capable of amounting to an abuse; and thirdly to satisfy the court that there are reasonable grounds for believing that such conduct has occurred. If the matter gets that far, then the court should require the judicial authority to provide an explanation. The court should not order extradition unless satisfied that no such abuse has taken place.

6.73 As stated above, the requested person bears the burden of satisfying the judge that, not only is the issue raised capable of amounting to an abuse, but also that there are reasonable grounds for believing that the abuse has occurred. It will be essential therefore for the requested person to bring cogent evidence of the abuse in order to satisfy the court that the conduct has occurred.

6.74 While the Administrative Court has stated that 'abuse of process in the extradition context is not confined to bad faith on the part of the requesting state'[47] it is clear that the circumstances in which abuse of process can be argued will be limited. In relation to Part 1 cases, the court has drawn a distinction between an abuse of the extradition process by the prosecuting authority and an abuse resulting from the misconduct or bad faith of the police of the requesting state in the investigation of the case or the preparation of evidence for trial. Abuse arising from misconduct or bad faith by the police is a matter to be resolved by the requesting state and will not be capable of preventing a person's extradition.[48] Where the requesting state seeks the 'extradition of someone for a collateral purpose, or when they know that the trial cannot succeed',[49] this will fall into the former category and will be capable of amounting to an abuse of the court's process.

---

45 *United States v Tollman* [2008] EWHC 184 (Admin).
46 *Haynes v Malta* [2009] EWHC 880 (Admin) at para 6.
47 *Janovic v Prosecutor General's Office, Lithuania* [2011] EWHC 710 (Admin) at para 18.
48 *Symeou v Public Prosecutor's Officer, Patras, Greece* [2009] EWHC 897 (Admin) at para 34.
49 At para 33.

Immigration status

6.75 If a requested person has made a claim for asylum after the certification of the warrant or request, he or she cannot be extradited while the asylum claim is pending.[50] The question of whether extradition proceedings should be adjourned pending the outcome of the asylum claim is currently moot: in the case of *R on the application of Chichvarkin v Secretary of State for the Home Department*[51] the Divisional Court stated that, in circumstances where an asylum claim is being actively considered by the SSHD and the extradition court is considering whether extradition would lead to a breach of a person's human rights, this would 'weigh heavily in favour of an adjournment of the extradition proceedings'.[52] See also, however, the case of *Kozlowski v District Court of Torun Poland*,[53] in which Ouseley J (in the face of a growing number of Polish appellants seeking to adjourn proceedings to await the outcome of asylum claims) warned against drawing a general point of principle from *Chichvarkin* and said that 'in cases involving Council of Europe and EU countries there ought to be a very firm approach not to grant adjournments'.[54]

6.76 The Refugee Convention prohibits the return of refugees to their home country.[55] While this is not explicitly covered in the EA 2003, it has been resolved by the Divisional Court in the case of *District Court in Ostroleka v Dytlow*.[56] If the requested person is a refugee whose extradition is sought by the home country, he or she should be discharged. It will be important to obtain the decision letter from the Home Office to satisfy the court that he or she is indeed a refugee.

6.77 The following chapter will go on to look at human rights considerations as grounds upon which extradition can be resisted.

---

50 EA 2003 ss39 and 121.
51 *R on the application of Chichvarkin v Secretary of State for the Home Department* [2010] EWHC 1858.
52 At para 61.
53 *Kozlowski v District Court of Torun, Poland* [2012] EWHC 1706 (Admin).
54 At para 20.
55 This is known as the principle of *non-refoulement*.
56 *District Court in Ostroleka, Second Criminal Division (A Polish Judicial Authority) v Dytlow* [2009] EWHC 1009 (Admin).

CHAPTER 7

Human rights

7.1	Introduction
7.3	Human rights in Part 1 cases
7.8	Human rights in Part 2 cases
7.9	Article 2 (the right to life) and article 3 (the prohibition of torture)
7.14	Article 5 (the right to liberty and security) and article 6 (the right to a fair trial)
7.21	Article 8 (right to respect for private and family life)

Introduction

7.1 In dealing with both Part 1 (EA 2003 s21) and Part 2 (s87) cases, the judge will be required to consider whether extradition would be compatible with a person's rights under the European Convention on Human Rights ('the Convention') within the meaning of the Human Rights Act 1998. If the judge decides the question in the negative, he or she must order the person's discharge.

7.2 Although in law the same considerations apply, the treatment of human rights by the courts differs in practice as between Part 1 and Part 2 cases. This chapter will begin by looking at how human rights considerations are applied in Part 1 and Part 2 cases. It will then go on to look at the specific human rights that are protected by the Convention.

Human rights in Part 1 cases

7.3 All EU countries have signed and ratified the Convention. The Framework Decision states that the EAW 'is the first concrete measure in the field of criminal law implementing the principle of mutual recognition, which the European Council referred to as the "cornerstone" of judicial cooperation.' It goes on to say that the mechanism of the EAW is 'based on a high level of confidence between Member States'.[1]

7.4 It is important to have this context in mind when considering human rights in Part 1 extradition cases. There is a presumption that EU countries will comply with their human rights obligations. As stated in the case of *Dabas*: 'The important underlying assumption of the Framework Decision is that member states, sharing common values and recognising common rights, can and should trust the integrity and fairness of each other's judicial institutions.'[2]

7.5 Nevertheless, the way in which human rights are considered in Part 1 cases has not always been consistent. There was a line of case-law that developed in 2010 in which it appeared that the presumption

---

1 Framework Decision 2002 paras 6 and 10 preamble.
2 *Dabas v High Court of Justice in Madrid, Spain* [2007] UKHL 6.

of compliance with human rights in EU countries was tantamount to being irrebuttable.³

7.6 There was, however, a shift following the case of *MSS v Belgium*,⁴ in which the European Court of Human Rights dealt with the case of an Afghan asylum-seeker who had been deported from Belgium to Greece, where he had been held in 'appalling' conditions. In that case, the court observed that:

> the existence of ... international treaties guaranteeing respect for fundamental rights in principle are not in themselves sufficient to ensure adequate protection against the risk of ill-treatment where, as in the present case, reliable sources have reported practices ... which are manifestly contrary to the principles of the Convention.

7.7 The Administrative Court followed this approach in the case of *Agius v Malta*,⁵ emphasising that section 21 imposed an obligation on the district judge to 'reach a decision as to whether extradition would be compatible with the appellant's Convention rights'. While maintaining that the starting point is the presumption (which is not easily displaced) that the requesting state will comply with its Convention obligations, the court stated it is 'capable of being rebutted by clear and cogent evidence, which establishes that ... extradition would not be compatible with the defendant's Convention rights'. The court went on to say⁶ that:

> In practical terms [...] the burden of displacing the assumption will be a heavy one, and it may well be the case that as a matter of fact successful reliance on section 21(1) will be the exception rather than the rule, but that does not mean that there is a legal obligation on an appellant relying on section 21(1) to demonstrate 'exceptional circumstances'.

---

3 See, for example, *Dabkowski v Poland* [2010] EWHC 1712 (Admin); *Jan Rot v District Court of Lublin, Poland* [2010] EWHC 1820 (Admin) and *Klimas v Prosecutor General's Office of Lithuania* [2010] EWHC 2076 (Admin). In the latter case, Mitting J said: 'Accordingly, and as a matter of principle, I would hold as I did in *Jan Rot* that when prison conditions in a Convention category 1 state are raised as an obstacle to extradition, the district judge need not, save in wholly extraordinary circumstances in which the constitutional order of the requesting state has been upset for example by a military coup or violent revolution examine the question at all ...'.
4 *MSS v Belgium*, Application No 30696/09, 21 January 2011.
5 *Agius v Court of Magistrates, Malta* [2011] EWHC 759 (Admin).
6 At para 19.

Human rights in Part 2 cases

7.8   All Council of Europe countries are also signatories to the Convention.[7] There is therefore also an assumption that non-EU Council of Europe countries will also be capable of offering adequate protection of a requested person's human rights.[8] Indeed, even for countries that have not signed the Convention, there will often be a presumption of compliance with international human rights norms. For many years, the courts have asserted that there are 'fundamental assumptions that the requesting state is acting in good faith and that the fugitive will receive a fair trial in the courts of the requesting state'.[9] Although this assumption can be rebutted by evidence, it will be all the more difficult to displace 'where the requesting state is one in which the United Kingdom has for many years reposed the confidence not only of general good relations, but also of successive bilateral treaties consistently honoured'.[10] An example of such a state is the United States. In practice, a court's willingness to find that a country will not comply with its human rights obligations will differ by country, according to its record of compliance. When seeking to persuade a court that a person should be discharged under section 87, it is therefore of the utmost importance to put before the court persuasive evidence of a lack of compliance with human rights obligations.

Article 2 (the right to life) and article 3 (the prohibition of torture)

7.9   Article 2 states that everyone's right to life shall be protected by law. Article 3 provides that no one shall be subjected to torture or

---

7 Norway, Albania, Turkey, Iceland, Switzerland, Liechtenstein, San Marino, Moldova, Macedonia, Ukraine, Russia, Georgia, Armenia, Azerbaijan, Bosnia and Herzegovina, Serbia, Monaco, Montenegro, Andorra and Croatia (on 1 July 2013 Croatia will accede to the European Union and become a category 1 territory for the purpose of EA 2003).

8 See *Gomes and Goodyer v Trinidad & Tobago* [2009] UKHL 21, para 35: 'Council of Europe countries in our view present no problem. All are subject to article 6 of the Convention and should readily be assumed capable of protecting an accused against an unjust trial – whether by an abuse of process jurisdiction like ours or in some other way.'

9 *Serbeh v Governor of HMP Brixton* [2002] EWHC 2356 (Admin) at para 31.

10 *Ahmad v USA* [2006] EWHC 2927 (Admin).

to inhuman or degrading treatment or punishment.[11] Challenges under article 2 have been brought where it is alleged that a person will be killed by other prison inmates (*Dewani*);[12] by gang members (*McLean*);[13] or where a person's extradition is sought by a country that uses the death penalty. In relation to article 3, requested persons have argued that their Convention rights will be violated by, for example, inter-prisoner violence arising from being targeted as a result of ethnicity (*Konuksever*);[14] the prison conditions in a particular country (*Krolik*);[15] or life imprisonment without parole (*Harkins and Edwards*).[16] As these examples show, the risk may be from the state, or may arise from threats by non-state actors.

7.10 In seeking to persuade a court that a requested person should not be extradited under these articles, the burden will be on the requested person to bring clear and cogent evidence showing that there are substantial grounds for believing that the person, if extradited, faces a real risk of either being killed[17] or being subjected to torture or to inhuman or degrading treatment.[18] Where the risk is from a non-state actor, it will be necessary to show that protection from the requesting state will be inadequate.[19]

7.11 Given the heavy burden on the requested person, it will not be enough to rely simply on the requested person's own evidence.[20] Witnesses of fact who can support the requested person's account may be appropriate, along with expert witnesses who can speak to the specific risk faced by the requested person. Case-law from the European Court of Human Rights can be used along with reports from governmental and non-governmental organisations, such as the US State Department and the Council of Europe Committee for the Prevention of Torture, to bolster the evidence of expert witnesses.

---

11 Where article 2 is argued, article 3 will frequently be argued alongside it, given that inhuman or degrading treatment will often be a corollary of a threat to life.
12 *Government of South Africa v Dewani* [2010] EWHC 3398 (Admin).
13 *McLean v High Court of Dublin, Ireland* [2008] EWHC 547 (Admin).
14 *Konuksever v Government of Turkey* [2012] EWHC 2166 (Admin).
15 *Krolik v Several Judicial Authorities of Poland* [2012] EWHC 2357 (Admin).
16 *Harkins and Edwards v UK* Application No 9146/07, 17 January 2012.
17 Although, as Lord Bingham points out in *R on the application of Ullah v Special Adjudicator* [2004] UKHL 26, the test that the court applied in the case of *Dehwari v Netherlands* (2000) 29 EHRR CD 74 was 'near certainty' rather than real risk: at para 24.
18 *Soering v UK* (1989) 11 EHRR 439 at para 91.
19 *R on the application of Bagdanavicius v Secretary of State for the Home Department* [2005] UKHL 38 at para 24.
20 *G v District Court of Czestochowa, Poland* [2011] EWHC 1597 (Admin).

7.12 The High Court, having encountered numerous appeals premised on poor prison conditions in Poland, provided in the case of *Krolik v Several Judicial Authorities of Poland*[21] for these cases as follows:
- Any appeal raising the issue must (1) clearly identify any new factual issues not considered in this appeal or earlier cases which are said to give rise to a breach of article 3 by reason of the conditions in Polish prisons, (2) set out a summary of the evidence relied on in support and (3) explain how it meets the criteria for evidence of the type to which we have referred at paragraphs 7.6 and 7.7.
- Any such appeal will be listed within days of it being lodged at the court. If there are no new factual issues and the evidence is not of the type identified, the court will consider whether it should be heard then and there and, if appropriate, dismissed.
- As it is highly unlikely that new factual issues will arise or that the type of evidence required will be provided, it is anticipated that there will be few, if any, further appeals that raise the issue.
- District judges should require a requested person or the advocate representing the requested person who seeks to raise an article 3 issue relying on Polish prison conditions to identify any new factual issues not considered in this appeal or earlier cases and whether the evidence in support is of the type to which we have referred. If the requested person or his advocate fails to do so, then the district judge should ordinarily be entitled to deal with the claim briefly by relying on the decisions of this court.

7.13 The Administrative Court has considered a wide range of factual issues in relation to prison conditions. The most common issue raised is overcrowding. In order to satisfy the first condition set out in the High Court guidance above, it will be necessary for the requested person to raise a novel issue relating to prisons in Poland. A Polish client should be advised of the difficulties that he or she will face in raising any argument on Polish prison conditions.

Article 5 (the right to liberty and security) and article 6 (the right to a fair trial)

7.14 Under article 5, everyone has the right to liberty and security of person. This is of course not an absolute right, and the provision

---

21 *Krolik v Several Judicial Authorities of Poland* [2012] EWHC 2357 (Admin).

7.15 Article 6 safeguards the right to a fair trial, and sets out the basic rights of those charged with a criminal offence. There is often an overlap between this article and the abuse of process jurisdiction.

7.16 Article 5 challenges will frequently arise in tandem with those under article 6, where, for example, it is suggested that, if a person is returned to the requesting state, they will be held in pre-trial detention for lengthy periods.[22]

7.17 In relation to both articles, the burden of proof will be on the requested person to show substantial grounds for believing that there is a real risk of a flagrant denial of the right to liberty and security. In the case of *R on the application of Ullah v Special Adjudicator*,[23] the House of Lords stated that 'where reliance is placed on article 6 it must be shown that a person has suffered or risks suffering a flagrant denial of a fair trial in the receiving state ... Successful reliance on article 5 would have to meet no less exacting a test.'[24]

7.18 Further guidance on this test can be found in the case-law. First, 'real risk' is less than the balance of probabilities. Real risk 'means a risk that is substantial and not merely fanciful; and it may be established by something less than proof of a 51 per cent probability'.[25] The meaning of 'flagrant' was elaborated on by Lord Bingham in *EM (Lebanon) v Secretary of State for the Home Department*,[26] quoting from a European Court of Human Rights case that stated that 'the use of the adjective is clearly intended to impose a stringent test of

---

22 The application of article 5 to those held in detention pending extradition, ie in the requested state, was recently examined in the case of *Lukaszewski v The District Court in Torun, Poland* [2012] UKSC 20 where it was argued that the article 5 rights of requested persons should operate to extend the period in which an appeal against an order for extradition could be served on the prosecution beyond that set out in the Civil Procedure Rules. The court held, following the decision in *MT (Algeria) v Secretary of State for Home Department* [2009] UKHL 10 that article 5 did not apply to the proceedings as they were not challenging detention per se, but challenging underlying decision to extradite the appellants. Nevertheless, as that case also points out, article 5 rights were relied on in the case *of R on the application of Kashamu v Governor of Brixton Prison* [2002] QB 887 to hold that the district judge should consider whether there had been abuse of process rendering the detention unlawful under article 5(4).
23 [2004] UKHL 26.
24 At para 24. Although that was an asylum case, the test nevertheless also applies in extradition cases. See para 24 of *Janovic v Prosecutor General's Office, Lithuania* [2011] EWHC 710 (Admin).
25 *Brown v Government of Rwanda* [2009] EWHC 770 at para 34.
26 *EM (Lebanon) v Secretary of State for the Home Department* [2008] UKHL 64.

unfairness going beyond mere irregularities or lack of safeguards in the trial procedures such as might result in a breach of article 6 if occurring within a contracting state itself'.[27]

7.19 For the reasons set out at the beginning of this chapter, there have been relatively few successful challenges to extradition under these articles. A notable recent exception can be found in the case of *Shawn Sullivan v USA*,[28] a successful challenge under article 5 where it was held that a man who risked being detained under a 'civil commitment order' faced a real risk of a flagrant denial of his rights because such an order fell outside the provisions of article 5.1(e)(the lawful detention of persons of unsound mind). In relation to article 6, the Divisional Court held in the case of *Office of the Prosecutor General of Turin v Barone*[29] that in circumstances where no steps had been taken to contradict the expert evidence of the defence (which sought to demonstrate that the trial was not compliant with article 6), a decision refusing to order extradition under section 21 would be inevitable. In the case of *Abu Qatada*,[30] a European Court of Human Rights decision on deportation, the court held[31] the admission of torture evidence:

> is manifestly contrary, not just to the provisions of article 6, but to the most basic international standards of a fair trial. It would make the whole trial not only immoral and illegal, but also entirely unreliable in its outcome. It would, therefore, be a flagrant denial of justice if such evidence were admitted in a criminal trial.

7.20 Expert evidence, such as a report or witness statement from an appropriately qualified lawyer, academic or NGO with knowledge of the justice system in the requesting state will almost always be required. Any other evidence of, for example, ways in which the requesting

---

27 *Mamatkulov and Askarov v Turkey* (2005) 41 EHRR 25, 537 at para OIII 14.
28 *Sullivan (Shawn) v Government of the United States of America* [2012] EWHC 1680 (Admin).
29 *Office of the Prosecutor General of Turin v Barone* [2010] EWHC 3004 (Admin). See also *Konuksever v Turkey* [2012] EWHC 2166 (Admin). In this case, the court found that there was a risk of a breach of the appellant's article 3 rights. They also, however, expressed concern over the procedural history and stated that the way the requesting state had proceeded 'is capable of being viewed as an abuse of process and as a breach of article 6', although failed to fully apply the test as set out in *Ullah*.
30 *Othman (Abu Qatada) v United Kingdom*, Application No 8139/09, [2012] ECHR 56 (17 January 2012).
31 At para 267. See also para 259 of that judgment for examples of cases where it has been accepted that certain forms of unfairness could amount to a flagrant denial of justice.

Article 8 (right to respect for private and family life)

7.21 Article 8 provides that everyone has a right to respect for his private and family life, his home and his correspondence. It goes on, however, to qualify that right, saying that:

> There shall be no interference by a public authority with the exercise of this right except as is in accordance with the law and is necessary in a democratic society in the interests of national security, public safety or the economic well-being of the country, for the prevention of disorder or crime, for the protection of health or morals, or for the protection of the rights and freedoms of others.

7.22 It is, therefore, a heavily qualified right and a number of cases have emphasised that there is a strong public interest in honouring extradition treaties.

7.23 In deciding whether a person's extradition would be compatible with his or her article 8 rights, the question 'is always whether the interference with the private and family lives of the extraditee and other members of his family is outweighed by the public interest in extradition'.[32] In assessing the proportionality of the interference, the court will take into account a number of considerations, among which are the gravity of the offence; time to be served (and how much time has been served in this country);[33] delay; and the effect of extradition on innocent members of an extraditee's family. The recent Supreme Court judgment in *HH*[34] cautioned against the assumption that there is an 'exceptionality test', while stating, however, that given the strong public interest in extradition, the cases in which extradition is held to be a disproportionate interference with a person's article 8 rights are likely to be exceptional.

7.24 In this judgment, Lady Hale discussed the information that the court requires in assessing a child's interests in the light of Article 8. She stated:

> If the children's interests are to be properly taken into account by the extraditing court, it will need to have some information about them.

---

32 As stated by Baroness Hale giving the leading judgment in the case of *HH v Deputy Prosecutor of the Italian Republic, Genoa* [2012] UKSC 25.
33 *Wysocki v Polish Judicial Authority* [2010] EWHC 3430 (Admin).
34 *HH v Deputy Prosecutor of the Italian Republic, Genoa* [2012] UKSC 25.

There is a good analogy with domestic sentencing practice, although in the first instance the information is likely to come from the parties, as there will be no pre-sentence report. The court will need to know whether there are dependent children, whether the parent's removal will be harmful to their interests and what steps can be taken to mitigate this. This should alert the court to whether any further information is needed. In the more usual case, where the person whose extradition is sought is not the sole or primary carer for the children, the court will have to consider whether there are any special features requiring further investigation of the children's interests, but in most cases it should be able to proceed with what it has.[35]

7.25 Lady Hale went on to say that:

The important thing is that everyone, the parties and their representatives, but also the courts, is alive to the need to obtain the information necessary in order to have regard to the best interests of the children as a primary consideration, and to take steps accordingly.[36]

7.26 In cases where the requested person is the sole carer of a child or where the extradition of both parents is sought, it is imperative that evidence be put before the court as to the consequences for the child of a separation from his or her parents and evidence from a child psychologist and/or social worker should be obtained. Guidance on the areas which such experts should cover can be found at paragraphs 82–86 of the judgment.

7.27 Practitioners should, however, be aware that the High Court has interpreted these paragraphs restrictively. In the case of *JP v District Court at Ústí Nad Labem, Czech Republic*,[37] for example, the High Court refused an adjournment to allow specialist reports to be obtained, stating that the evidence of the mother and family members was sufficient to allow the court to consider how the interests of the children would be affected.

7.28 Practitioners will find that this is the most common objection to extradition raised by requested persons when first appearing at WMC. Solicitors must therefore ensure that clients are given realistic advice about their likelihood of success if they do seek to raise it.

---

35 *HH v Deputy Prosecutor of the Italian Republic, Genoa* [2012] UKSC 25 at para 82.
36 At para 86.
37 *JP v District Court at Ústí Nad Labem, Czech Republic* [2012] EWHC 2603 (Admin).

CHAPTER 8
The initial hearing in EAW cases

8.1	Introduction
8.2	Provisional or certified EAW request?
8.7	**The initial hearing**
8.11	Service of the EAW
8.14	Production before the appropriate judge
8.24	Identity
8.32	Appealing service, production and identity
8.34	Other issues before consent
8.38	Consent
8.41	**Issues to be raised at the extradition hearing to resist extradition**
8.43	Case management forms and directions
8.51	**Bail**
8.57	**The uncontested extradition hearing**
8.63	**Competing EAW requests**
8.65	**Removal where no appeal lodged**

Introduction

8.1 This chapter covers the initial hearing that takes place following a requested person's arrest under Part 1 of EA 2003. Part 1 of the Act governs EAWs. This chapter will consider:
- procedural requirements;
- challenging production and service;
- identification issues;
- requested persons facing domestic proceedings/sentence;
- issues to be raised to challenge extradition;
- bail;
- proceeding to an uncontested extradition hearing;
- competing EAW requests;
- removal where no appeal.

Provisional or certified EAW request?

8.2 The most common way for a person to be arrested under EA 2003 is by way of a certified[1] EAW. If that happens the procedure as set out in paragraph 8.7 below is followed.

8.3 However, arrest under EA 2003 Part 1 can also be provisional. A provisional arrest takes place where a constable, customs officer or a service policeman has reasonable grounds for believing that a Part 1 warrant (EAW) has been or will be issued by a category 1 territory.[2]

8.4 A person arrested under a provisional EAW must be brought before the appropriate judge within 48 hours of arrest and must be given a copy of the warrant as soon as practicable after arrest. An EAW and SOCA certificate must also be produced to the judge within 48 hours of arrest.

8.5 If the person is brought before the court within 48 hours but the EAW and SOCA certificate have not been so produced, the judge may extend the period by a further 48 hours if the judge decides (on the balance of probabilities) that production of the documents could not reasonably be complied with within the initial 48-hour period.

8.6 The provisional arrest is used where SOCA has yet to certify an issued EAW.

---

1 SOCA is responsible for certifying EAWs.
2 EA 2003 s5.

The initial hearing

8.7 The initial hearing starts when the requested person is brought before the appropriate judge.

8.8 In almost all cases the requested person will appear in custody. As in all court proceedings, persons brought before the court will be asked to give their name and date of birth. The requested person will have an interpreter present with them to assist in translation if required.

8.9 Once the requested person has been identified, the CPS representative acting on behalf of the judicial authority will introduce him or herself and the person acting on behalf of the requested person.

8.10 The judicial authority (ie the CPS representative) will confirm that the court has a copy of the EAW and the arrest statement. The judicial authority will then summarise the EAW and provide the court with the circumstances of arrest. The court will be asked to find that the requested person has been served with a copy of the EAW as soon as practicable after arrest[3] and produced before the appropriate judge as soon as practicable.[4]

Service of the EAW

8.11 Section 4(2) states that a copy of the warrant must be given to the person as soon as practicable after his or her arrest. If this section is not complied with and the person applies to the judge to be discharged, the judge *may* order his or her discharge.[5]

8.12 The arrest statement will usually state when the EAW was served upon the requested person. It may be the case that the arresting officer merely gives the EAW to the person upon arrest and then immediately takes it from that person and places it in his or her property bag while the requested person is in custody. It appears that this would be sufficient for the purpose of the EA 2003. The warrant must be in the language of the state requesting the person's extradition and also in English. Furthermore, the SOCA certificate should be attached. There is no requirement that the warrant be in the native language of the requested person.

8.13 If the requested person has not been served with the EAW then an application should be made to the judge for discharge. It should

---

3 EA 2003 s4(2).
4 EA 2003 s4(3).
5 EA 2003 s4(4).

be noted, however, that although EA 2003 s4(4) gives the judge discretion whether to discharge, this is not normally exercised in favour of discharge. Judges will look at what prejudice has actually been suffered by the EAW not being served upon the requested person and will often seek to remedy the problem by ensuring that a copy of the EAW is given to the requested person in the dock. The duty solicitor will also have had an opportunity to provide advice to the requested person on the content of the EAW before going into court.

Production before the appropriate judge

8.14 Section 4(3) states that the person must be brought as soon as practicable before the appropriate judge. If this requirement is not complied with and the person applies to the judge to be discharged, the judge *must* order his or her discharge.[6] Unlike section 4(4) the judge has no discretion and must discharge if they find that the person has not been produced before the judge as soon as practicable.

8.15 What is deemed to be 'as soon as practicable' is a factual determination that will differ from case to case and from judge to judge. The leading authority on production is *Nikonovs v Governor of Brixton Prison*.[7] The facts of that case were set out in paragraph 4 of the judgment:

> At 5.45 on the morning of Saturday 17 September GSL Court Services, who were responsible for conveying Mr Nikonovs to court, telephoned the Boston Custody Suite to say that Mr Nikonovs would not be collected until Monday as Bow Street Magistrates Court was not open over the weekend. In fact this was an error, the court was open on Saturday. In the event Mr Nikonovs was not brought before a judge at Bow Street until 14:00 hours on Monday 19 September, which was nearly 66 hours after his arrest at Boston police station and some 74 hours after his arrest at his home.

8.16 The judge at the magistrates' court refused to discharge Nikonovs who subsequently sought a writ of *habeas corpus ad subjiciendum*. The High Court granted the writ of *habeas corpus* and discharged Nikonovs. As part of their reasoning the court stated that: 'the criterion is practicable rather than the more elastic reasonably practicable' and:[8]

---

6   EA 2003 s4(5).
7   [2005] EWHC 2405 (Admin).
8   At para 21.

No one suggests it was not practicable to bring him to London that day. He could have been brought to Bow Street and the district judge was very unhappy that he was not. He was not, in the event, brought before District Judge Wickham at Bow Street until 14:00 hours on the Monday afternoon. In these circumstances I have no hesitation in concluding that the applicant was not brought before an appropriate judge as soon as practicable.

8.17 This approach appears to have been tempered more recently by the High Court in the case of *Huczko v Governor of HMP Wandsworth*.[9] This was also a case where a writ of *habeas corpus ad subjiciendum* was sought following the refusal of the judge to order the requested person's discharge. In this case, Huczko was arrested and taken the following day to Hammersmith Magistrates' Court in West London. This was an error, as he should have been taken to WMC in order to be produced before an appropriate judge. Huczko was detained for four hours at Hammersmith Magistrates' Court until it was appreciated that he should have been taken to WMC. He was transferred to the correct court where he arrived at about 1 pm. He was then brought before a judge just after 4 pm. The judge found that, despite the human error, he had been produced within 18 hours of his arrest and therefore as soon as practicable. The Divisional Court agreed.

8.18 The 'referral' time at WMC for receiving new cases is 12.30 pm. After that time a case can only be accepted if it is referred to an appropriate judge and the judge agrees to accept the late arrival. If the judge refuses then the person will be lodged overnight in a London police station to be produced the following day.

8.19 When deciding whether to argue that a person has not been brought before an appropriate judge as soon as practicable, it is important to consider the following:

- What time was the person arrested?
- Was the arrest a planned arrest or unexpected?
- What time did the person arrive at the police station and when was his detention authorised?
- When were arrangements made for the collection of the requested person to be taken to court?
- What time was the person transported from the police station to the court?
- How far was the distance between the police station and the court?

---

9 [2012] All ER (D) 47 (Jun).

- Was the case referred to an appropriate judge the previous day after the cut-off?
- If so what information was conveyed to the court about the estimated time of arrival and what was the response of the judge?
- Did anything occur during the transportation to the court that unexpectedly delayed the arrival?

8.20 Only after considering these questions will a duty solicitor be able realistically to determine whether or not to challenge the person's production.

8.21 As guidance, if it has taken two working days to get to court, production should be challenged. If the person was produced before the appropriate judge on the day of arrest or even the following day, unless the distance to be travelled was short, an argument that the person was not produced as soon as practicable will usually be untenable.

8.22 After the CPS representative acting on behalf of the judicial authority has made the introductions the judge will ask the defence representative if there are any challenges to service and production. If there are, submissions should be made there and then. Once the case has moved beyond the initial hearing these issues cannot be revisited.[10] If there are no challenges, then the judicial authority will ask the judge to move on to the issue of identity.

8.23 If the defence submissions on either service of the EAW or production at court are successful then the person is discharged from the extradition request. This does not mean that the EAW is automatically withdrawn and that the person is immune from extradition. A new EAW can be issued and certified by SOCA and proceedings would then start again. It does, however, provide the requested person with an opportunity to try and compromise the EAW (see chapter 12).

Identity

8.24 The appropriate judge must decide whether the person brought before him is the person who is referred to in the EAW. Very often identity will not be in dispute – the requested person will have already given details of their identity on arrest and when asked by the court – but it may be challenged by the defence.

8.25 The appropriate judge must determine identity on the balance of probabilities.[11]

10 *Hilali v The National Court, Madrid* [2006] EWHC 1239 (Admin).
11 EA 2003 s7(3).

8.26 There are many sources from which the court can determine identity. As already mentioned above, the requested person will have given their details when asked by the court. The appropriate judge will also have recourse to the arrest statement and the details that were given to the police upon arrest. Furthermore, identity documents may have been seized. Finally the PNC may determine their true identity if the requested person has been the subject of a livescan check.

8.27 If identity is still in doubt, the judicial authority may seek a set of fingerprints from the requesting state in order to compare them with those taken upon arrest.

8.28 EAWs also contain a section in box A that allows for the judicial authority to enter details about the requested persons 'distinctive marks' or to provide a description. Many judicial authorities take advantage of this and provide a full description including known tattoos and scars.

8.29 EAWs may be accompanied by a photograph of the person sought that could help the appropriate judge determine identity.

8.30 If the judge decides that the person before him is not the person in respect of whom the warrant was issued, he or she must order discharge. If the judge concludes that it is the correct person then the case must proceed to EA 2003 s8 and the issue of consent.

8.31 The requested person must be warned that if identity is unsuccessfully challenged, this may affect the weight to be attached to his or her evidence at the extradition hearing.[12]

Appealing service, production and identity

8.32 Appeals under the EA 2003 in EAW cases are brought under section 26 (for the defence) and section 28 (for the issuing judicial authority). Sections 26 and 28 relate to appeals regarding decisions made at the extradition hearing. Sections 4 to 8 are considered to be issues dealt with at the 'initial hearing' and therefore not subject to the statutory appeal provisions of section 26 or 28. A decision cannot be reopened under Magistrates' Courts Act 1980 s142, as would be the case in criminal proceedings.[13]

8.33 The only way of challenging an adverse decision under sections 4 to 8 is by way of a judicial review or, if the person is in custody,

---

12 *Adedeji v Public Prosecutor's Office, Germany* [2012] EWHC 3237 (Admin).
13 *Klimeto v Westminster Magistrates' Court* [2013] 1 WLR 420.

applying for a writ *of habeas corpus ad subjiciendum*. This approach was approved by the High Court in the case of *Nikonovs* above.

Other issues before consent

8.34 If the person before the court is subject to a charge in the United Kingdom then the extradition hearing *must* be adjourned prior to dealing with consent[14] until the charge is disposed of. Consent will not be taken and the court will proceed to deal with bail.

8.35 If the person before the court is subject to a sentence of imprisonment in the United Kingdom then the judge *may* adjourn the extradition hearing until the sentence of imprisonment has been served. A judge can adjourn the hearing for up to six months before the matter has to be brought back before the court. Again, under section 8B consent will not be taken.

8.36 Sections 8A and 8B were introduced into legislation in order to prevent a requested person escaping prosecution in the United Kingdom or escaping a sentence by consenting to extradition and being removed from the jurisdiction before being prosecuted or completing their sentence.[15]

8.37 If a requested person is subject to a lengthy sentence of imprisonment, the CPS will obtain instructions from the judicial authority as to whether it wishes to seek the requested person's temporary extradition – this is known as 'temporary surrender'. The requesting state will be required to provide an undertaking stating that the requested person will be kept in custody pending their trial and returned to the United Kingdom after proceedings have concluded in that state. If the court agrees to temporary surrender, the requested person will be returned to the United Kingdom to serve the remainder of the sentence.

Consent

8.38 Once the court has progressed through sections 4 to 7 of the Act the next issue to be dealt with is that of consent. The consent procedure was discussed in chapter 5. The clerk of the court will put the consent procedure to the requested person, who will be asked to indicate whether he or she wishes to consent to their extradition. If the requested person consents to their extradition they will be asked to

---

14 EA 2003 s8A.
15 *R on the application of Governor of Wandsworth Prison v Kinderis* [2008] QB 347.

sign the consent form. The interpreter will translate this. It is advisable to ask the court for a copy of the signed consent order to keep on the requested person's file.

8.39   A person consenting to extradition will waive appeal rights and specialty protection, and will be extradited within ten days of having given consent. This ten-day period can be extended upon an application from the judicial authority if it is not possible to effect removal within that time.

8.40   Where requested persons do not consent to their extradition they will be informed that they can change their mind at any time. The court will next ask the advocate to indicate whether any issues will be raised or whether the matter can proceed to an uncontested hearing.

Issues to be raised at the extradition hearing to resist extradition

8.41   If there are any issues to raise these should be outlined by the advocate at the initial hearing. These issues may come under intense scrutiny from the judge and the advocate must be prepared to fully justify why the issue to be raised is tenable, why time is required to prepare the case and why it is in the interests of justice to adjourn.

8.42   The issues raised to challenge extradition may be one or more of the following:

- validity of the EAW (s2);
- the offence(s) contained in the EAW are not extradition offences (s10);
- one (or more) of the bars to extradition (ss11–19);
- conviction in absence (s20);
- extradition would be incompatible with Convention rights (s21);
- physical/mental health of requested person (s25).

Case management forms and directions

8.43   From 2 January 2013 it became a standard direction in extradition proceedings that, for cases that are to be contested, the defence advocate should complete a case management form at the initial hearing. The case management form can be found at appendix F. The form warns the advocate that 'the information you provide must be accurate as it may be checked, and it may be referred to at a later hearing'. The form must therefore be completed accurately.

8.44 Should issues arise later in the proceedings that were not included in the form it is important to notify both the court and the CPS as soon as they arise so that all parties are on notice in advance of the extradition hearing.

8.45 Having identified the issues to be contested, the court will then proceed to fix a date for the extradition hearing to take place. If the issues appear complex the court may set a review date before fixing a final hearing date. A judge will often be allocated to the case to ensure judicial continuity in case management.

8.46 The advocate will need to provide a realistic time estimate in order to assist the court in finding a date for the hearing. By way of example, a section 10 extradition offence argument could take as little as 30 minutes, whereas a substantial issue where expert evidence is to be called could last a day or two.

8.47 Once a date is fixed the court will make directions. These will include directions for the service of a skeleton argument, defence evidence (if any), and a proof of evidence. In extradition proceedings, where the requested person is to be called to give evidence, a signed proof of evidence has to be served in advance (see paragraph 9.24). This allows the CPS acting on behalf of the judicial authority to seek instructions on issues raised within the statement. It can also then be adopted in evidence by the requested person, drastically reducing the amount of time required for examination in chief. The standard directions state that a signed proof of evidence must be served within 14 days of the grant of legal aid (within 28 days if the requested person is in custody).

8.48 A skeleton argument will also be required in most, if not all, contested cases. The preparation of the skeleton argument and other documents for the extradition hearing will be explored in chapter 9.

8.49 When agreeing to directions, it is important to remember that it may take at least a week for the requested person's legal aid application to be determined. Work is unlikely to start straight away on a case unless the requested person is paying privately and has put the representative in funds.

8.50 On occasions the duty solicitor may have too many cases to deal with to allow time for the completion of the case management form for each case. The court makes allowance for this and the last question on the form asks: 'have you had sufficient time to advise your client on potential challenges? If not why not?' It is acceptable to indicate 'no' and in these cases the court will direct that the case management form be completed and submitted within seven days of the initial hearing or by the second hearing, whichever is sooner.

Bail

8.51 The final issue for the court to determine at the initial hearing is that of bail. Bail applications in all proceedings, but especially so in extradition proceedings, need to be structured. As discussed in chapter 5, there are enquiries specific to extradition proceedings that the court will make of the advocate if bail is to be granted. It is important to have a good bail package in place and for that reason telephone calls will very often need to be made to family members in order to obtain a security or locate travel documents.

8.52 There is no presumption in favour of bail in conviction cases and, in reality, a requested person is unlikely to be granted bail without a security.

8.53 The conditions usually imposed in extradition cases include:
- security/surety or both (pre-release condition);
- surrender/retention of travel documents (pre-release condition);
- residence;
- not to apply for international travel documents;
- reporting to a police station;
- curfew;
- geographical restriction.

8.54 All securities need to be paid in at WMC and sureties are taken at the same court. Assistance is provided at the first floor helpdesk. Those offering securities do not need to attend court if they can deposit the funds via an electronic transfer. In this situation the proposed security contacts the WMC bail department, which will provide them with the court's bank details and reference number. If a security is to be paid in cash, the person offering the security will need to bring proof of identity (passport/ID card/driver's licence) to court together with proof of address (bank statement/utility bill). A surety will need to attend court with proof of identity and proof of funds being offered.

8.55 If a male requested person is remanded into custody he will be taken to HMP Wandsworth unless he is assessed on arrival at the prison to be a category A prisoner, in which case he will be transferred to HMP Belmarsh. Female requested persons remanded into custody will go to HMP Holloway.

8.56 If the requested person is remanded into custody it is important to inform family, friends or partners (if instructed to do so) that HMP Wandsworth operates induction visits on Mondays to Thursdays between 8 am and 9 am. These visits do not have to be booked in advance and are only for prisoners who have been in custody for seven days at the most.

The uncontested extradition hearing

8.57 If there are no issues to be raised on behalf of the requested person – or the person wishes to return to the requesting state but does not consent to his or her extradition – the matter will very often proceed to an uncontested extradition hearing there and then and it is therefore important for the advocate to be prepared for this to happen.

8.58 The court has to be satisfied of the following before ordering extradition:
- the extradition request is a valid request within the meaning of EA 2003 s2;
- the offences contained in the EAW are extradition offences;
- there are no bars to extradition;
- there is no conviction in absence, or the requested person accepts deliberately absenting themselves (conviction cases only);
- extradition would be compatible with the requested person's Convention rights within the meaning of the Human Rights Act 1998.

8.59 At an uncontested extradition hearing the prosecutor acting on behalf of the judicial authority will conduct most of the hearing, taking the judge through the warrant. The prosecutor will refer to sections 64 or 65 in establishing extradition offences and will submit that no bars to extradition are raised and that extradition would be compatible with the requested person's Convention rights.

8.60 The judge will ask the advocate on behalf of the requested person if there are any representations to be made. Having received confirmation that there are none, the judge will make the extradition order pursuant to section 21(3) of the Act.

8.61 The judge should then inform the requested person that he or she has seven days to appeal the decision to order extradition (see chapter 11). If no appeal is lodged, then arrangements are made for extradition within the ten days that follow the end of the seven-day period. The requested person will also be informed that due to the numbers awaiting extradition, this period can be – and very often is – extended on application to the court. If the requested person is not removed in the relevant period and there has been no extension of time application granted, then the court must order their discharge unless reasonable cause can be shown for the delay.[16]

8.62 The requested person – if remanded in custody – will be informed that every day spent in custody awaiting extradition will be deducted

---
16 EA 2003 s35(5).

from any sentence outstanding in the requesting state, or if convicted the time will count against any sentence of imprisonment imposed. This information is transmitted to the requesting judicial authority by SOCA on surrender of the requested person.

Competing EAW requests

8.63 There are rare occasions when an EAW has been issued by two different category 1 territories. If during the relevant period[17] the judge is informed that there are competing EAW requests he or she may:
- order further proceedings on the warrant under consideration to be deferred until the other warrant has been disposed of, if the warrant under consideration has not been disposed of;
- order the person's extradition on the warrant under consideration to be deferred until the other warrant has been disposed of, if an order for extradition has been made on the warrant under consideration.

8.64 The appropriate judge when deciding the above must take account of:[18]
- the relative seriousness of the offence concerned;
- the place where each offence was committed (or was alleged to have been committed);
- the date on which each warrant was issued;
- whether in the case of each offence, the person is accused or alleged to be unlawfully at large after conviction.

Removal where no appeal lodged

8.65 If there is no appeal against the decision to order extradition, removal must take place within the ten days that follow the end of the seven-day period permitted for lodging an appeal. This period can be extended if the judge and the judicial authority agree a later date. If the person is not removed within the required period then the person must be discharged if an application is made to the appropriate judge unless reasonable cause is shown for the delay.[19]

17 The relevant period starts when the person is brought before the appropriate judge and ends when the person is extradited or discharged: EA 2003 s44(3).
18 EA 2003 s44(7).
19 EA 2003 s35(3).

Figure 8.1: Procedure following arrest on a certified EAW

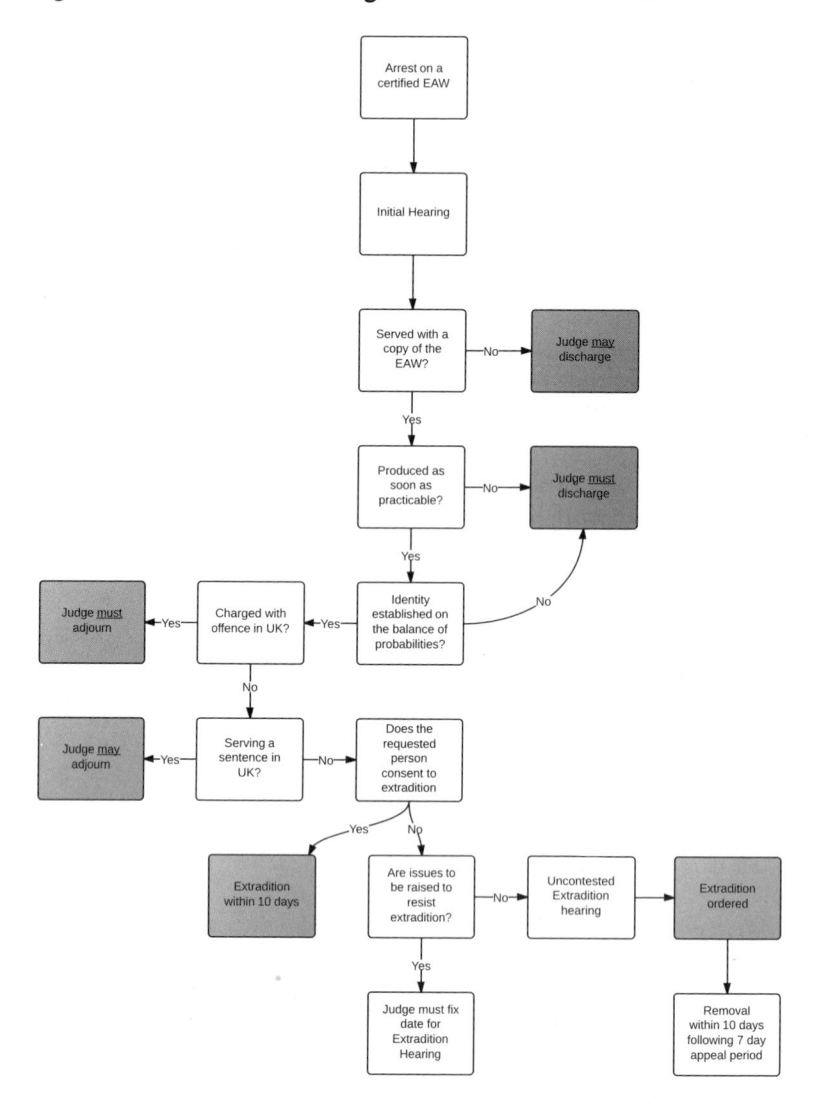

CHAPTER 9

Preparing for the contested hearing

9.1	Introduction
9.2	Visiting the client in custody
9.4	Use of interpreters
9.7	Case management and court directions
9.11	Taking instructions
9.14	Rule against double jeopardy
9.15	Extraneous considerations
9.16	Passage of time
9.19	Human rights considerations
9.20	Conviction in absence
9.21	Physical or mental health
9.22	Statement of issues
9.24	Drafting a proof of evidence
9.27	Witness statements
9.28	Obtaining expert evidence
9.34	Objective evidence
9.35	Further information from the issuing state
9.36	Disclosure

continued

9.37	Drafting a skeleton argument
9.38	Preparation of the bundle
9.40	Certificate for counsel

Introduction

9.1 Preparing even the most straightforward case for a contested hearing is likely to take some hours, particularly when time is factored in to allow for interpreters and travel to HMP Wandsworth to take instructions from those remanded in custody. It is important to consider these factors when setting a timetable for a contested hearing in court. This chapter will look at the casework that may need to be undertaken prior to any hearing.

Visiting the client in custody

9.2 It will often take time for a prison visit to be arranged, and the booking of a visit should therefore be prioritised. It can take over half an hour to gain entry to the visiting area, so it is always worth arriving at the prison well before the visit is due to start. The use of an interpreter will necessarily reduce the time available for the exchange of information, and a 'double visit' may be required.

9.3 While the relevant law and procedure will have been explained to the requested person at the first hearing, it will often be worth running through this again, in order to ensure the requested person has a proper understanding. In addition, lawyers will find that there are a large number of prisoners from Poland and the Baltic states on remand in extradition cases, many of whom have developed considerable knowledge about extradition. If the requested person has had an opportunity to speak to others in the prison, it may be necessary to deal with issues that other prisoners have advised him or her to raise, eg article 3 in relation to prison conditions in Poland, or the impact of an asylum claim on extradition.

Use of interpreters

9.4 Criminal defence practitioners should be familiar with the Law Society practice note on 'Use of Interpreters in Criminal Cases',[1] which applies equally to extradition as to other types of criminal proceedings. The quality of interpreters provided by the court can vary greatly,

---

1 www.lawsociety.org.uk/advice/practice-notes/interpreters-in-criminal-cases/ (24 January 2012).

and those representing requested persons will be aware of the need to ensure, as far as is possible, that the interpreter is competent.

9.5 Some requested persons may be confident in everyday speech, but not at a hearing that involves complicated legal concepts and terminology. It may be that he or she did not have an interpreter at the first hearing, but feels that one would be necessary for the extradition hearing. The court is familiar with such requests being made.

9.6 When seeing requested persons (or defence witnesses) outside court, the interpreter will need to be arranged by the solicitor. If the client is legally aided, the Legal Aid Agency will pay a maximum of £25 per hour for an interpreter (or £32 per hour outside London).[2] If the interpreter's fees fall within this rate, there will be no need to apply for prior authority. If, however, it proves impossible to find an interpreter who will work at this rate (in the case, for example, of a rare language), an application for prior authority should be made on form CRM4, demonstrating that the case is exceptional.

Case management and court directions

9.7 In most contested cases, the following documents will need to be prepared for service on the court and the prosecution:
- statement of issues;
- proof of evidence;
- witness statements;
- expert reports;
- objective evidence;
- skeleton argument.

9.8 This chapter will look at the preparation of each of these in turn. Prior to the extradition hearing, all documents in the case should be put together into a joint bundle to be served on the court.

9.9 At the initial hearing, directions will often be set for the service of the above documents, although in more complex cases (and in Part 2 cases) these directions may be made at a subsequent hearing. If the case is not straightforward (and most cases where there is an arguable point will not be) there may be one or indeed several case management hearings. A review hearing may be listed at the initial hearing, or more commonly the case will be listed at the request of one of the parties prior to the extradition hearing.

2 Criminal Legal Aid (Remuneration) Regulations 2013 Sch 5.

Preparing for the contested hearing

9.10 If there are difficulties in complying with the directions, it is essential to make a written application to the court to extend time for service. Ignoring such directions may lead the court to consider wasted costs. Although it is possible to make applications administratively in criminal proceedings, the practice of the IJO is to list all such applications (including applications to vary bail) in court. Where the application is agreed by the other side or is not contentious, it is possible to request that attendance be excused; but where the application is disputed, attendance at court will obviously be preferable.

Taking instructions

9.11 Some basic instructions should already have been taken at the initial hearing, covering the areas set out in the checklists at appendices D and E. The requested person should be asked whether they have, or can get hold of, any documentary evidence (for example papers from the court in the requesting state). People often retain important documents and may not realise their significance. Those in custody will sometimes have friends or family who can assist in obtaining any documentation. Full background instructions should be taken when preparing for the contested hearing covering:

- family background and current circumstances;
- education;
- employment;
- health;
- immigration history;
- reason for coming to the United Kingdom;
- reason for leaving the requesting state;
- previous convictions in this or any other jurisdiction;
- concerns regarding extradition to the requesting state.

9.12 As with any client, the areas that will be covered will be led, to some extent, by the particular circumstances of that client. It is, of course, always important to foster a relationship with the client that encourages him or her to raise any issues that he or she thinks relevant, and it is good practice to ask the requested person whether there is anything that he or she can think of that has not been covered.

9.13 It may be necessary to take instructions directed towards the particular bar that the requested person wishes to raise. Clearly, there are some areas where a client's instructions will be of less importance. For example if a person is arguing that prison conditions in a particular country will result in a breach of his or her article 3 rights, there may be little or indeed nothing that he or she can add to the expert reports, and it may be in such a case that no proof of evidence need be served. If, however, that person does have first-hand experience of prison conditions, or if he or she falls within a category of individual cited as being at risk in the reports (for example because of illness or race), this is something that should be covered when taking instructions. In view of the most commonly raised bars, suggested areas to discuss with the requested person are covered below.

Rule against double jeopardy

9.14 Full instructions should be taken on the circumstances of the previous conviction/acquittal, together with any sentence imposed and the extent to which it has been served. It will also be important to obtain any documentary evidence from the court in the requesting state that dealt with the case – a local lawyer will be able to facilitate this. A signed letter of consent to enable the gathering of such information from third parties should be obtained.

Extraneous considerations

9.15 Relying on either limb, the requested person should be asked about any past experience of prejudice or punishment experienced by him or her on account of race, religion, nationality, gender, sexual orientation or political opinion.

Passage of time

9.16 It will be essential to take detailed instructions on the reasons why the requested person left the jurisdiction in order to deal with any assertion that the requested person has deliberately fled the jurisdiction. The warrant may give an indication as to whether the requesting state will assert that the requested person is a fugitive. If the person faces an accusation warrant, it will be necessary to probe his or her knowledge (if any) of the offence and its aftermath. If, for example, the person was arrested and later released, why did he or she subsequently leave the jurisdiction? Was he or she under any obligation to return or abide by any bail conditions? Similarly for a conviction warrant the requested person should be asked whether he or she knew that he or she had been convicted and, if so, why he or she left the jurisdiction. Was he or she given any assurance that led him or her

Preparing for the contested hearing 123

to believe that he or she was allowed to leave? Documentary evidence in support will lend weight to the requested person's case.

9.17 The second area that should be covered in detail is the person's current circumstances as this will go to the question of oppression. How has his or her life changed since the time of the alleged offence, in particular with regards to family, employment and health? Does he or she now have familial responsibilities such that extradition would cause particular hardship to a vulnerable person? An expert report from, for example, a social worker may be helpful in such a case.

9.18 In addition to this, requested persons should be asked whether they know of any reason why their extradition would be unjust, ie whether there are essential witnesses who are no longer available.

Human rights considerations

9.19 With regard to articles 2, 3, 5 and 6, there will often be limited instructions that can be taken from the requested person (see paragraph 9.9 above) beyond his or her past experience of conditions in the requesting state. For article 8, however, detailed instructions should be taken on the requested person's personal and family circumstances, covering areas similar to those set out in paragraph 9.14 above.

Conviction in absence

9.20 If the requested person was absent from his or her trial, instructions should be taken on his or her knowledge (or lack of knowledge) of the trial, covering the same areas as those set out in paragraph 9.13 above. If instructions establish that he or she was not deliberately absent and knew nothing of the criminal investigation, the requested person is unlikely to be able to provide any useful instructions on whether or not he or she will be entitled to a retrial: this will be a question for an expert to address. If the requested person was arrested or involved in the preliminary parts of the investigation, this should be covered.

Physical or mental health

9.21 While this is an area that will always require medical reports to be commissioned, it will often be the case (depending on the precise medical condition of the requested person) that useful instructions can be taken on the history of the requested person's medical complaints along with the effects that that condition has had on his or her life. In suicide risk cases, a full history of previous incidents of self-harm or attempts should be taken in addition to information on psychiatric diagnoses. Again, a signed authority for the release of medical records should be obtained from the client as well as details of the relevant GP, treating doctor and hospitals.

Statement of issues

9.22 A statement of issues will not be required in straightforward cases. Its purpose is to notify the court and primarily the prosecution of the grounds on which extradition is contested. A statement of issues should set out the very basic facts about the EAW or request, along with the challenges to be raised and an outline of the facts that support the grounds on which extradition is contested.

9.23 It is essential that it sets out any point on which the prosecution may wish to seek further information from the requesting state. If it does not, this may well lead to delay as the prosecution may seek time to obtain information to address issues that are raised late in proceedings. If it becomes apparent that an issue has arisen after the statement of issues has been served, it is good practice to notify the prosecution of this issue in writing at the first opportunity.

Drafting a proof of evidence

9.24 The proof of evidence is a crucial document in extradition proceedings. Particular time and care should be taken in its preparation. There are no rules or guidelines that dictate its form or content. While the court will direct that a 'proof of evidence' be served, this does not mean that a full statement setting out all of the client's instructions need necessarily be provided to the court. A proof of evidence in extradition cases is different from that which would be taken in usual criminal proceedings and that would be used by the defence team and not disclosed to the court or the other side. A proof of evidence for service in extradition proceedings will be more like a witness statement served in civil proceedings.

9.25 In terms of form, practice among solicitors varies – some favour serving the proof in the form of a section 9 statement;[3] others will serve it as a statement with numbered paragraphs signed and dated

---

3 Criminal Justice Act 1967.

by the client. The authors prefer the latter approach. Given that there is no requirement to serve the statement in section 9 format, there is no good reason for the requested person to provide a statement that carries a risk of prosecution for perjury if he or she does deviate from it under cross-examination. The proof should be set out in chronological order with subject headings at appropriate points. It is important that it is in the requested person's own words and that any comment that could be seen as legal argument is avoided.

9.26 The content of the proof should set out relevant background information, along with current circumstances and the particular detail pertaining to the grounds upon which extradition is contested (as set out in paragraphs 9.14–9.21). There is no need to serve a full statement setting out detail that is irrelevant, and district judges dealing with cases that are frequently document heavy are unlikely to welcome lengthy biographical histories. Nevertheless, it is important that any fact that may be raised by the requested person in evidence is covered in the proof, and it may therefore be preferable to lean towards inclusion of detail if in doubt. Although no statutory inference will be drawn from failure to mention facts in a proof, requested persons should be aware that where facts not included are then elicited in live evidence, this may undermine their credibility. If there are parts of a client's case that are particularly problematic, it is tactically better to deal with this in the proof rather than to leave an obvious gap that will be exploited in cross-examination.

Witness statements

9.27 Witnesses in extradition hearings range from friends and family of the requested person to professionals in the requesting state with, for example, knowledge of proceedings in that jurisdiction. Witness statements should be served in section 9 form, given that there will always be a possibility that the witness will not attend the extradition hearing.

Obtaining expert evidence

9.28 Expert evidence will usually be used in two areas. First, it is used in support of arguments about the situation (legal or political) in the requesting state, when challenging extradition on either extraneous considerations or human rights grounds. Secondly, experts are commonly relied upon to support cases where a requested person's personal circumstances are relevant to an issue in the case, for example doctors who can provide a report for the purposes of sections 25/81 or psychologists who can comment on the impact of a separation between parent and child for the purposes of an argument on ECHR article 8.

9.29 Where a requested person is legally aided, an application for prior authority should be made using the form CRM4 to cover the expert's costs. Online applications for prior authority are usually dealt with much more quickly than those made in hard copy and, from 1 April 2013, all CRM4s must be made online. The hourly rates are set out in the Criminal Legal Aid (Remuneration) Regulations 2013 at Schedule 5. If it is impossible to find an expert who can produce a report at the rates set out in the Order the Legal Aid Agency may increase the rates in exceptional circumstances. Exceptional circumstances are defined by the LAA as:

> where the expert's evidence is key to the client's case and either –
> a) the complexity of the material is such that an expert with a high level of seniority is required; or
> b) the material is of such a specialised and unusual nature that only very few experts are available to provide the necessary evidence.[4]

9.30 If prior authority is refused, legally aided clients can, in certain circumstances, pay for experts reports.[5]

9.31 As in other proceedings, an expert's duty is to the court, and he or she must be objective. Part 33 of the Criminal Procedure Rules applies to expert witnesses in extradition cases and a copy of this should be provided to any expert along with the letter of instruction. Rule 33.3 sets out information that all expert reports should contain. Compliance with the rules should be verified upon receipt of the report. It is important that the statement includes enough detail for a court to be able to establish that the expert has complied with his or her duties.

9.32 Letters of instruction should enclose the warrant or request along with any further information received from the prosecution, the proof of evidence and any pertinent witness statements. It may be useful in some cases for the expert to be provided with relevant case-law. The letter of instruction should set out a brief background before going through the questions to be addressed. These questions should be as specific as possible, and should direct the expert towards answering

---

4 See LAA *Guidance on Remuneration of Expert Witnesses* April 2013.
5 2010 Standard Criminal Contract Specification Part A, para 8.52.

Preparing for the contested hearing

9.33 questions that are not addressed in the objective evidence. Funding matters and the timeframe should also be covered. It is advisable to require experts to submit reports at least a week prior to the deadline in order to allow sufficient time to address any issues. In drafting a letter of instruction, it is important to bear in mind that the letter and enclosures, as well as any correspondence between the solicitor and the expert, may be seen by the court and/or the prosecution.

9.33 Solicitors will be responsible for paying the costs of the commissioning of expert reports. Where a client is legally aided and the expert's attendance at court is required, this will be covered by the court. The rates for travel and attendance for expert witnesses are minimal,[6] and can only be claimed after attendance. It can take the court many months to process the expert's claim for payment. For this reason it is frequently impossible to secure the attendance of experts based in other jurisdictions. Furthermore, there is currently no provision to allow witnesses in extradition proceedings to appear by video-link,[7] although it is anticipated that a forthcoming statutory instrument will change this.

Objective evidence

9.34 Reports from international organisations, if available, should be served as part of the bundle in appropriate cases. If, for example, a requested person is arguing that his or her extradition will result in a breach of his or her human rights, reports from such organisations as Amnesty International, the US State Department or the European Committee for the Prevention of Torture will reinforce other evidence. Although criticism from independent international bodies may carry some weight, the court will also require expert evidence that is tailored to the specific facts of the case.

---

6 See the Guide to Allowances under Part V of the Costs in Criminal Cases (General) Regulations 1986 SI No 1335, available at www.justice.gov.uk, for the applicable rates of payment.
7 Criminal Justice Act 1988 s32 and the Criminal Justice Act 2003 s51 set out the circumstances in which a witness can give evidence by video-link. Evidence has, however, been received by video-link in some cases, such as that of *Government of the Republic of South Africa v Shrien Dewani* [2012] EWHC 842 (Admin).

Further information from the issuing state

9.35 The court in this country cannot compel the requesting state to provide further information. It may, however, direct that further information, if it is to be provided, should be served by a particular date. While there is no obligation on the requesting state to serve further information, it is sometimes provided following service of defence documents where the requesting state 'wishes to resist the implications of evidence advanced and proffered by an appellant ...'.[8] Note, however, that a requesting state may well rely on the presumption that it will comply with its Convention obligations and serve no information in response. When it is provided, further information is frequently served very late in proceedings. Even if the CPS has acted diligently in communicating requests for information, the requesting state itself can be dilatory in responding. In some cases, there will be no comment that the requested person can usefully make on the further information, but he or she should nevertheless be provided with the opportunity to do so. If it is a case in which expert reports have been commissioned, the expert's views on the further information should also be solicited – this may require a further application for prior authority if an addendum report is necessary.

Disclosure

9.36 The CPS does not have a general duty of disclosure as it does when conducting prosecutions in English criminal proceedings. However, the CPS owes the court a duty of candour and good faith.[9] It is accepted that, while it is for the requesting state to determine which evidence to put forward in support of its request for extradition, the CPS in accordance with its duty to the court must disclose evidence (but only if such material is brought to the attention of the CPS by the requesting state) which destroys, renders worthless or very severely undermines the evidence on which it relies.[10]

---

8 *Baksys v Ministry of Justice of the Republic of Lithuania* [2007] EWHC 2838 (Admin) at para 11.
9 *Knowles Jr v United States of America and another* [2006] UKPC 38 at para 35.
10 At para 35.

Drafting a skeleton argument

9.37 A skeleton argument is usually served well in advance of the extradition hearing. Those used to drafting skeleton arguments in usual criminal proceedings will recognise the format: in short, it should set out the facts, followed by the law, then the submissions. The headings below provide a suggested structure for a skeleton argument:

1) introduction and procedural chronology:
   - details of the EAW (relevant dates, accusation/conviction, offence);
   - court proceedings since initial hearing;
2) issues for the court to determine:
   - set out the challenges to be raised;
3) the law:
   - set out the statutory provisions and relevant case-law relied upon. It may be necessary to set out more of the case-law than in criminal proceedings;
4) submissions:
   - apply the law to the facts;
5) conclusion.

Preparation of the bundle

9.38 A bundle, preferably indexed with tabs and page numbering, should be served on the court prior to the extradition hearing. It should include all the documents set out in paragraph 9.7, along with the documents relied upon by the prosecution (usually EAW/extradition request, further information and skeleton argument) and the relevant statutory provisions and case-law. If a joint bundle is to be prepared it should be properly paginated and indexed. The general running order for such a joint bundle will be:

1) opening note/skeleton argument of the judicial authority;
2) EAW/extradition request;
3) witness statements from the judicial authority;
4) expert reports;
5) further information from judicial authority;
6) defence skeleton argument;
7) proof of requested person;
8) witness statements;
9) expert reports;
10) authorities (with key passages highlighted).

9.39 Current practice at WMC is to assign a specific district judge to hear a case prior to the extradition hearing. When sending the bundle to the court, it should be accompanied by a covering letter requesting that it be placed before the relevant district judge so that he or she has time to read it prior to the extradition hearing. The court and the CPS should be served with the bundle electronically (as a PDF) where possible.

Certificate for counsel

9.40 Where a case is publicly funded, a certificate for counsel (including, in appropriate cases, Queen's Counsel) can be granted for extradition proceedings in the magistrates' court. The relevant legislation is the Criminal Defence Service (General) (No 2) Regulations 2001. Regulation 12 reads:

> (1) A representation order for the purposes of proceedings before a magistrates' court may only include representation by an advocate in the case of:
> (a) any indictable offence, including an offence which is triable either way; or
> (b) extradition hearings under the Extradition Act 2003
> where the court is of the opinion that, because of circumstances which make the proceedings unusually grave or difficult, representation by both a litigator and an advocate would be desirable.

9.41 It is important to note that the Regulations use the word 'desirable' rather than, for example, 'necessary'. In order to apply for a certificate for counsel, a written application should be submitted to WMC setting out the facts of the case and the reason that the proceedings are unusually grave or difficult. The application can be supplemented by a written advice from counsel.

CHAPTER 10

The contested extradition hearing

10.1	Introduction
10.2	Receivable and admissible documents
10.5	Burden and standard of proof
10.6	Requests for further information
10.8	Applications to adjourn
10.12	Housekeeping
10.16	Who goes first?
10.19	Calling your client – evidence in chief
10.28	Expert evidence
10.32	Adducing other evidence
10.34	Submissions
10.38	Judgment
10.42	Ex tempore judgment
10.43	Information provided to the requested person after judgment

Introduction

10.1 The extradition hearing can vary in length depending on the complexity of the issues to be argued and the amount of evidence that is to be called. Straightforward issues can be argued in 30 minutes whereas complex Part 2 cases may require several days of the court's time.

Receivable and admissible documents

10.2 An EAW is a receivable document that is admissible in proceedings under the Act.[1] But what about other documents adduced by the judicial authority/requesting state in the course of the proceedings?

10.3 Section 202(2) and (3) state that any other document issued in a category 1 or 2 territory may be received in evidence if it has been 'duly authenticated'. Duly authenticated is defined in subsection (4). A document is duly authenticated if one of the following apply:

- it purports to be signed by a judge, magistrate or officer of the territory;
- it purports to be certified, whether by seal or otherwise, by the ministry or department of the territory responsible for justice or for foreign affairs;
- it purports to be authenticated by the oath or affirmation of a witness.

10.4 A document that is not duly authenticated is not precluded from being admitted into evidence in extradition proceedings. However, less weight may be attached to it.

Burden and standard of proof

10.5 Unless any express provisions in the Act apply, the burden and standard of proof must be applied as if the person who is facing extradition is accused of an offence and the judicial authority/requesting state is the prosecution.[2]

---

1 EA 2003 s202(1).
2 EA 2003 s206.

Requests for further information

10.6 The CPS decides what will be disclosed. Domestic rules of disclosure do not apply to extradition proceedings.[3] However, the CPS owes the court a duty of candour and good faith.

10.7 Although the appropriate judge can request further information from the CPS acting on behalf of the judicial authority/requesting state, he or she cannot compel them to provide it. Failure to provide a response could, however, lead to an inference being drawn as to why it has not been produced.

Applications to adjourn

10.8 Applications to adjourn should not be left until the day of the extradition hearing unless unavoidable. The court will be reluctant to lose court time, especially given the courts' listing difficulties. The court is unlikely to consider sympathetically an application to adjourn the extradition hearing if it is made on the day of the hearing. However, if an application to adjourn on the day of the extradition hearing is essential, it must be made on notice.

10.9 The CPS acting on behalf of the judicial authority/requesting state should be put on notice of an intention to seek an adjournment as soon as the need arises. The reasons that an adjournment is sought, and the proposed timetable for the case going forward should the court grant the application to adjourn, should be set out. If the CPS do not oppose the application or are 'neutral' to it, the application is more likely to be granted. In that case, the court will expect the parties to have agreed directions.

10.10 Ordinarily, the court should be notified in writing of an application to adjourn the extradition hearing. The letter should clearly outline the reason an adjournment is required and state why it is in the interests of justice that the case be adjourned. The court will be referred to any previous applications to adjourn and will consider whether the parties have complied with directions set by the court. It is therefore important to apply to vary the directions where they cannot be complied with.

10.11 Where an application to adjourn is made on the day of the extradition hearing, advocates should be prepared for the application to

3 *R on the application of Raissi v Secretary of State for the Home Department* [2008] EWCA Civ 72, [2008] QB 836.

be refused and for the hearing to proceed. Challenges to the refusal to grant adjournments are made by way of judicial review but the Administrative Court will be slow to interfere in a decision by the appropriate judge.

Housekeeping

10.12 Before the extradition hearing begins the advocate should ensure that both the court and the CPS have all the documents that are to be relied upon. Ideally, these should all be in an indexed and paginated joint bundle (see chapter 9). A spare copy of the bundle should be brought to the hearing in case it has not made its way to the appropriate judge hearing the case. If the judge has not had sight of the bundle or has not read it, the court should be invited to rise to allow the judge to read the skeleton arguments.

10.13 If the judge has considered the skeleton arguments, he or she should be taken through the bundle. The relevance of each document in the bundle should be explained.

10.14 The order in which live witnesses are to be called should be outlined. If there is a witness who is to be called 'out of turn', the reason for this should be explained to the court.

10.15 Finally, if the time estimate does not appear sufficient, the court should be informed so that the judge can decide whether to begin to hear the case and adjourn the proceedings part-heard or to adjourn to a day when the hearing can be heard in full.

Who goes first?

10.16 Those acting on behalf of the judicial authority/requesting state will open the hearing and take the court through the EAW/extradition request. They will outline the issues that are raised by the requested person and invite the court to find matters not contested in their favour.

10.17 If the burden is on the judicial authority to prove the issue under EA 2003 then they will go first in making their submission to the court. For example, the burden is on the judicial authority to prove to the criminal standard that the conduct contained in the EAW/extradition request is an extradition offence.

10.18 In all other situations, it will be the requested person's case that is heard first, with his or her evidence called first.

Calling your client – evidence in chief

10.19 Before the requested person gives evidence it is important to ensure that no other witness of fact is sitting in the courtroom. Any witness of fact should be asked to leave while the requested person is giving his or her testimony. This does not apply to expert witnesses who can sit in court throughout the proceedings while other evidence is being heard.

10.20 If the requested person is in custody he or she will be brought to the witness box by the gaolers. If the requested person is on bail he or she will be asked to make his or her way to the witness box by the court usher.

10.21 It is important that the requested person has with him or her the proof of evidence and any other documents that will be referred to. If the court has a bundle of evidence for the hearing the requested person should also be provided with one.

10.22 As with many types of proceedings, the requested person will be asked to affirm or to swear on oath. If the requested person is assisted by an interpreter the interpreter will also be sworn in.

10.23 The advocate should ask the requested person to confirm his or her name and date of birth. The requested person should then be asked if the proof of evidence that has been drafted is his or her statement and confirm that it is true to the best of his or her knowledge and belief. The requested person should be asked to confirm that it is his or her signature on each page of the statement and then asked if he or she wishes the proof of evidence to be adopted as their evidence in chief.

10.24 Depending on the issues raised, there may be no supplementary questions for the requested person or he or she may be asked to address issues not covered in the proof of evidence.

10.25 The advocate should be careful not to frustrate the court by asking questions where the answers are clearly contained in the proof of evidence: the judge should have read the papers ahead of the extradition hearing. If it is clear that the judge has not had an opportunity to read the papers in advance of the hearing, it may be necessary to summarise the main points covered in the proof of evidence with the requested person. If there is information that has been served by the judicial authority/requesting state subsequent to the proof of evidence being served, then this will need to be addressed by the requested person in their oral evidence.

10.26 If there is a break in the proceedings and the requested person is in the middle of giving evidence it is important to remember that the evidence cannot be discussed.

10.27 Once the requested person has finished giving his evidence in chief he or she will be exposed to cross-examination from the judicial authority and is also likely to be questioned by the judge. Re-examination follows should there be a need for it.

Expert evidence

10.28 If relying upon expert evidence, the report of such experts should have been served ahead of the hearing to allow the judicial authority an opportunity to respond and adduce its own evidence in rebuttal.

10.29 The reports of experts can be adopted into evidence – in the same manner as that presented by the requested person – and this can drastically reduce the time an expert spends in the witness box. The expert should have a copy of the report when giving evidence and any other documents that he or she will be asked to consider. If there is a bundle, this should be provided to the expert before giving evidence.

10.30 With the permission of the court it is possible to lead experts through their qualifications and experience before addressing the main conclusion and findings of a report. If the judicial authority/requesting state does not contest the expertise of an expert there will be no need to go through their qualifications.

10.31 It is important that the expert addresses any points made by the judicial authority/requesting state in further information served in the proceedings if this has not been addressed in an addendum report. Once the expert has finished giving their evidence in chief he or she may be subjected to questions from both the court and the judicial authority/requesting state.

Adducing other evidence

10.32 If other evidence is to be adduced, the time to do it is after the requested person and expert (if applicable) have given their evidence.

10.33 Other evidence could take the form of section 9 witness statements[4] to be read, or objective reports. If there are lengthy objective reports to be relied upon, relevant passages in the judge's bundle should be highlighted to ensure that they are easily found when reference is made to them. Relevant passages should be read out to the court.

---

4 Criminal Justice Act (CJA) 1967.

Submissions

10.34 Once all the evidence has been called/adduced then it is time for submissions to be made. The skeleton argument that has already been served should address the submissions on behalf of the requested person. This is an opportunity to expand upon the main arguments and address the evidence that has been heard.

10.35 The court should be addressed as to the relevant law. If the applicability of the law is agreed between the requested person and the judicial authority/requesting state then this could be agreed in a section 10 admission.[5]

10.36 The advocate should apply the facts of the case to the law. It may be necessary to distinguish the facts of the current case from the reported case-law. When referring to reported cases the court should be taken to the relevant passages. If the passage relied upon is not too lengthy, it should be read to the court. Again, highlighting key passages in the authorities in the bundle will bring them to the judge's attention in pre-hearing reading.

10.37 Very often judges will be careful to avoid making decisions that will 'open the floodgates'. It is therefore important not to make general sweeping assertions (ie a fair trial is not possible in Malta) but rather to emphasise the points in the case being presented that are unique (ie a fair trial in Malta is not possible for this particular requested person because …).

Judgment

10.38 After both the requested person and the judicial authority have made submissions, the judge will give his or her ruling. It is normal practice in contested extradition hearings for the judge to reserve judgment to another date. This allows the judge to consider both the oral submissions made at the contested hearing and to consider the written material served.

10.39 If judgment is reserved a written ruling will be handed down. This is normally read out in full in open court. It is the practice of some judges to read the findings of fact and the conclusion rather than the whole judgment.

5 CJA 1967.

10.40   If there are any factual errors in the judgment these should be noted and brought to the attention of the judge once it has been read out in full. The amendments (if any) can then be made by hand.

10.41   A copy of the written ruling will be provided to the parties and there is therefore no need to take a detailed note.

Ex tempore judgment

10.42   If the issue raised at the contested extradition hearing is straightforward the judge may give an *ex tempore* judgment. This will not be in writing; therefore as full a note as possible should be taken. If the matter is to be appealed a summary of the judgment should be agreed between the parties so that it can be provided to the Administrative Court Office with the notice of appeal (see chapter 11 on appeals).

Information provided to the requested person after judgment

10.43   After reading out the judgment, the judge will then explain to the requested person the effect of his or her decision. If the result is to order the person's extradition (in a Part 1 case) or to send the case to the SSHD (in a Part 2 case) the judge will explain the timeframe for appealing. He or she will then remand the person in custody or on bail.

10.44   If the decision of the judge is to order the person's discharge, and the CPS gives an indication to the judge of an intention to appeal the decision, then the judge must continue to remand the person in custody or on bail. If no such indication is given, and the requested person is in custody he or she will be released. If the requested person was subject to bail conditions then those conditions will cease to apply.

CHAPTER 11

Appeals

11.1	Introduction
11.6	Legal aid
11.11	Appeals under Part 1 of the Act
11.15	Preparing the appeal
	Form N161 • Grounds of appeal
11.22	Lodging and service of the appeal
11.28	Appeals under Part 2 of the Act
11.32	Appeals in cases where risk of suicide is in issue
11.33	Appeals against the decision of the appropriate judge
11.34	Appeals against the decision of the SSHD
11.35	Out-of-time appeals
11.39	Case management conference – Part 2 cases only
11.44	Compliance with directions made by the High Court
11.47	Applications to adjourn
11.50	Bundles for the appeal hearing
11.52	Withdrawing the appeal
11.53	Withdrawing representation
11.60	Applying to extend the representation order

continued

11.68	Introduction of new evidence
11.75	Court's powers on appeal in Part 1 cases
11.78	Appeal against discharge at the extradition hearing
11.80	Court's powers on appeal in Part 2 cases
11.83	Appeal against discharge at the extradition hearing
11.86	Appeal against the decision of the SSHD to order extradition
11.91	Appeals to the Supreme Court
11.95	Making the application to certify a point of law
11.101	Supervening events
11.106	Removal following dismissal of appeal
11.108	Application to the European Court of Human Rights for rule 39 interim measures

Introduction

11.1 Both the requested person whose extradition has been ordered and the issuing state have a statutory right of appeal against adverse decisions made at the extradition hearing. There is no permission stage.

11.2 In EAW cases the appeal is against the decision of the appropriate judge who either ordered extradition or ordered the person's discharge.

11.3 In Part 2 cases the appeal can be against the decision of the appropriate judge to send the case to the SSHD and/or the decision of the SSHD to order extradition or a decision by either to order the person's discharge from the extradition request.

11.4 The timeframe in which an appeal must be lodged and served differs depending on the part of the Act under which proceedings are brought. The timeframe is tight and unforgiving if not adhered to. Only in exceptional circumstances can an application to appeal out of time be heard.

11.5 Appeals to the High Court under EA 2003 are also governed by the Civil Procedure Rules, in particular CPR Practice Direction 52D para 21.1. Practitioners must comply with these Rules and Practice Directions.

Legal aid

11.6 In order to apply for legal aid in the High Court in extradition proceedings a form CRM14 must be submitted to the Administrative Court Office (ACO). There is no means testing in the High Court for extradition appeals and therefore the delays that are sometimes experienced in the magistrates' court do not occur once the case reaches the appeal stage.

11.7 CRM14s that were previously submitted to the magistrates' court will not be accepted.

11.8 The CRM14 should be submitted at the same time that the appeal is lodged so that the issuing fee of £235 can be recovered as a disbursement. The case lawyers at the ACO have delegated powers to grant a representation order. A copy of the representation order will usually be received by the legal representative two to three days after a CRM14 is submitted.

11.9 A representation order will be granted for a solicitor and junior counsel. In order to obtain a representation order for leading counsel alone or for leading counsel and junior counsel, an application must be made to extend the representation order (see paragraph 11.65 below).

11.10 The representation order can also be extended to cover disbursements such as experts' fees and interpreters' fees (see paragraph 11.60 below).

Appeals under Part 1 of the Act

11.11 If a person's extradition is ordered then that person has seven days in which to appeal the decision to the High Court. The seven days start with the day the extradition order is made. If, for example, the order is made on a Tuesday, the appeal must be filed and served by the following Monday. If the decision was made on a Monday the deadline will be the following Monday as the seventh day falls on a Sunday. Similarly, if the seventh day falls on a bank holiday the deadline moves to the next working day.[1]

11.12 The appeal must be issued by the High Court *and* served[2] upon the CPS acting on behalf of the judicial authority within the seven-day time limit. The Supreme Court in *Lukaszewski v The District Court in Torun, Poland*[3] considered the question of the form the notice of appeal must take when served on the other party.

11.13 In the lead judgment in *Lukaszewski*, Lord Mance stated:[4]

> In my view, a generous approach can and should be taken of this, bearing in mind the shortness of the permitted period and the fact that what really matters is that an appeal should have been filed and all respondents should be on notice of this, sufficient to warn them that they should not proceed with extradition pending an appeal. This should not however be taken as licence to appellants to give informal notices of appeal. Any potential appellant serving anything other than a complete copy of the sealed Form N161 will need to seek and will depend upon obtaining the court's permission to cure the position under the rules.

11.14 It is therefore best practice for practitioners to avoid the need to obtain the court's permission to cure 'informal' notices of appeal, by lodging and serving as much information as possible within the relevant

---

1 *Mucelli v The Government of Albania* [2009] UKHL 2.
2 The House of Lords decision in *Mucelli v The Government of Albania* also held that the notice of appeal must also be served on the CPS within the relevant period (seven days for Part 1 cases; 14 days for Part 2 cases).
3 [2012] UKSC 20.
4 At para 18.

timeframe. It should be noted that in the case of *Lukaszewski*, three of the appellants were unrepresented; the court is likely to be less sympathetic where an appellant is represented. See paragraph 11.40 below on out-of-time appeals.

Preparing the appeal

11.15 The following documents should be put together in a bundle to be lodged at the High Court:
- form N161 – appellant's notice;
- grounds of appeal;
- EAW;
- judgment of the appropriate judge.

11.16 The court will require three copies of the above and the CPS will also require one copy. In total five bundles should be prepared.

11.17 The appellant will be covered by the representation order in the lower court for the preparation and filing of the appellant's notice and grounds of appeal. The CRM14 and a copy of the representation order from the magistrates' court (if applicable) should also accompany the appeal documents.

Form N161

11.18 The form can be completed online and then printed. It cannot be saved online. The form itself is relatively straightforward. Form N161 can be found at appendix G.

11.19 It is important to state at section 8 of form N161 the date of the person's arrest.[5] Under EA 2003 s31 an appeal under Part 1 of the Act[6] must begin to be heard within 40 days of the person's arrest. This is not normally possible, particularly as extradition proceedings in the magistrates' court are frequently heard outside this period. The High Court will therefore extend the period in which the appeal is to be heard as being in the interests of justice.

11.20 Form N161 should be signed either by the appellant or a solicitor of the firm lodging the appeal. Any documents not included at the time of lodging that should ordinarily be included (such as a copy of the EAW or a copy of the judge's ruling) should be provided as soon

---

5 Endorsing the date of arrest is a requirement of CPR Practice Direction 52D para 21.1(3)(b) although failure to provide this information is not fatal.
6 CPR Practice Direction 52D para 21.1(3)(c).

as possible and an indication given in section 11 of form N161 as to when it can be provided.

Grounds of appeal

11.21 The grounds of appeal should accompany the appellant's notice. It need not be a lengthy document but should identify the grounds upon which the appeal is brought. See below.

IN THE HIGH COURT OF ENGLAND & WALES   CASE NO:
QUEEN'S BENCH DIVISION
ADMINISTRATIVE COURT

BETWEEN

THE REQUESTED PERSON

Appellant

v

THE REQUESTING STATE

Respondent

GROUNDS OF APPEAL

The appellant was arrested on ....

On ...... District Judge ...... ordered the requested person's extradition/sent the case to the Secretary of State for the Home Department. [The Secretary of State for the Home Department ordered extradition on ......]

The appellant relies upon the following grounds of appeal:

That (pursuant to s26 and 14 Extradition Act 2003) the District Judge should have decided the question of whether it would be oppressive by reason of the passage time differently, and had he done so he would have been required to order the appellant's discharge.

Lodging and service of the appeal

11.22 Once the bundles have been prepared they should then be taken to the Royal Courts of Justice on the Strand, London, along with a cheque for the court fee of £235, made payable to 'HMCTS', to be lodged.

11.23 If the fee is being paid by cash it must be paid at the fees office before the appeal is lodged, where the appellant's notice will be stamped to show the fee has been paid. A receipt will also be provided. The documents should then be taken to the ACO where staff will 'seal' the appellant's notice by stamping it with the court seal and retain three copies of the bundles.

11.24 Once the appeal has been lodged the court may give a date for the listing of the appeal there and then. If the court does fix a date the time estimate given will be usually 30 minutes. If this will be insufficient the ACO should be notified at the time the appeal is lodged.

11.25 If a date is not fixed for the appeal at the time of lodging, then the court will place the appeal into the Administrative Court 'warned list' and a date will subsequently be fixed for the hearing. It is important to notify the court of the time estimate for the hearing and details of counsel so that the list office can liaise with counsel's clerks. Failure to give these details could result in the case being listed when instructed counsel is not available.

11.26 Once the documents have been sealed they must be served by the appellant upon the CPS within the same seven-day period. It is best to serve these documents by fax (0203 357 0055/0056) to ensure service the same day. When serving by fax, it is important to ensure that a 'transmission ok' receipt is received. Alternatively, the CPS will accept service by email to scd.extradition@cps.gsi.gov.uk. Again, it will be important to request a 'read receipt'. A copy should also be served on the IJO at WMC.[7]

11.27 Ordinarily High Court proceedings take precedence over proceedings in the lower courts in relation to counsel's availability.

Appeals under Part 2 of the Act

11.28 Under Part 2 of the Act it is the appropriate judge that sends the case to the SSHD, who then has a two-month period in which to make the extradition order, starting on the day on which the case is sent to the

---

7 CPR Practice Direction 52D para 3.4(1).

11.29 SSHD.[8] Once the extradition order has been signed by the SSHD, the requested person has 14 days in which to lodge the appeal starting from the date he or she is informed of the SSHD's decision.

11.29 An appeal can be against either the decision of the appropriate judge or the SSHD or both. The following documents should be put together in a bundle in order to be lodged at the High Court:

- form N161 – appellant's notice;
- grounds of appeal;
- extradition request;
- judgment of the appropriate judge;
- decision of the SSHD ordering extradition.

11.30 The notice of appeal and grounds of appeal must be lodged with the ACO and the sealed documents must be then be served within the 14 days on both the CPS acting on behalf of the judicial authority and the SSHD.

11.31 Appeals under Part 2 of the Act should begin within 76 days of filing of the appellant's notice. Again, this can be extended by the High Court 'in the interests of justice'.

Appeals in cases where risk of suicide is in issue

11.32 In January 2013 the President of the Queen's Bench Division stated that an appeal in a case where the risk of suicide is an issue should be heard within as short a timescale as practicable.[9] He stated that such appeals should be listed for hearing within two to three weeks of the notice of appeal being lodged at the ACO. Practitioners should be aware that in such cases the skeleton argument should be served with the notice of appeal (where possible) and in any event within 7–14 days of the appeal being lodged

Appeals against the decision of the appropriate judge

11.33 An appeal against the decision of the appropriate judge may be brought on a question of law or fact. An appeal against the decision

8 See *Zaporozhchenko v Westminster Magistrates' Court* [2011] EWHC 34 (Admin).
9 *Poland v Wolkowicz; Poland v Biskup & Lithuania v Rizleriene* [2013] EWHC 102 (Admin).

of the appropriate judge may be lodged and issued before the SSHD has made her decision but cannot be heard by the High Court until after the SSHD has made her decision. It is normal practice to appeal the decision once the SSHD has made her order.

Appeals against the decision of the SSHD

11.34 As above the appeal may be brought on a question of law or fact. If there is to be an appeal against the SSHD the Home Office should be served with the sealed appeal documents. Once the appeal has been issued and served, the Treasury Solicitor will be appointed to act on behalf of the SSHD and they will in turn instruct their own counsel.

Out-of-time appeals

11.35 Prior to the case of *Lukaszewski* (see above) the High Court had no jurisdiction to hear out-of-time appeals. However, it is now possible for appeals lodged out of time by citizens of the United Kingdom to be considered. Lord Mance stated:[10]

> I consider that, in the case of a citizen of the United Kingdom like Mr Halligen, the statutory provisions concerning appeals can and should all be read subject to the qualification that the court must have a discretion in exceptional circumstances to extend time for both filing and service, where such statutory provisions would otherwise operate to prevent an appeal in a manner conflicting with the right of access to an appeal process held to exist under article 6(1) in *Tolstoy Miloslavsky*. The High Court must have the power in any individual case to determine whether the operation of the time limits would have this effect. If and to the extent that it would do so, it must have power to permit and hear an out of time appeal which a litigant personally has done all he can to bring and notify timeously.

11.36 Exceptional circumstances are only likely to apply to unrepresented appellants. It is difficult to envisage circumstances in which an out-of-time appeal, which has been brought by a legally represented appellant, would be allowed to be heard.

11.37 If it can be avoided, appeals should not be brought at the last minute, so that if there are any problems they can be resolved in good time without the risk of the appeal being time-barred.

10 [2012] UKSC 20 at para 39.

11.38 Where appeals must be lodged as a matter of urgency, that is on the seventh day of the permitted period, it is possible to obtain permission from the ACO to lodge the appeal by fax. The ACO will require a faxed undertaking to be returned with the documents that are available. The terms of the undertaking will oblige the solicitor to lodge any missing or unavailable documents, including the court fee, within 24 hours. The ACO will ask for an explanation as to why the appeal cannot be lodged in person and why the appeal is being lodged at a late stage.

Case management conference – Part 2 cases only

11.39 In all Part 2 appeals a case management conference will be held 35 days after the appeal has been lodged. Unlike Part 1 cases, a date will not be fixed for the appeal hearing at the time of lodging the appeal.

11.40 The case management conference will be held before a Master or Deputy Master of the Administrative Court. The purpose of the case management hearing is to provide effective management of the appeal so as to ensure that the appeal takes place on the date fixed for hearing. Five days before the case management conference the parties will be expected to send to the court office a document marked for the attention of the master that provides the following information:

- a time estimate for the appeal hearing including delivery of the judgment;
- names of counsel and a list of dates to avoid for listing of the substantive appeal;
- a list of issues for the case management conference (if any);
- a list of the legal points to be taken at the appeal (together with any relevant authorities, with page references to passages relied on);
- a chronology of events;
- a list of the essential documents for the advance reading of the court;
- the case for any further evidence to be adduced, having regard to the provisions of the Practice Guidance dated December 2012 (see paragraph 11.60 below);
- a date for the exchange of evidence that the parties may be permitted to rely upon;
- a date for replies following exchange of evidence;
- a date for the parties to provide joint bundles;
- any further directions necessary for the appeal to proceed without delay that the master ought to consider.

11.41 The purpose of providing dates to avoid and a time estimate five days in advance of the case management conference is to enable the list office to fix a date for the appeal so that all parties at the conference have an opportunity to consider whether it allows sufficient time for the preparation of the appeal. If insufficient time has been set aside for the appeal hearing an application should be made at the case management conference for the date to be vacated and refixed. The reason that more time is required should be identified in the documents to be provided to the master ahead of the conference.

11.42 The court will expect the parties to the appeal to reach agreement (as far as is possible) as to the directions to be applied that are necessary to ensure that the appeal will be heard on the date fixed.

11.43 Case management conferences take place in open court and therefore only barristers or solicitors with higher rights of audience may appear. The case management conference will usually be listed to commence at 9.30 am.

Compliance with directions made by the High Court

11.44 It is important to comply with all directions made by the High Court (as with any court). Where a direction cannot be complied with, the court should be notified of the reasons why and an extension sought in a formal application by lodging form PF244 – application notice.

11.45 It is usual practice where full grounds of appeal are not submitted with the notice of appeal for the court to make an 'unless order'. The court will direct that the appellant is to lodge full grounds of appeal and a summary of his argument (skeleton argument) within a certain time or the case will be listed for strike out or determination of the appeal on its merits with the evidence available at that date. Usually the order will allow 14 days for compliance from the date of the order.

11.46 Whenever corresponding with the ACO it is important to ensure that the case reference number is included so that court staff can identify the case more easily. Misspelt names can cause delays and result in misfiling. If documents are to be sent to the judge's clerk these should be copied to the extradition team by email: Administrativecourtoffice.extradition@hmcts.x.gsi.gov.uk.

Applications to adjourn

11.47 Once a date has been fixed, it can only be vacated on written application to the court. A fee is applicable if the application to vacate is made within 14 days of the hearing date. If the other party consents then a fee of £45 is due. If the other party does not consent, a fee of £80 is payable. Before making the application to adjourn, solicitors should obtain the view of the other side. It may be that the judicial authority/requesting state consents to the adjournment, which will greatly increase the appellant's chances of obtaining the adjournment.

11.48 Any application to adjourn should be made on form PF244 and be accompanied by a signed witness statement. If the issue is relatively straightforward the witness statement can be contained within the PF244. A draft order should also be attached to the application notice setting out the orders sought. The application notice should be lodged with the ACO and served upon the CPS/Home Office (for Part 2 matters).

11.49 An application to adjourn will normally be dealt with on the papers by a single judge although an oral hearing may be directed.

Bundles for the appeal hearing

11.50 The bundles for the appeal hearing should be prepared and served on the court/parties at least three weeks before the date fixed for the appeal hearing. If the appeal is to be heard by a single judge two bundles should be provided to the court. If the case has been allocated to a Divisional Court, three bundles will be required.

11.51 It is usual practice for counsel to prepare and serve the bundles.

Withdrawing the appeal

11.52 An appellant can withdraw the appeal at any time.[11] In order to do so, a consent order should be drafted (in the format given below) and signed by all parties to the appeal. Once signed it should then be lodged at the ACO together with the fee of £45 (recoverable as a disbursement on taxation).

---

11 The court will dismiss the appeal on receipt of a consent order signed by all parties: CPR Practice Direction 52A para 6.1.

IN THE HIGH COURT OF ENGLAND & WALES
QUEEN'S BENCH DIVISION
ADMINISTRATIVE COURT   CASE NO:

BETWEEN

THE REQUESTED PERSON
                                                Appellant
v

THE REQUESTING STATE
                                                Respondent

CONSENT ORDER

UPON CONSIDERATION OF THE DOCUMENTS LODGED BY THE APPELLANT WITHDRAWING THE APPEAL

AND IT BEING DECLARED THAT NEITHER THE APPELLANT NOR THE RESPONDENT IS A CHILD OR PATIENT

IT IS ORDERED THAT:

1. The appeal be dismissed

2. [The appellant be remanded in custody/remanded on bail pending his removal]

3. There be no order for costs save for a detailed assessment of the legally aided party's public funding certificate

    Signed

    Appellant   Respondent

Withdrawing representation

11.53 Sometimes it may be necessary to come 'off the record'. This may be because the legal representative is professionally embarrassed or because the legal representative has advised that the appeal is no longer tenable. A solicitor may have obtained a representation order in order to advise an unrepresented appellant as to the merits of his appeal and subsequently advised negatively.

11.54 If an appellant has been advised that there is no merit in the appeal but does not accept the advice and does not consent to the appeal being withdrawn then the solicitors will need to apply to come off the record. Legal representatives should not pursue an unmeritorious appeal.

11.55 In order to apply to come off record, a PF244 should be lodged at the ACO along with the £80 court fee informing the court that the solicitor wishes to apply to come off the record with immediate effect. If the appellant wishes to dispense with his or her legal representation and represent him or herself this should be achieved by completing form N434 (notice of change of solicitor). It will be necessary to obtain the requested person's signature in order to use the N434. No court fee is payable if this form is used.

11.56 If the appellant intends to represent him or herself and wishes to be present at his or her appeal hearing then the ACO will need to be informed of this so that a production warrant can be sent to the prison if he or she is in custody or correspondence can be sent to the appellant's address if on bail. The ACO has started to arrange for appeal hearings to take place by way of a video-link if the appellant is representing him or herself and is in custody. However, this cannot always be arranged and therefore the appellant may be produced in person. If the appellant requires an interpreter this information should also be provided to the ACO so that they can make the relevant arrangements.

11.57 The court should be notified of a representative's intention to come off the record as soon as negative advice has been provided to the client. A late or delayed notification is not something the court looks upon favourably and should be avoided at all costs. A late application to come off the record may be refused by the court and the representative ordered to attend court in order to explain why it has been made so late.

11.58 A late application to come off the record can cause inconvenience for the ACO, especially if the person is in custody, resulting in the need for a production order and an interpreter to be booked.

11.59 If the appellant wishes to obtain a second opinion on the advice received then a form N434 will need to be completed as above. However, the court is live to the fact that many appellants seek to delay their appeal by so-called 'solicitor shopping'.

Applying to extend the representation order

11.60 In December 2012 the Administrative Court issued Practice Guidance for parties wishing to request an extension of a representation order to cover the cost of a) obtaining expert evidence, b) the translation of documents or c) representation by both leading and junior counsel.

11.61 Disbursements may be incurred without seeking approval of the court, but they must be justified on taxation. A note from counsel to be submitted on taxation may assist.

11.62 A request for any of the costs mentioned above should be made in writing, either by letter or e-mail, quoting the CO reference, and should be sent to the ACO.

11.63 The request should be supported by evidence and accompanied by a statement of truth.

11.64 According to the Practice Guidance (Administrative Court: applications to extend representation orders in extradition appeals) a party wishing to make an application to cover a disbursement must include the following information in their application:

- assurance that the evidence sought has not been considered in any previous appeals determined by the appellate courts;
- explanation as to why the evidence was not called at the extradition hearing in the WMC and what evidence can be produced to support that;
- explanation as to why the new evidence would have resulted in the district judge deciding a question before him at the extradition hearing differently and whether, if he or she had done so, the district judge would have been required to make a different order as to discharge of the requested person;
- statement of when the need for the new evidence first became known;
- explanation of any delay in making the request;
- explanation as to what relevant factual, as opposed to expert evidence, is being given by whom to create the factual basis for the expert's opinion;

- explanation as to why this particular area of expertise is relevant: for example why a child psychologist should be appointed as opposed to a social worker;
- full breakdown of all costs involved, including any VAT or other tax payable, including alternative quotes or explaining why none are available;
- provision of a list of all previous extensions of the representation order and the approval of expenditure to date;
- provision of a timetable for the production of the evidence and its anticipated effect on the time estimate and hearing date.

11.65 An application to extend the representation order to cover representation by both junior and leading counsel must include information:
- identifying the substantial novel or complex issues of law or fact in the case;
- explaining why these may only be adequately presented by a Queen's Counsel;
- whether a Queen's Counsel has been instructed on behalf of the respondent;
- explaining any delay in making the request.

11.66 The application must be supported by an advice from junior or leading counsel.

11.67 A Master of the Administrative Court will consider the above applications on the papers although he or she may order that the matter be dealt with at a case management conference. In Part 2 cases the applications should be included in the information to be provided to the Master ahead of the case management conference so that the issue(s) can be determined at the conference.

Introduction of new evidence

11.68 There are strict rules on the introduction of new evidence being adduced on appeal. The introduction of fresh evidence was considered in the case of *The Szombathely City Court v Fenyvesi*.[12]

11.69 The Divisional Court considered the provisions in EA 2003 s29(4), in particular where evidence was available on appeal that was not available at the extradition hearing. The court held that 'not available at the extradition hearing' was to be interpreted as evidence that either did not exist at the time of the extradition hearing, or that was

12 [2009] EWHC 231 (Admin).

not at the disposal of the party wishing to adduce it and that he or she could not with reasonable diligence have produced.

11.70 Following the case of *Fenyvesi* a party wishing to adduce fresh evidence must submit a witness statement explaining why the evidence was not available at the extradition hearing.

11.71 When considering whether to admit fresh evidence the court must consider it to be decisive; in other words the court must be satisfied that the evidence would have resulted in the appropriate judge deciding the relevant question differently.

11.72 Appellants should not 'keep their powder dry' and adduce evidence on appeal or raise new issues that could have been presented before the appropriate judge at first instance. However, there is a material difference between seeking to adduce fresh evidence on appeal that could have been available before the appropriate judge and raising a new issue that was not argued at first instance. In *Hoholm v Government of Norway*[13] Stanley Burnton LJ held:

> it seems to me to be significant that section 104 distinguishes between a new issue and new evidence. I would therefore hold that where an issue was available to be raised by an appellant on the evidence adduced at the extradition hearing, she is in general, if not always, entitled to raise that issue on appeal to this Court, even though the issue was not raised at that hearing. In any event, I see no good reason why the Appellant should not be permitted to argue the issue before this Court. Extradition is an infringement of liberty, and while the Court is concerned to ensure that those who are the subject of conforming requests for extradition are lawfully extradited, the legal requirements for extradition are safeguards that must be observed.

11.73 It is therefore possible to raise an issue on appeal (such as dual criminality, validity of the warrant) that was not raised at the extradition hearing, provided no new evidence is to be adduced. If new evidence is to be adduced then the criteria in *Fenyvesi* will need to be satisfied.

11.74 If a new issue and/or fresh evidence are to be raised on appeal that was not raised at the extradition hearing by previous legal representatives and if specific criticism of the previous legal representatives is being levelled, then the guidance set out in *Sondy v Crown Prosecution Service*[14] will need to be followed. Openshaw J stated:

> In my judgment, the practice commonly followed in the Court of Appeal Criminal Division should have been followed here; the

---

13 [2009] EWHC 1513 (Admin).
14 [2010] EWHC 108 (Admin).

appellant should have been formally invited to waive his privilege and, whether he did so or not, the lawyers should have been asked by the court to deal with the points made against them, having regard to whether privilege has been waived or not. If the appellant did not waive privilege, then of course an adverse inference could in any event be drawn against him.

Court's powers on appeal in Part 1 cases

11.75 On appeal under section 26 the High Court may either allow or dismiss the appeal. The court can only allow the appeal if the conditions in section 27(3) or (4) are satisfied.

11.76 The conditions in section 27(3) are that:
- the appropriate judge ought to have decided a question before him or her at the extradition hearing differently;
- if the judge had decided the question in the way he or she ought to have done, he or she would have been required to order the person's discharge.

The conditions in section 27(4) are that:
- an issue is raised that was not raised at the extradition hearing or evidence is available that was not available at the extradition hearing;
- the issue or evidence would have resulted in the appropriate judge deciding a question before him or her at the extradition hearing differently;
- if the judge had decided the question in that way, he or she would have been required to order the person's discharge.

11.77 On allowing the appeal the court must order the person's discharge and quash the order for his or her extradition.[15]

Appeal against discharge at the extradition hearing

11.78 If the judicial authority has appealed the decision of the appropriate judge to discharge the requested person then the appeal is brought under section 28. On appeal under section 28 the High Court may either allow the appeal or dismiss it. Section 29(3) and (4) mirror those stated above in section 27(3) and (4).

---

15 EA 2003 s27(5).

11.79 If the appeal is allowed the court must quash the order discharging the requested person and remit the case back to the judge, directing the judge to proceed, as he or she would have been required to had he or she decided the relevant question differently at the extradition hearing.[16]

Court's powers on appeal in Part 2 cases

11.80 On appeal under section 103 (appeal against the decision of the appropriate judge) the court may a) allow the appeal, b) direct the judge to decide again a question (or questions) which he or she decided at the extradition hearing, or c) dismiss the appeal.[17]

11.81 The court may only allow the appeal if one of the conditions in section 104(3) or the conditions in subsection (4) are satisfied. The conditions in subsection (3) are:

- the judge ought to have decided a question before him or her at the extradition hearing differently;
- if the judge had decided the question in the way he or she ought to have done, he or she would have been required to order the person's discharge.

The conditions in subsection (4) are:

- an issue is raised that was not raised at the extradition hearing or evidence is available that was not available at the extradition hearing;
- the issue or evidence would have resulted in the judge deciding a question before him or her at the extradition hearing differently;
- if the judge had decided the question in that way, he or she would have been required to order the person's discharge.

11.82 If the court allows the appeal then it must make an order for the person's discharge and quash the order for his or her extradition.[18]

Appeal against discharge at the extradition hearing

11.83 On appeal under section 105 the High Court may allow the appeal, direct the judge to decide the relevant question again or dismiss the

---

16 EA 2003 s29(5)(a)–(c).
17 EA 2003 s104(1)(a)–(c).
18 EA 2003 s104(5).

appeal.[19] The court may allow the appeal only if the conditions in subsection (4) or the conditions in subsection (5) are satisfied.

11.84 If the appeal is allowed the court must quash the order discharging the person; remit the case to the judge; and direct the judge to proceed as he or she would have been required to do if he or she had decided the relevant question differently at the extradition hearing.

11.85 If the court makes a direction that the judge is to decide the relevant question again and the judge subsequently decides the relevant question differently he or she must proceed, as he or she would have been required to do had he or she decided that question differently at the extradition hearing. If the court makes a direction that the judge is to decide the relevant question again and the judge does not subsequently decide the relevant question differently, the appeal must be taken to have been dismissed by a decision of the High Court.

Appeal against the decision of the SSHD to order extradition

11.86 The requested person may also appeal against the decision of the SSHD to order extradition and the category 2 territory can appeal the decision of the SSHD to discharge the person from the extradition request.

11.87 On appeal the High Court may either allow the appeal or dismiss the appeal (s109(1)).

11.88 The court may allow the appeal only if the conditions in section 109(3) or the conditions in subsection (4) are satisfied. The conditions in subsection (3) are that:

- the SSHD ought to have decided a question before her differently;
- if the SSHD had decided the question in the way she ought to have done, she would not have ordered the person's extradition.

The conditions in subsection (4) are that:

- an issue is raised that was not raised when the case was being considered by the SSHD or information is available that was not available at that time;
- the issue or information would have resulted in the SSHD deciding a question before her differently;
- if the SSHD had decided the question in that way, she would not have ordered the person's extradition.

---

19 EA 2003 s106(1)(a)–(c).

11.89 If the court allows the appeal it must order the person's discharge and quash the order for extradition.[20]

11.90 The same conditions apply to an appeal against the decision of the SSHD under section 110 to order the person's discharge. If the appeal is allowed against the decision to discharge the person the court must quash the order discharging the person and order the person's extradition.[21]

Appeals to the Supreme Court

11.91 In order to appeal to the Supreme Court, the High Court must have certified that there is a point of law of general public importance involved in the decision and it must appear to the court granting leave that the point is one that ought to be considered by the Supreme Court.[22]

11.92 An application to certify a point of law must be made within 14 days starting with the day on which the High Court makes its decision on the appeal.[23] An application to certify is dealt with on the papers. Only in exceptional circumstances would the court agree to an oral hearing. However, the decision will always be pronounced in open court (no attendance required) so there is no confusion as to when time runs from for removal/appeal to the Supreme Court.

11.93 If the High Court certifies that there is a point of law of general public importance it can then also grant leave to appeal or refuse leave to appeal. If the High Court refuses leave to appeal then an application for leave can be made to the Supreme Court within 14 days starting with the day on which the High Court refuses to grant leave.[24] It is rare for the High Court to grant leave to appeal to the Supreme Court.

11.94 The Supreme Court has no power to grant a representation order. If a point of law of general public importance is certified, an application for a representation order to be extended to cover an application to the Supreme Court for leave to appeal should be made at the time of certification.

---

20 EA 2003 s109(5).
21 EA 2003 s111(5).
22 EA 2003 s114(4).
23 EA 2003 s114(5).
24 EA 2003 s114(6).

Making the application to certify a point of law

11.95 A formal application must be submitted (form PF244) with the fee of £80. It is usual for counsel to draft the application to certify and for it to be attached to the application notice.

11.96 Although the application must be made within 14 days, there is no time limit within which the application must be determined by the High Court.

11.97 If leave is granted by the High Court then the appeal must be lodged with the Supreme Court within 28 days of the date when the High Court granted leave.[25]

11.98 If leave to appeal is granted by the Supreme Court the appeal must also be lodged with them within 28 days of leave being granted.

11.99 The Supreme Court has strict rules and Practice Directions relating to appeals brought before it and the reader is referred to the Supreme Court website for further information.[26]

11.100 The Supreme Court has the power to allow an appeal, dismiss an appeal or remit the matter back to the High Court.

Supervening events

11.101 If the appeal concludes and a supervening event occurs then fresh representations should be made to the SSHD to persuade her to reconsider the order for extradition by engaging her human rights obligations. Any adverse decision of the SSHD can be subject to judicial review proceedings. An undertaking not to effect removal until the new representations have been considered should be sought at the same time from the SSHD. If the SSHD refuses to provide such an undertaking it will be necessary to obtain an injunction from the High Court in order to prevent removal.

11.102 The reader should be aware that the Crime and Courts Bill contains an amendment to the EA 2003, which removes the SSHD's obligation to consider human rights issues that arise after a person's appeal rights have been exhausted. Instead, the requested person will be required to lodge an appeal in the High Court.

11.103 In Part 1 cases, once an appeal has concluded and become final, an injunction against SOCA to prevent a person's removal must be obtained if it is necessary either to make representations or to reopen

---

25 EA 2003 s114(7).
26 www.supremecourt.gov.uk/procedures/index.html.

the statutory appeal. An application for an injunction is made to the High Court using form PF244.

11.104 A case can only be reopened after an appeal has been determined if the criteria in CPR Part 52.17(1) are satisfied. This will not be easily achieved. Part 52.17(1) states:

> (1) The Court of Appeal or the High Court will not reopen a final determination of any appeal unless –
> (a) it is necessary to do so in order to avoid real injustice;
> (b) the circumstances are exceptional and make it appropriate to reopen the appeal; and
> (c) there is no alternative effective remedy.

11.105 There is no right to an oral hearing of an application for permission to reopen a final decision unless, exceptionally, the judge so directs.

Removal following dismissal of appeal

11.106 If an appeal is dismissed then the time for removal does not start until the 14-day period permitted for an application to certify a point of law of general public importance has expired. If there is no application within this period then in Part 1 cases the person must be removed within ten days of the 14-day period ending. In Part 2 cases the person must be removed within 28 days of the 14-day period ending.

11.107 If the person has not been removed within the period set out above and no extension has been granted then the person must be discharged if an application is made to the appropriate judge (WMC) unless reasonable cause is shown for the delay.[27]

Application to the European Court of Human Rights for rule 39 interim measures

11.108 On exhaustion of all domestic avenues of appeal, an appellant can apply to the ECtHR under rule 39 of the Rules of Court. The ECtHR will only grant Rule 39 relief in exceptional circumstances. In 2012, 722 applications for Rule 39 relief were made from the UK and only 13 of these applications were granted.[28] If an application is

---

27 EA 2003 s36(8) for Part 1 cases and EA 2003 s118(7) for Part 2 cases.
28 Figures provided by the ECtHR website: www.echr.coe.int/NR/rdonlyres/91C30C84-EFAF-4979-BBD6-C730D6380196/0/Art_39_TAB_2008_2012.pdf.

granted, the ECtHR will issue interim measures against the United Kingdom against the removal of the person until the ECtHR directs otherwise.

11.109 The ECtHR will only impose interim measures where, having reviewed all the relevant information, it considers that the applicant faces a real risk of serious, irreversible harm if the measure is not applied.

11.110 Any application for rule 39 interim measure must state reasons and, in particular, must specify in detail the grounds on which the applicant's particular fears are based, the nature of the alleged risks and the Convention provisions that are alleged to have been violated or will be violated if the measures are not imposed.

11.111 The application must be accompanied by the final decision of the domestic court (if available).

11.112 The expected date and time of removal must be provided in the application together with the applicant's place of detention if in custody. If the final decision of the court is imminent and there is a risk of immediate removal, an application for rule 39 interim measures can be made without the need to await the final decision of the domestic court, but the application must indicate that the request is subject to an adverse decision of the domestic court.

11.113 The ECtHR recommends that an application for rule 39 interim measures should be sent by fax and all requests should be marked in bold on the face of the request:

Rule 39 – Urgent
Person to contact (name and contact details)
Date and time of removal and destination

11.114 The ECtHR has a dedicated fax number for sending requests for rule 39 interim measures: + 33 (0)3 88 41 39 00.[29]

11.115 Applications are only received between Monday to Friday from 8 am to 4.30 pm.[30]

11.116 The result of the application will be communicated to the parties relatively quickly and, if such application is refused, there are no further steps that can be taken to prevent removal unless a supervening event occurs.

---

29 Correct as of 11 March 2013. Those wishing to apply for rule 39 interim measures from the ECtHR should check the court website for up to date contact information: www.echr.coe.int/ECHR.

30 The times given are local time (GMT+1).

CHAPTER 12
Ancillary matters

12.1	Introduction
12.2	Compromising the extradition request
12.6	'Iron letters'
12.7	Transfer of prisoners
12.12	Funding and billing

Introduction

12.1 This chapter seeks to deal with matters that are outside the scope of EA 2003, but nonetheless are matters that practitioners need to be aware of when conducting (and concluding) extradition proceedings.

Compromising the extradition request

12.2 As the preceding pages show, resisting extradition is notoriously difficult. Very often a requested person will be more likely to avoid extradition by attempting to persuade the requesting state to withdraw the request for extradition. In order to do this, it will be necessary to secure the assistance of a lawyer in the requesting state. This lawyer can then apply to the court for the case to be dealt with without the requested person having to return. For example on an 'accusation warrant' it may be possible for the requested person to plead guilty and be sentenced to a non-custodial sentence in his or her absence. In a conviction case, it may be possible for a lawyer in the requesting state to apply to the court to suspend or defer a sentence of imprisonment.

12.3 A lawyer in the requesting state will not be funded by the representation order: it is very often the requested person or his or her family who fund this. Very occasionally lawyers may agree to carry out the work on a *pro bono* basis, particularly where the requested person is a former client.

12.4 Practitioners may sometimes be asked to assist in finding a lawyer in the requesting state. Given the likelihood of language difficulties, it is unlikely that a lawyer in this country will be able to offer any real help unless he or she has had previous dealings with a lawyer in the issuing state. It is therefore worth retaining details of those lawyers who have been effective in securing the withdrawal of a warrant for future use.

12.5 The court is often reluctant to adjourn extradition proceedings while attempts are being made to compromise a warrant. In order to persuade the court to adjourn, the defence will have to demonstrate that the attempt to compromise is at an advanced stage and stands a chance of success. Evidence from the lawyer instructed in the requesting state will assist such an application.

'Iron letters'

12.6 Some jurisdictions will withdraw an extradition request on an application by the requested person to a court upon payment of a security to guarantee the requested person's return. This is known as an 'iron letter'. Although it can result in the withdrawal of the extradition request it requires the requested person to appear voluntarily at the court in the requesting state when summoned to appear (unlike the scenarios at paragraph 12.2). Arranging for an iron letter to be issued will require close liaison with a lawyer in the requesting state – it will only be issued after a bail security has been deposited in the requesting state. After this has been paid in, the extradition request will be withdrawn resulting in the discharge of the requested person in the United Kingdom.

Transfer of prisoners

12.7 It is, in some cases, possible for a sentence to be transferred across jurisdictions. Where, for example, a British person is serving a sentence of imprisonment in another state, the Repatriation of Prisoners Act 1984 (RPA 1984) will in some cases allow that person to be repatriated to complete that sentence in the United Kingdom. Using these provisions, it is possible to transfer a sentence of a requested person prior to his or her extradition, thus obviating the need for return.

12.8 Currently there are significant practical difficulties involved in negotiating such a transfer of a sentence; however, with increasing judicial co-operation between EU member states it is anticipated that this alternative to extradition will become more common. It should be noted that article 4(6) of the Framework Decision provides an optional bar to extradition 'where the requested person is staying in, or is a national or a resident of the executing member state and that state undertakes to execute the sentence or detention order in accordance with its domestic law'. The United Kingdom has not however implemented this bar.

12.9 RPA 1984 s1(1) sets out the circumstances in which a transfer can take place as follows:

> (a) the United Kingdom is a party to international arrangements providing for the transfer between the United Kingdom and a country or territory outside the British Islands of persons to whom subsection (7) below applies, and

(b) the relevant Minister and the appropriate authority of that country or territory have each agreed to the transfer under those arrangements of a particular person (in this Act referred to as 'the prisoner'), and

(c) the prisoner has consented to being transferred in accordance with those arrangements.

12.10 The international arrangements referred to under RPA 1984 s1(1)(a) are as follows:

- Council of Europe Convention on Transfer of Sentenced Persons and the Additional Protocol;[1]
- the Commonwealth Scheme for the Transfer of Convicted Offenders;
- bilateral agreements;
- EU Framework Decision 2008/909/JHA. This replaced the Europe Convention referred to above in relation to the repatriation of prisoners between EU member states from 5 December 2011.

12.11 EU Framework Decision 2008/909/JHA aims to facilitate the transfer of prisoners across EU member states[2] and those representing requested persons facing a custodial sentence should, in appropriate cases, make efforts for a sentence to be transferred to this country. While RPA 1984 envisages the transfer of British nationals, the Framework Decision expands the scope of those who can be transferred to residents as well.[3] This will inevitably require the assistance of a lawyer in the requesting state, along with negotiations with 'the relevant minister' as set out in RPA 1984 s1(1)(b), ie the Secretary of State for Justice. Requests for transfer are dealt with by the Cross Border Transfer Section of the National Offender Management Service (NOMS), an executive agency of the Ministry of Justice.

Funding and billing

12.12 Where a case is privately funded, for all cases commencing after 1 October 2012, it will be possible to obtain an order for costs from central funds if the requested person is discharged; but costs will be capped at legal aid rates.[4]

1 ETS 112.
2 Poland has a five-year derogation from 6 December 2011.
3 Article 4(1).
4 Schedule 7 of the Legal Aid, Sentencing and Punishment of Offenders Act 2012.

12.13 All extradition cases conducted in the magistrates' court that are the subject of public funding are to be submitted for taxation to the Legal Aid Agency within three months of conclusion. A CRM7 must be completed for all cases and lodged with the file of papers. If a certificate for counsel has been granted in the proceedings then counsel's claim for costs must be completed on a CRM8 and submitted at the same time as the CRM7.

12.14 Given that the claim will be for a non-standard fee, it is possible to apply for an uplift in costs.[5] An enhancement to the hourly rate will be allowed if:

- the work was done with exceptional competence, skill or expertise; or
- the work was done with exceptional dispatch; or
- the case involved exceptional circumstances or complexity.

12.15 In deciding whether to grant an enhancement in fees, and in determining the appropriate percentage enhancement, the LAA will have regard to:

- the degree of responsibility;
- the care, speed and economy with which the case was prepared;
- the novelty, weight and complexity of the case.

12.16 The percentage enhancement is capped at 100 per cent, except where proceedings relate to serious or complex fraud, where the relevant hourly rate will not be enhanced by more than 200 per cent.

12.17 If applying for an enhancement, a covering letter stating why the case meets the above criteria should be sent to the LAA when the claim is submitted.

12.18 Cases that have concluded before the Administrative Court must be submitted for taxation to the Senior Courts Cost Office (SCCO) at the Royal Courts of Justice (DX 44454 Strand). It is usual for a bill of costs to be drafted by an experienced costs draftsman. The bill of costs, representation order and disbursement invoices are the only documents that need to be sent to the SCCO.

12.19 Again, an uplift can be applied to the solicitors costs. Counsel instructed in these cases are able to submit their bills directly to the SCCO and need not be submitted at the same time as the solicitor submits his or her bill.

12.20 Publicly funded judicial review proceedings will be funded under a civil legal aid certificate. Firms without a civil legal aid contract but holding a 2010 Standard Crime Contract are entitled to apply for

5 Criminal Contract Specification Part B, para 10.100.

community legal services certificates for this work: judicial review and *habeas corpus* are classified as 'associated Civil Work carried out under the provisions governing civil legal aid in Part 1 of the Act [LASPO]'.[6] Practitioners must ensure that they adhere to the Funding Code criteria as set out on the LAA website. Applications should be made using forms CIV APP1 and the relevant means form (usually CIV MEANS 1 or 2) and sent to the regional LAA office. An advice from counsel setting out the merits of the case will usually be required. It can take many weeks for such applications to be processed. If the application is urgent, the form CIV APP 6 should be faxed or emailed to the Special Cases Unit of the Legal Aid Agency, currently based in Brighton. The more detailed CIV APP1 must be submitted to the regional office within five working days of the grant of a certificate. A certificate will then be issued that permits work to a given stage of the case and with a limitation on costs. If the work is to proceed beyond that permitted in the funding certificate, a further application should be made to the LAA using form CIV APP8. This form should also be used to apply to extend funding to cover the cost of experts or leading counsel.

6 See 2010 Standard Crime Contract – Specification para 1.5.

APPENDICES

A Framework Decision on the European Arrest Warrant   171

B Extradition Act 2003 ss1–25, 64, 65, 70–75, 137–138   191

C EAW validity checklist   215

D EAW first appearance checklist   217

E Bail checklist   219

F Case management form   221

G Application notice – Form N161   223

APPENDIX A

Framework Decision on the European Arrest Warrant and the surrender procedures between member states

2002/584/JHA: Council Framework Decision of 13 June 2002 on the European arrest warrant and the surrender procedures between member states: statements made by certain member states on the adoption of the Framework Decision[1]

THE COUNCIL OF THE EUROPEAN UNION,

Having regard to the Treaty on European Union, and in particular Article 31(a) and (b) and Article 34(2)(b) thereof,

Having regard to the proposal from the Commission,

Having regard to the opinion of the European Parliament,

Whereas:

(1) According to the Conclusions of the Tampere European Council of 15 and 16 October 1999, and in particular point 35 thereof, the formal extradition procedure should be abolished among the Member States in respect of persons who are fleeing from justice after having been finally sentenced and extradition procedures should be speeded up in respect of persons suspected of having committed an offence.

(2) The programme of measures to implement the principle of mutual recognition of criminal decisions envisaged in point 37 of the Tampere European Council Conclusions and adopted by the Council on 30 November 2000, addresses the matter of mutual enforcement of arrest warrants.

(3) All or some Member States are parties to a number of conventions in the field of extradition, including the European Convention on extradition of 13 December 1957 and the European Convention on the suppression of terrorism of 27 January 1977. The Nordic States have extradition laws with identical wording.

(4) In addition, the following three Conventions dealing in whole or in part with extradition have been agreed upon among Member States and form part of

---

[1] *Official Journal* L 190, 18/07/2002 P. 0001–0020. Available at http://eur-lex.europa.eu/LexUriServ/LexUriServ.do?uri=CELEX:32002F0584:en:HTML.

the Union acquis: the Convention of 19 June 1990 implementing the Schengen Agreement of 14 June 1985 on the gradual abolition of checks at their common borders (regarding relations between the Member States which are parties to that Convention), the Convention of 10 March 1995 on simplified extradition procedure between the Member States of the European Union and the Convention of 27 September 1996 relating to extradition between the Member States of the European Union.

(5) The objective set for the Union to become an area of freedom, security and justice leads to abolishing extradition between Member States and replacing it by a system of surrender between judicial authorities. Further, the introduction of a new simplified system of surrender of sentenced or suspected persons for the purposes of execution or prosecution of criminal sentences makes it possible to remove the complexity and potential for delay inherent in the present extradition procedures. Traditional cooperation relations which have prevailed up till now between Member States should be replaced by a system of free movement of judicial decisions in criminal matters, covering both pre-sentence and final decisions, within an area of freedom, security and justice.

(6) The European arrest warrant provided for in this Framework Decision is the first concrete measure in the field of criminal law implementing the principle of mutual recognition which the European Council referred to as the 'cornerstone' of judicial cooperation.

(7) Since the aim of replacing the system of multilateral extradition built upon the European Convention on Extradition of 13 December 1957 cannot be sufficiently achieved by the Member States acting unilaterally and can therefore, by reason of its scale and effects, be better achieved at Union level, the Council may adopt measures in accordance with the principle of subsidiarity as referred to in Article 2 of the Treaty on European Union and Article 5 of the Treaty establishing the European Community. In accordance with the principle of proportionality, as set out in the latter Article, this Framework Decision does not go beyond what is necessary in order to achieve that objective.

(8) Decisions on the execution of the European arrest warrant must be subject to sufficient controls, which means that a judicial authority of the Member State where the requested person has been arrested will have to take the decision on his or her surrender.

(9) The role of central authorities in the execution of a European arrest warrant must be limited to practical and administrative assistance.

(10) The mechanism of the European arrest warrant is based on a high level of confidence between Member States. Its implementation may be suspended only in the event of a serious and persistent breach by one of the Member States of the principles set out in Article 6(1) of the Treaty on European Union, determined by the Council pursuant to Article 7(1) of the said Treaty with the consequences set out in Article 7(2) thereof.

(11) In relations between Member States, the European arrest warrant should replace all the previous instruments concerning extradition, including the provisions of Title III of the Convention implementing the Schengen Agreement which concern extradition.

(12) This Framework Decision respects fundamental rights and observes the principles recognised by Article 6 of the Treaty on European Union and reflected in the Charter of Fundamental Rights of the European Union, in particular Chapter VI thereof. Nothing in this Framework Decision may be interpreted as prohibiting refusal to surrender a person for whom a European arrest warrant has been issued when there are reasons to believe, on the basis of objective elements, that the said arrest warrant has been issued for the purpose of prosecuting or punishing a person on the grounds of his or her sex, race, religion, ethnic origin, nationality, language, political opinions or sexual orientation, or that that person's position may be prejudiced for any of these reasons.

This Framework Decision does not prevent a Member State from applying its constitutional rules relating to due process, freedom of association, freedom of the press and freedom of expression in other media.

(13) No person should be removed, expelled or extradited to a State where there is a serious risk that he or she would be subjected to the death penalty, torture or other inhuman or degrading treatment or punishment.

(14) Since all Member States have ratified the Council of Europe Convention of 28 January 1981 for the protection of individuals with regard to automatic processing of personal data, the personal data processed in the context of the implementation of this Framework Decision should be protected in accordance with the principles of the said Convention,

HAS ADOPTED THIS FRAMEWORK DECISION:

CHAPTER 1
GENERAL PRINCIPLES

Article 1
Definition of the European arrest warrant and obligation to execute it

1. The European arrest warrant is a judicial decision issued by a Member State with a view to the arrest and surrender by another Member State of a requested person, for the purposes of conducting a criminal prosecution or executing a custodial sentence or detention order.

2. Member States shall execute any European arrest warrant on the basis of the principle of mutual recognition and in accordance with the provisions of this Framework Decision.

3. This Framework Decision shall not have the effect of modifying the obligation to respect fundamental rights and fundamental legal principles as enshrined in Article 6 of the Treaty on European Union.

Article 2
Scope of the European arrest warrant

1. A European arrest warrant may be issued for acts punishable by the law of the issuing Member State by a custodial sentence or a detention order for a maximum period of at least 12 months or, where a sentence has been passed or a detention order has been made, for sentences of at least four months.

2. The following offences, if they are punishable in the issuing Member State

by a custodial sentence or a detention order for a maximum period of at least three years and as they are defined by the law of the issuing Member State, shall, under the terms of this Framework Decision and without verification of the double criminality of the act, give rise to surrender pursuant to a European arrest warrant:
- participation in a criminal organisation,
- terrorism,
- trafficking in human beings,
- sexual exploitation of children and child pornography,
- illicit trafficking in narcotic drugs and psychotropic substances,
- illicit trafficking in weapons, munitions and explosives,
- corruption,
- fraud, including that affecting the financial interests of the European Communities within the meaning of the Convention of 26 July 1995 on the protection of the European Communities' financial interests,
- laundering of the proceeds of crime,
- counterfeiting currency, including of the euro,
- computer-related crime,
- environmental crime, including illicit trafficking in endangered animal species and in endangered plant species and varieties,
- facilitation of unauthorised entry and residence,
- murder, grievous bodily injury,
- illicit trade in human organs and tissue,
- kidnapping, illegal restraint and hostage-taking,
- racism and xenophobia,
- organised or armed robbery,
- illicit trafficking in cultural goods, including antiques and works of art,
- swindling,
- racketeering and extortion,
- counterfeiting and piracy of products,
- forgery of administrative documents and trafficking therein,
- forgery of means of payment,
- illicit trafficking in hormonal substances and other growth promoters,
- illicit trafficking in nuclear or radioactive materials,
- trafficking in stolen vehicles,
- rape,
- arson,
- crimes within the jurisdiction of the International Criminal Court,
- unlawful seizure of aircraft/ships,
- sabotage.

3. The Council may decide at any time, acting unanimously after consultation of the European Parliament under the conditions laid down in Article 39(1) of the Treaty on European Union (TEU), to add other categories of offence to the list contained in paragraph 2. The Council shall examine, in the light of the report submitted by the Commission pursuant to Article 34(3), whether the list should be extended or amended.

4. For offences other than those covered by paragraph 2, surrender may be subject to the condition that the acts for which the European arrest warrant has

been issued constitute an offence under the law of the executing Member State, whatever the constituent elements or however it is described.

Article 3
Grounds for mandatory non-execution of the European arrest warrant

The judicial authority of the Member State of execution (hereinafter 'executing judicial authority') shall refuse to execute the European arrest warrant in the following cases:

1. if the offence on which the arrest warrant is based is covered by amnesty in the executing Member State, where that State had jurisdiction to prosecute the offence under its own criminal law;
2. if the executing judicial authority is informed that the requested person has been finally judged by a Member State in respect of the same acts provided that, where there has been sentence, the sentence has been served or is currently being served or may no longer be executed under the law of the sentencing Member State;
3. if the person who is the subject of the European arrest warrant may not, owing to his age, be held criminally responsible for the acts on which the arrest warrant is based under the law of the executing State.

Article 4
Grounds for optional non-execution of the European arrest warrant

The executing judicial authority may refuse to execute the European arrest warrant:

1. if, in one of the cases referred to in Article 2(4), the act on which the European arrest warrant is based does not constitute an offence under the law of the executing Member State; however, in relation to taxes or duties, customs and exchange, execution of the European arrest warrant shall not be refused on the ground that the law of the executing Member State does not impose the same kind of tax or duty or does not contain the same type of rules as regards taxes, duties and customs and exchange regulations as the law of the issuing Member State;
2. where the person who is the subject of the European arrest warrant is being prosecuted in the executing Member State for the same act as that on which the European arrest warrant is based;
3. where the judicial authorities of the executing Member State have decided either not to prosecute for the offence on which the European arrest warrant is based or to halt proceedings, or where a final judgment has been passed upon the requested person in a Member State, in respect of the same acts, which prevents further proceedings;
4. where the criminal prosecution or punishment of the requested person is statute-barred according to the law of the executing Member State and the acts fall within the jurisdiction of that Member State under its own criminal law;
5. if the executing judicial authority is informed that the requested person has been finally judged by a third State in respect of the same acts provided that, where there has been sentence, the sentence has been served or is currently

being served or may no longer be executed under the law of the sentencing country;
6. if the European arrest warrant has been issued for the purposes of execution of a custodial sentence or detention order, where the requested person is staying in, or is a national or a resident of the executing Member State and that State undertakes to execute the sentence or detention order in accordance with its domestic law;
7. where the European arrest warrant relates to offences which:
    (a) are regarded by the law of the executing Member State as having been committed in whole or in part in the territory of the executing Member State or in a place treated as such; or
    (b) have been committed outside the territory of the issuing Member State and the law of the executing Member State does not allow prosecution for the same offences when committed outside its territory.

Article 5
Guarantees to be given by the issuing Member State in particular cases

The execution of the European arrest warrant by the executing judicial authority may, by the law of the executing Member State, be subject to the following conditions:

1. where the European arrest warrant has been issued for the purposes of executing a sentence or a detention order imposed by a decision rendered in absentia and if the person concerned has not been summoned in person or otherwise informed of the date and place of the hearing which led to the decision rendered in absentia, surrender may be subject to the condition that the issuing judicial authority gives an assurance deemed adequate to guarantee the person who is the subject of the European arrest warrant that he or she will have an opportunity to apply for a retrial of the case in the issuing Member State and to be present at the judgment;
2. if the offence on the basis of which the European arrest warrant has been issued is punishable by custodial life sentence or life-time detention order, the execution of the said arrest warrant may be subject to the condition that the issuing Member State has provisions in its legal system for a review of the penalty or measure imposed, on request or at the latest after 20 years, or for the application of measures of clemency to which the person is entitled to apply for under the law or practice of the issuing Member State, aiming at a non-execution of such penalty or measure;
3. where a person who is the subject of a European arrest warrant for the purposes of prosecution is a national or resident of the executing Member State, surrender may be subject to the condition that the person, after being heard, is returned to the executing Member State in order to serve there the custodial sentence or detention order passed against him in the issuing Member State.

Article 6
Determination of the competent judicial authorities

1. The issuing judicial authority shall be the judicial authority of the issuing

Member State which is competent to issue a European arrest warrant by virtue of the law of that State.
2. The executing judicial authority shall be the judicial authority of the executing Member State which is competent to execute the European arrest warrant by virtue of the law of that State.
3. Each Member State shall inform the General Secretariat of the Council of the competent judicial authority under its law.

Article 7
Recourse to the central authority
1. Each Member State may designate a central authority or, when its legal system so provides, more than one central authority to assist the competent judicial authorities.
2. A Member State may, if it is necessary as a result of the organisation of its internal judicial system, make its central authority(ies) responsible for the administrative transmission and reception of European arrest warrants as well as for all other official correspondence relating thereto.

Member State wishing to make use of the possibilities referred to in this Article shall communicate to the General Secretariat of the Council information relating to the designated central authority or central authorities. These indications shall be binding upon all the authorities of the issuing Member State.

Article 8
Content and form of the European arrest warrant
1. The European arrest warrant shall contain the following information set out in accordance with the form contained in the Annex:
   (a) the identity and nationality of the requested person;
   (b) the name, address, telephone and fax numbers and e-mail address of the issuing judicial authority;
   (c) evidence of an enforceable judgment, an arrest warrant or any other enforceable judicial decision having the same effect, coming within the scope of Articles 1 and 2;
   (d) the nature and legal classification of the offence, particularly in respect of Article 2;
   (e) a description of the circumstances in which the offence was committed, including the time, place and degree of participation in the offence by the requested person;
   (f) the penalty imposed, if there is a final judgment, or the prescribed scale of penalties for the offence under the law of the issuing Member State;
   (g) if possible, other consequences of the offence.
2. The European arrest warrant must be translated into the official language or one of the official languages of the executing Member State. Any Member State may, when this Framework Decision is adopted or at a later date, state in a declaration deposited with the General Secretariat of the Council that it will accept a translation in one or more other official languages of the Institutions of the European Communities.

CHAPTER 2
SURRENDER PROCEDURE

Article 9
Transmission of a European arrest warrant

1. When the location of the requested person is known, the issuing judicial authority may transmit the European arrest warrant directly to the executing judicial authority.
2. The issuing judicial authority may, in any event, decide to issue an alert for the requested person in the Schengen Information System (SIS).
3. Such an alert shall be effected in accordance with the provisions of Article 95 of the Convention of 19 June 1990 implementing the Schengen Agreement of 14 June 1985 on the gradual abolition of controls at common borders. An alert in the Schengen Information System shall be equivalent to a European arrest warrant accompanied by the information set out in Article 8(1).

   For a transitional period, until the SIS is capable of transmitting all the information described in Article 8, the alert shall be equivalent to a European arrest warrant pending the receipt of the original in due and proper form by the executing judicial authority.

Article 10
Detailed procedures for transmitting a European arrest warrant

1. If the issuing judicial authority does not know the competent executing judicial authority, it shall make the requisite enquiries, including through the contact points of the European Judicial Network, in order to obtain that information from the executing Member State.
2. If the issuing judicial authority so wishes, transmission may be effected via the secure telecommunications system of the European Judicial Network.
3. If it is not possible to call on the services of the SIS, the issuing judicial authority may call on Interpol to transmit a European arrest warrant.
4. The issuing judicial authority may forward the European arrest warrant by any secure means capable of producing written records under conditions allowing the executing Member State to establish its authenticity.
5. All difficulties concerning the transmission or the authenticity of any document needed for the execution of the European arrest warrant shall be dealt with by direct contacts between the judicial authorities involved, or, where appropriate, with the involvement of the central authorities of the Member States.
6. If the authority which receives a European arrest warrant is not competent to act upon it, it shall automatically forward the European arrest warrant to the competent authority in its Member State and shall inform the issuing judicial authority accordingly.

Article 11
Rights of a requested person

1. When a requested person is arrested, the executing competent judicial authority shall, in accordance with its national law, inform that person of the

European arrest warrant and of its contents, and also of the possibility of consenting to surrender to the issuing judicial authority.
2. A requested person who is arrested for the purpose of the execution of a European arrest warrant shall have a right to be assisted by a legal counsel and by an interpreter in accordance with the national law of the executing Member State.

Article 12
Keeping the person in detention

When a person is arrested on the basis of a European arrest warrant, the executing judicial authority shall take a decision on whether the requested person should remain in detention, in accordance with the law of the executing Member State. The person may be released provisionally at any time in conformity with the domestic law of the executing Member State, provided that the competent authority of the said Member State takes all the measures it deems necessary to prevent the person absconding.

Article 13
Consent to surrender

1. If the arrested person indicates that he or she consents to surrender, that consent and, if appropriate, express renunciation of entitlement to the 'speciality rule', referred to in Article 27(2), shall be given before the executing judicial authority, in accordance with the domestic law of the executing Member State.
2. Each Member State shall adopt the measures necessary to ensure that consent and, where appropriate, renunciation, as referred to in paragraph 1, are established in such a way as to show that the person concerned has expressed them voluntarily and in full awareness of the consequences. To that end, the requested person shall have the right to legal counsel.
3. The consent and, where appropriate, renunciation, as referred to in paragraph 1, shall be formally recorded in accordance with the procedure laid down by the domestic law of the executing Member State.
4. In principle, consent may not be revoked. Each Member State may provide that consent and, if appropriate, renunciation may be revoked, in accordance with the rules applicable under its domestic law. In this case, the period between the date of consent and that of its revocation shall not be taken into consideration in establishing the time limits laid down in Article 17. A Member State which wishes to have recourse to this possibility shall inform the General Secretariat of the Council accordingly when this Framework Decision is adopted and shall specify the procedures whereby revocation of consent shall be possible and any amendment to them.

Article 14
Hearing of the requested person

Where the arrested person does not consent to his or her surrender as referred to in Article 13, he or she shall be entitled to be heard by the executing judicial authority, in accordance with the law of the executing Member State.

Article 15
Surrender decision

1. The executing judicial authority shall decide, within the time-limits and under the conditions defined in this Framework Decision, whether the person is to be surrendered.
2. If the executing judicial authority finds the information communicated by the issuing Member State to be insufficient to allow it to decide on surrender, it shall request that the necessary supplementary information, in particular with respect to Articles 3 to 5 and Article 8, be furnished as a matter of urgency and may fix a time limit for the receipt thereof, taking into account the need to observe the time limits set in Article 17.
3. The issuing judicial authority may at any time forward any additional useful information to the executing judicial authority.

Article 16
Decision in the event of multiple requests

1. If two or more Member States have issued European arrest warrants for the same person, the decision on which of the European arrest warrants shall be executed shall be taken by the executing judicial authority with due consideration of all the circumstances and especially the relative seriousness and place of the offences, the respective dates of the European arrest warrants and whether the warrant has been issued for the purposes of prosecution or for execution of a custodial sentence or detention order.
2. The executing judicial authority may seek the advice of Eurojust when making the choice referred to in paragraph 1.
3. In the event of a conflict between a European arrest warrant and a request for extradition presented by a third country, the decision on whether the European arrest warrant or the extradition request takes precedence shall be taken by the competent authority of the executing Member State with due consideration of all the circumstances, in particular those referred to in paragraph 1 and those mentioned in the applicable convention.
4. This Article shall be without prejudice to Member States' obligations under the Statute of the International Criminal Court.

Article 17
Time limits and procedures for the decision to execute the European arrest warrant

1. A European arrest warrant shall be dealt with and executed as a matter of urgency.
2. In cases where the requested person consents to his surrender, the final decision on the execution of the European arrest warrant should be taken within a period of 10 days after consent has been given.
3. In other cases, the final decision on the execution of the European arrest warrant should be taken within a period of 60 days after the arrest of the requested person.
4. Where in specific cases the European arrest warrant cannot be executed

within the time limits laid down in paragraphs 2 or 3, the executing judicial authority shall immediately inform the issuing judicial authority thereof, giving the reasons for the delay. In such case, the time limits may be extended by a further 30 days.

5. As long as the executing judicial authority has not taken a final decision on the European arrest warrant, it shall ensure that the material conditions necessary for effective surrender of the person remain fulfilled.
6. Reasons must be given for any refusal to execute a European arrest warrant.
7. Where in exceptional circumstances a Member State cannot observe the time limits provided for in this Article, it shall inform Eurojust, giving the reasons for the delay. In addition, a Member State which has experienced repeated delays on the part of another Member State in the execution of European arrest warrants shall inform the Council with a view to evaluating the implementation of this Framework Decision at Member State level.

Article 18
Situation pending the decision

1. Where the European arrest warrant has been issued for the purpose of conducting a criminal prosecution, the executing judicial authority must:
   (a) either agree that the requested person should be heard according to Article 19;
   (b) or agree to the temporary transfer of the requested person.
2. The conditions and the duration of the temporary transfer shall be determined by mutual agreement between the issuing and executing judicial authorities.
3. In the case of temporary transfer, the person must be able to return to the executing Member State to attend hearings concerning him or her as part of the surrender procedure.

Article 19
Hearing the person pending the decision

1. The requested person shall be heard by a judicial authority, assisted by another person designated in accordance with the law of the Member State of the requesting court.
2. The requested person shall be heard in accordance with the law of the executing Member State and with the conditions determined by mutual agreement between the issuing and executing judicial authorities.
3. The competent executing judicial authority may assign another judicial authority of its Member State to take part in the hearing of the requested person in order to ensure the proper application of this Article and of the conditions laid down.

Article 20
Privileges and immunities

1. Where the requested person enjoys a privilege or immunity regarding jurisdiction or execution in the executing Member State, the time limits referred to in Article 17 shall not start running unless, and counting from the day when,

the executing judicial authority is informed of the fact that the privilege or immunity has been waived.

The executing Member State shall ensure that the material conditions necessary for effective surrender are fulfilled when the person no longer enjoys such privilege or immunity.

2. Where power to waive the privilege or immunity lies with an authority of the executing Member State, the executing judicial authority shall request it to exercise that power forthwith. Where power to waive the privilege or immunity lies with an authority of another State or international organisation, it shall be for the issuing judicial authority to request it to exercise that power.

Article 21
Competing international obligations

This Framework Decision shall not prejudice the obligations of the executing Member State where the requested person has been extradited to that Member State from a third State and where that person is protected by provisions of the arrangement under which he or she was extradited concerning speciality. The executing Member State shall take all necessary measures for requesting forthwith the consent of the State from which the requested person was extradited so that he or she can be surrendered to the Member State which issued the European arrest warrant. The time limits referred to in Article 17 shall not start running until the day on which these speciality rules cease to apply. Pending the decision of the State from which the requested person was extradited, the executing Member State will ensure that the material conditions necessary for effective surrender remain fulfilled.

Article 22
Notification of the decision

The executing judicial authority shall notify the issuing judicial authority immediately of the decision on the action to be taken on the European arrest warrant.

Article 23
Time limits for surrender of the person

1. The person requested shall be surrendered as soon as possible on a date agreed between the authorities concerned.
2. He or she shall be surrendered no later than 10 days after the final decision on the execution of the European arrest warrant.
3. If the surrender of the requested person within the period laid down in paragraph 2 is prevented by circumstances beyond the control of any of the Member States, the executing and issuing judicial authorities shall immediately contact each other and agree on a new surrender date. In that event, the surrender shall take place within 10 days of the new date thus agreed.
4. The surrender may exceptionally be temporarily postponed for serious humanitarian reasons, for example if there are substantial grounds for believing that it would manifestly endanger the requested person's life or health. The execution of the European arrest warrant shall take place as soon as these grounds have ceased to exist. The executing judicial authority shall immediately inform

the issuing judicial authority and agree on a new surrender date. In that event, the surrender shall take place within 10 days of the new date thus agreed.
5. Upon expiry of the time limits referred to in paragraphs 2 to 4, if the person is still being held in custody he shall be released.

Article 24
Postponed or conditional surrender
1. The executing judicial authority may, after deciding to execute the European arrest warrant, postpone the surrender of the requested person so that he or she may be prosecuted in the executing Member State or, if he or she has already been sentenced, so that he or she may serve, in its territory, a sentence passed for an act other than that referred to in the European arrest warrant.
2. Instead of postponing the surrender, the executing judicial authority may temporarily surrender the requested person to the issuing Member State under conditions to be determined by mutual agreement between the executing and the issuing judicial authorities. The agreement shall be made in writing and the conditions shall be binding on all the authorities in the issuing Member State.

Article 25
Transit
1. Each Member State shall, except when it avails itself of the possibility of refusal when the transit of a national or a resident is requested for the purpose of the execution of a custodial sentence or detention order, permit the transit through its territory of a requested person who is being surrendered provided that it has been given information on:
   (a) the identity and nationality of the person subject to the European arrest warrant;
   (b) the existence of a European arrest warrant;
   (c) the nature and legal classification of the offence;
   (d) the description of the circumstances of the offence, including the date and place.

   Where a person who is the subject of a European arrest warrant for the purposes of prosecution is a national or resident of the Member State of transit, transit may be subject to the condition that the person, after being heard, is returned to the transit Member State to serve the custodial sentence or detention order passed against him in the issuing Member State.
2. Each Member State shall designate an authority responsible for receiving transit requests and the necessary documents, as well as any other official correspondence relating to transit requests. Member States shall communicate this designation to the General Secretariat of the Council.
3. The transit request and the information set out in paragraph 1 may be addressed to the authority designated pursuant to paragraph 2 by any means capable of producing a written record. The Member State of transit shall notify its decision by the same procedure.
4. This Framework Decision does not apply in the case of transport by air without a scheduled stopover. However, if an unscheduled landing occurs, the

issuing Member State shall provide the authority designated pursuant to paragraph 2 with the information provided for in paragraph 1.

5. Where a transit concerns a person who is to be extradited from a third State to a Member State this Article will apply mutatis mutandis. In particular the expression 'European arrest warrant' shall be deemed to be replaced by 'extradition request'.

CHAPTER 3
EFFECTS OF THE SURRENDER

Article 26
Deduction of the period of detention served in the executing Member State

1. The issuing Member State shall deduct all periods of detention arising from the execution of a European arrest warrant from the total period of detention to be served in the issuing Member State as a result of a custodial sentence or detention order being passed.
2. To that end, all information concerning the duration of the detention of the requested person on the basis of the European arrest warrant shall be transmitted by the executing judicial authority or the central authority designated under Article 7 to the issuing judicial authority at the time of the surrender.

Article 27
Possible prosecution for other offences

1. Each Member State may notify the General Secretariat of the Council that, in its relations with other Member States that have given the same notification, consent is presumed to have been given for the prosecution, sentencing or detention with a view to the carrying out of a custodial sentence or detention order for an offence committed prior to his or her surrender, other than that for which he or she was surrendered, unless in a particular case the executing judicial authority states otherwise in its decision on surrender.
2. Except in the cases referred to in paragraphs 1 and 3, a person surrendered may not be prosecuted, sentenced or otherwise deprived of his or her liberty for an offence committed prior to his or her surrender other than that for which he or she was surrendered.
3. Paragraph 2 does not apply in the following cases:
   (a) when the person having had an opportunity to leave the territory of the Member State to which he or she has been surrendered has not done so within 45 days of his or her final discharge, or has returned to that territory after leaving it;
   (b) the offence is not punishable by a custodial sentence or detention order;
   (c) the criminal proceedings do not give rise to the application of a measure restricting personal liberty;
   (d) when the person could be liable to a penalty or a measure not involving the deprivation of liberty, in particular a financial penalty or a measure in lieu thereof, even if the penalty or measure may give rise to a restriction of his or her personal liberty;
   (e) when the person consented to be surrendered, where appropriate at the

same time as he or she renounced the speciality rule, in accordance with Article 13;
   (f) when the person, after his/her surrender, has expressly renounced entitlement to the speciality rule with regard to specific offences preceding his/her surrender. Renunciation shall be given before the competent judicial authorities of the issuing Member State and shall be recorded in accordance with that State's domestic law. The renunciation shall be drawn up in such a way as to make clear that the person has given it voluntarily and in full awareness of the consequences. To that end, the person shall have the right to legal counsel;
   (g) where the executing judicial authority which surrendered the person gives its consent in accordance with paragraph 4.
4. A request for consent shall be submitted to the executing judicial authority, accompanied by the information mentioned in Article 8(1) and a translation as referred to in Article 8(2). Consent shall be given when the offence for which it is requested is itself subject to surrender in accordance with the provisions of this Framework Decision. Consent shall be refused on the grounds referred to in Article 3 and otherwise may be refused only on the grounds referred to in Article 4. The decision shall be taken no later than 30 days after receipt of the request.

   For the situations mentioned in Article 5 the issuing Member State must give the guarantees provided for therein.

Article 28
Surrender or subsequent extradition

1. Each Member State may notify the General Secretariat of the Council that, in its relations with other Member States which have given the same notification, the consent for the surrender of a person to a Member State other than the executing Member State pursuant to a European arrest warrant issued for an offence committed prior to his or her surrender is presumed to have been given, unless in a particular case the executing judicial authority states otherwise in its decision on surrender.
2. In any case, a person who has been surrendered to the issuing Member State pursuant to a European arrest warrant may, without the consent of the executing Member State, be surrendered to a Member State other than the executing Member State pursuant to a European arrest warrant issued for any offence committed prior to his or her surrender in the following cases:
   (a) where the requested person, having had an opportunity to leave the territory of the Member State to which he or she has been surrendered, has not done so within 45 days of his final discharge, or has returned to that territory after leaving it;
   (b) where the requested person consents to be surrendered to a Member State other than the executing Member State pursuant to a European arrest warrant. Consent shall be given before the competent judicial authorities of the issuing Member State and shall be recorded in accordance with that State's national law. It shall be drawn up in such a way as to make clear that the person concerned has given it voluntarily and in full awareness of

the consequences. To that end, the requested person shall have the right to legal counsel;

(c) where the requested person is not subject to the speciality rule, in accordance with Article 27(3)(a), (e), (f) and (g).

3. The executing judicial authority consents to the surrender to another Member State according to the following rules:
   (a) the request for consent shall be submitted in accordance with Article 9, accompanied by the information mentioned in Article 8(1) and a translation as stated in Article 8(2);
   (b) consent shall be given when the offence for which it is requested is itself subject to surrender in accordance with the provisions of this Framework Decision;
   (c) the decision shall be taken no later than 30 days after receipt of the request;
   (d) consent shall be refused on the grounds referred to in Article 3 and otherwise may be refused only on the grounds referred to in Article 4.

   For the situations referred to in Article 5, the issuing Member State must give the guarantees provided for therein.

4. Notwithstanding paragraph 1, a person who has been surrendered pursuant to a European arrest warrant shall not be extradited to a third State without the consent of the competent authority of the Member State which surrendered the person. Such consent shall be given in accordance with the Conventions by which that Member State is bound, as well as with its domestic law.

Article 29
Handing over of property

1. At the request of the issuing judicial authority or on its own initiative, the executing judicial authority shall, in accordance with its national law, seize and hand over property which:
   (a) may be required as evidence, or
   (b) has been acquired by the requested person as a result of the offence.

2. The property referred to in paragraph 1 shall be handed over even if the European arrest warrant cannot be carried out owing to the death or escape of the requested person.

3. If the property referred to in paragraph 1 is liable to seizure or confiscation in the territory of the executing Member State, the latter may, if the property is needed in connection with pending criminal proceedings, temporarily retain it or hand it over to the issuing Member State, on condition that it is returned.

4. Any rights which the executing Member State or third parties may have acquired in the property referred to in paragraph 1 shall be preserved. Where such rights exist, the issuing Member State shall return the property without charge to the executing Member State as soon as the criminal proceedings have been terminated.

Article 30
Expenses

1. Expenses incurred in the territory of the executing Member State for the execution of a European arrest warrant shall be borne by that Member State.
2. All other expenses shall be borne by the issuing Member State.

CHAPTER 4
GENERAL AND FINAL PROVISIONS

Article 31
Relation to other legal instruments

1. Without prejudice to their application in relations between Member States and third States, this Framework Decision shall, from 1 January 2004, replace the corresponding provisions of the following conventions applicable in the field of extradition in relations between the Member States:
   (a) the European Convention on Extradition of 13 December 1957, its additional protocol of 15 October 1975, its second additional protocol of 17 March 1978, and the European Convention on the suppression of terrorism of 27 January 1977 as far as extradition is concerned;
   (b) the Agreement between the 12 Member States of the European Communities on the simplification and modernisation of methods of transmitting extradition requests of 26 May 1989;
   (c) the Convention of 10 March 1995 on simplified extradition procedure between the Member States of the European Union;
   (d) the Convention of 27 September 1996 relating to extradition between the Member States of the European Union;
   (e) Title III, Chapter 4 of the Convention of 19 June 1990 implementing the Schengen Agreement of 14 June 1985 on the gradual abolition of checks at common borders.
2. Member States may continue to apply bilateral or multilateral agreements or arrangements in force when this Framework Decision is adopted in so far as such agreements or arrangements allow the objectives of this Framework Decision to be extended or enlarged and help to simplify or facilitate further the procedures for surrender of persons who are the subject of European arrest warrants.

   Member States may conclude bilateral or multilateral agreements or arrangements after this Framework Decision has come into force in so far as such agreements or arrangements allow the prescriptions of this Framework Decision to be extended or enlarged and help to simplify or facilitate further the procedures for surrender of persons who are the subject of European arrest warrants, in particular by fixing time limits shorter than those fixed in Article 17, by extending the list of offences laid down in Article 2(2), by further limiting the grounds for refusal set out in Articles 3 and 4, or by lowering the threshold provided for in Article 2(1) or (2).

   The agreements and arrangements referred to in the second subparagraph may in no case affect relations with Member States which are not parties to them.

Member States shall, within three months from the entry into force of this Framework Decision, notify the Council and the Commission of the existing agreements and arrangements referred to in the first subparagraph which they wish to continue applying.

Member States shall also notify the Council and the Commission of any new agreement or arrangement as referred to in the second subparagraph, within three months of signing it.

3. Where the conventions or agreements referred to in paragraph 1 apply to the territories of Member States or to territories for whose external relations a Member State is responsible to which this Framework Decision does not apply, these instruments shall continue to govern the relations existing between those territories and the other Members States.

Article 32
Transitional provision

1. Extradition requests received before 1 January 2004 will continue to be governed by existing instruments relating to extradition. Requests received after that date will be governed by the rules adopted by Member States pursuant to this Framework Decision. However, any Member State may, at the time of the adoption of this Framework Decision by the Council, make a statement indicating that as executing Member State it will continue to deal with requests relating to acts committed before a date which it specifies in accordance with the extradition system applicable before 1 January 2004. The date in question may not be later than 7 August 2002. The said statement will be published in the Official Journal of the European Communities. It may be withdrawn at any time.

Article 33
Provisions concerning Austria and Gibraltar

1. As long as Austria has not modified Article 12(1) of the 'Auslieferungs- und Rechtshilfegesetz' and, at the latest, until 31 December 2008, it may allow its executing judicial authorities to refuse the enforcement of a European arrest warrant if the requested person is an Austrian citizen and if the act for which the European arrest warrant has been issued is not punishable under Austrian law.

2. This Framework Decision shall apply to Gibraltar.

Article 34
Implementation

1. Member States shall take the necessary measures to comply with the provisions of this Framework Decision by 31 December 2003.

2. Member States shall transmit to the General Secretariat of the Council and to the Commission the text of the provisions transposing into their national law the obligations imposed on them under this Framework Decision. When doing so, each Member State may indicate that it will apply immediately this Framework Decision in its relations with those Member States which have given the same notification.

The General Secretariat of the Council shall communicate to the Member States and to the Commission the information received pursuant to Article 7(2), Article 8(2), Article 13(4) and Article 25(2). It shall also have the information published in the Official Journal of the European Communities.

3. On the basis of the information communicated by the General Secretariat of the Council, the Commission shall, by 31 December 2004 at the latest, submit a report to the European Parliament and to the Council on the operation of this Framework Decision, accompanied, where necessary, by legislative proposals.
4. The Council shall in the second half of 2003 conduct a review, in particular of the practical application, of the provisions of this Framework Decision by the Member States as well as the functioning of the Schengen Information System.

Article 35
Entry into force

This Framework Decision shall enter into force on the twentieth day following that of its publication in the Official Journal of the European Communities.

Done at Luxembourg, 13 June 2002.

For the Council

The President

M. Rajoy Brey

ANNEX
EUROPEAN ARREST WARRANT(1)

This warrant has been issued by a competent judicial authority. I request that the person mentioned below be arrested and surrendered for the purposes of conducting a criminal prosecution or executing a custodial sentence or detention order.

(1) This warrant must be written in, or translated into, one of the official languages of the executing Member State, when that State is known, or any other language accepted by that State.

Statements made by certain Member States on the adoption of the Framework Decision
Statements provided for in Article 32

Statement by France:
Pursuant to Article 32 of the framework decision on the European arrest warrant and the surrender procedures between Member States, France states that as executing Member State it will continue to deal with requests relating to acts committed before 1 November 1993, the date of entry into force of the Treaty on European Union signed in Maastricht on 7 February 1992, in accordance with the extradition system applicable before 1 January 2004.

Statement by Italy:
Italy will continue to deal in accordance with the extradition rules in force with all requests relating to acts committed before the date of entry into force of the framework decision on the European arrest warrant, as provided for in Article 32 thereof.

Statement by Austria:
Pursuant to Article 32 of the framework decision on the European arrest warrant and the surrender procedures between Member States, Austria states that as executing Member State it will continue to deal with requests relating to punishable acts committed before the date of entry into force of the framework decision in accordance with the extradition system applicable before that date.

Statements provided for in Article 13(4)

Statement by Belgium:
The consent of the person concerned to his or her surrender may be revoked until the time of surrender.

Statement by Denmark:
Consent to surrender and express renunciation of entitlement to the speciality rule may be revoked in accordance with the relevant rules applicable at any time under Danish law.

Statement by Ireland:
In Ireland, consent to surrender and, where appropriate, express renunciation of the entitlement to the 'specialty' rule referred to in Article 27(2) may be revoked. Consent may be revoked in accordance with domestic law until surrender has been executed.

Statement by Finland:
In Finland, consent to surrender and, where appropriate, express renunciation of entitlement to the 'speciality rule' referred to in Article 27(2) may be revoked. Consent may be revoked in accordance with domestic law until surrender has been executed.

Statement by Sweden:
Consent or renunciation within the meaning of Article 13(1) may be revoked by the party whose surrender has been requested. Revocation must take place before the decision on surrender is executed.

APPENDIX B

Extradition Act 2003 ss1–25, 64, 65, 70–75, 137–138

PART 1: EXTRADITION TO CATEGORY 1 TERRITORIES

Introduction

Extradition to category 1 territories

1 (1) This Part deals with extradition from the United Kingdom to the territories designated for the purposes of this Part by order made by the Secretary of State.
  (2) In this Act references to category 1 territories are to the territories designated for the purposes of this Part.
  (3) A territory may not be designated for the purposes of this Part if a person found guilty in the territory of a criminal offence may be sentenced to death for the offence under the general criminal law of the territory.

Part 1 warrant and certificate

2 (1) This section applies if the designated authority receives a Part 1 warrant in respect of a person.
  (2) A Part 1 warrant is an arrest warrant which is issued by a judicial authority of a category 1 territory and which contains–
    (a) the statement referred to in subsection (3) and the information referred to in subsection (4), or
    (b) the statement referred to in subsection (5) and the information referred to in subsection (6).
  (3) The statement is one that–
    (a) the person in respect of whom the Part 1 warrant is issued is accused in the category 1 territory of the commission of an offence specified in the warrant, and
    (b) the Part 1 warrant is issued with a view to his arrest and extradition to the category 1 territory for the purpose of being prosecuted for the offence.
  (4) The information is–
    (a) particulars of the person's identity;
    (b) particulars of any other warrant issued in the category 1 territory for the person's arrest in respect of the offence;
    (c) particulars of the circumstances in which the person is alleged to have committed the offence, including the conduct alleged to constitute the offence, the time and place at which he is alleged to have committed the offence and any provision of the law of the category 1 territory under which the conduct is alleged to constitute an offence;

(d) particulars of the sentence which may be imposed under the law of the category 1 territory in respect of the offence if the person is convicted of it.
(5) The statement is one that–
  (a) the person in respect of whom the Part 1 warrant is issued has been convicted of an offence specified in the warrant by a court in the category 1 territory, and
  (b) the Part 1 warrant is issued with a view to his arrest and extradition to the category 1 territory for the purpose of being sentenced for the offence or of serving a sentence of imprisonment or another form of detention imposed in respect of the offence.
(6) The information is–
  (a) particulars of the person's identity;
  (b) particulars of the conviction;
  (c) particulars of any other warrant issued in the category 1 territory for the person's arrest in respect of the offence;
  (d) particulars of the sentence which may be imposed under the law of the category 1 territory in respect of the offence, if the person has not been sentenced for the offence;
  (e) particulars of the sentence which has been imposed under the law of the category 1 territory in respect of the offence, if the person has been sentenced for the offence.
(7) The designated authority may issue a certificate under this section if it believes that the authority which issued the Part 1 warrant has the function of issuing arrest warrants in the category 1 territory.
(8) A certificate under this section must certify that the authority which issued the Part 1 warrant has the function of issuing arrest warrants in the category 1 territory.
(9) The designated authority is the authority designated for the purposes of this Part by order made by the Secretary of State.
(10) An order made under subsection (9) may–
  (a) designate more than one authority;
  (b) designate different authorities for different parts of the United Kingdom.

Arrest

Arrest under certified Part 1 warrant

3 (1) This section applies if a certificate is issued under section 2 in respect of a Part 1 warrant issued in respect of a person.
  (2) The warrant may be executed by a constable or a customs officer in any part of the United Kingdom.
  (3) The warrant may be executed by a service policeman anywhere, but only if the person is subject to service law or is a civilian subject to service discipline.
  (5) The warrant may be executed even if neither the warrant nor a copy of it is in the possession of the person executing it at the time of the arrest.

Person arrested under Part 1 warrant

4 (1) This section applies if a person is arrested under a Part 1 warrant.
  (2) A copy of the warrant must be given to the person as soon as practicable after his arrest.

(3) The person must be brought as soon as practicable before the appropriate judge.
(4) If subsection (2) is not complied with and the person applies to the judge to be discharged, the judge may order his discharge.
(5) If subsection (3) is not complied with and the person applies to the judge to be discharged, the judge must order his discharge.
(6) A person arrested under the warrant must be treated as continuing in legal custody until he is brought before the appropriate judge under subsection (3) or he is discharged under subsection (4) or (5).

Provisional arrest

5 (1) A constable, a customs officer or a service policeman may arrest a person without a warrant if he has reasonable grounds for believing–
  (a) that a Part 1 warrant has been or will be issued in respect of the person by an authority of a category 1 territory, and
  (b) that the authority has the function of issuing arrest warrants in the category 1 territory.
 (2) A constable or a customs officer may arrest a person under subsection (1) in any part of the United Kingdom.
 (3) A service policeman may arrest a person under subsection (1) only if the person is subject to service law or is a civilian subject to service discipline.
 (4) If a service policeman has power to arrest a person under subsection (1) he may exercise the power anywhere.

Person arrested under section 5

6 (1) This section applies if a person is arrested under section 5.
 (2) The person must be brought before the appropriate judge within 48 hours starting with the time when the person is arrested.
 (2A) The documents specified in subsection (4) must be produced to the judge within 48 hours starting with the time when the person is arrested but this is subject to any extension under subsection (3B).
 (2B) Subsection (3) applies if–
  (a) the person has been brought before the judge in compliance with subsection (2); but
  (b) documents have not been produced to the judge in compliance with subsection (2A).
 (3) The person must be brought before the judge when the documents are produced to the judge.
 (3A) While the person is before the judge in pursuance of subsection (2), the authority of the category 1 territory may apply to the judge for an extension of the 48 hour period mentioned in subsection (2A) by a further 48 hours.
 (3B) The judge may grant an extension if the judge decides that subsection (2A) could not reasonably be complied with within the initial 48 hour period.
 (3C) The judge must decide whether that subsection could reasonably be so complied with on a balance of probabilities.
 (3D) Notice of an application under subsection (3A) must be given in accordance with rules of court.
 (4) The documents are–
  (a) a Part 1 warrant in respect of the person;
  (b) a certificate under section 2 in respect of the warrant.

(5) A copy of the warrant must be given to the person as soon as practicable after his arrest.
(5A) Subsection (5B) applies if–
   (a) the person is before the judge in pursuance of subsection (2); and
   (b) the documents specified in subsection (4) have not been produced to the judge.
(5B) The judge must remand the person in custody or on bail (subject to subsection (6)).
(6) If subsection (2), (2A) or (3) is not complied with and the person applies to the judge to be discharged, the judge must order his discharge.
(7) If subsection (5) is not complied with and the person applies to the judge to be discharged, the judge may order his discharge.
(8) The person must be treated as continuing in legal custody until he is brought before the appropriate judge under subsection (2) or he is discharged under subsection (6) or (7).
(8A) In calculating a period of 48 hours for the purposes of this section no account is to be taken of–
   (a) any Saturday or Sunday;
   (b) Christmas Day;
   (c) Good Friday; or
   (d) any day falling within subsection (8B).
(8B) The following days fall within this subsection–
   (a) in Scotland, any day prescribed under section 8(2) of the Criminal Procedure (Scotland) Act 1995 as a court holiday in the court of the appropriate judge;
   (b) in any part of the United Kingdom, any day that is a bank holiday under the Banking and Financial Dealings Act 1971 in that part of the United Kingdom.
(9) Subsection (10) applies if–
   (a) a person is arrested under section 5 on the basis of a belief that a Part 1 warrant has been or will be issued in respect of him;
   (b) the person is discharged under subsection (6) or (7).
(10) The person must not be arrested again under section 5 on the basis of a belief relating to the same Part 1 warrant.

The initial hearing

Identity of person arrested
7 (1) This section applies if–
   (a) a person arrested under a Part 1 warrant is brought before the appropriate judge under section 4(3), or
   (b) a person arrested under section 5 is brought before the appropriate judge under section 6 and section 6(2A) is complied with in relation to him.
(2) The judge must decide whether the person brought before him is the person in respect of whom–
   (a) the warrant referred to in subsection (1)(a) was issued, or
   (b) the warrant referred to in section 6(4) was issued.
(3) The judge must decide the question in subsection (2) on a balance of probabilities.

(4) If the judge decides the question in subsection (2) in the negative he must order the person's discharge.
(5) If the judge decides that question in the affirmative he must proceed under section 8.
(6) In England and Wales, the judge has the same powers (as nearly as may be) as a magistrates' court would have if the proceedings were the summary trial of an information against the person.
(7) In Scotland–
  (a) the judge has the same powers (as nearly as may be) as if the proceedings were summary proceedings in respect of an offence alleged to have been committed by the person; but
  (b) in his making any decision under subsection (2) evidence from a single source shall be sufficient.
(8) In Northern Ireland, the judge has the same powers (as nearly as may be) as a magistrates' court would have if the proceedings were the hearing and determination of a complaint against the person.
(9) If the judge exercises his power to adjourn the proceedings he must remand the person in custody or on bail.
(10) If the person is remanded in custody, the appropriate judge may later grant bail.

Remand etc

8 (1) If the judge is required to proceed under this section he must–
  (a) fix a date on which the extradition hearing is to begin;
  (b) inform the person of the contents of the Part 1 warrant;
  (c) give the person the required information about consent;
  (d) remand the person in custody or on bail.
(2) If the person is remanded in custody, the appropriate judge may later grant bail.
(3) The required information about consent is–
  (a) that the person may consent to his extradition to the category 1 territory in which the Part 1 warrant was issued;
  (b) an explanation of the effect of consent and the procedure that will apply if he gives consent;
  (c) that consent must be given before the judge and is irrevocable.
(4) The date fixed under subsection (1) must not be later than the end of the permitted period, which is 21 days starting with the date of the arrest referred to in section 7(1)(a) or (b).
(5) If before the date fixed under subsection (1) (or this subsection) a party to the proceedings applies to the judge for a later date to be fixed and the judge believes it to be in the interests of justice to do so, he may fix a later date; and this subsection may apply more than once.
(6) Subsections (7) and (8) apply if the extradition hearing does not begin on or before the date fixed under this section.
(7) If the person applies to the judge to be discharged the judge must order his discharge, unless reasonable cause is shown for the delay.
(8) If no application is made under subsection (7) the judge must order the person's discharge on the first occasion after the date fixed under this section

when the person appears or is brought before the judge, unless reasonable cause is shown for the delay.

Person charged with offence in United Kingdom before extradition hearing

8A(1) This section applies if–
   (a) a person has been brought before the appropriate judge under section 4(3) or 6(2) but the extradition hearing has not begun; and
   (b) the judge is informed that the person is charged with an offence in the United Kingdom.
(2) The judge must order further proceedings in respect of the extradition to be adjourned until one of these occurs–
   (a) the charge is disposed of;
   (b) the charge is withdrawn;
   (c) proceedings in respect of the charge are discontinued;
   (d) an order is made for the charge to lie on the file, or in relation to Scotland, the diet is deserted *pro loco et tempore*.
(3) If a sentence of imprisonment or another form of detention is imposed in respect of the offence charged, the judge may order further proceedings in respect of the extradition to be adjourned until the person is released from detention pursuant to the sentence (whether on licence or otherwise).

Person serving sentence in United Kingdom before extradition hearing

8B(1) This section applies if–
   (a) a person has been brought before the appropriate judge under section 4(3) or 6(2) but the extradition hearing has not begun; and
   (b) the judge is informed that the person is in custody serving a sentence of imprisonment or another form of detention in the United Kingdom.
(2) The judge may order further proceedings in respect of the extradition to be adjourned until the person is released from detention pursuant to the sentence (whether on licence or otherwise).
(3) In a case where further proceedings in respect of the extradition are adjourned under subsection (2)–
   (a) section 131 of the Magistrates' Courts Act 1980 (remand of accused already in custody) has effect as if a reference to 28 clear days in subsection (1) or (2) of that section were a reference to six months;
   (b) Article 47(2) of the Magistrates' Courts (Northern Ireland) Order 1981 (period of remand in custody) has effect as if a reference to 28 days in–
      (i) sub-paragraph (a)(iii), or
      (ii) the words after sub-paragraph (b),
   were a reference to six months.

The extradition hearing

Judge's powers at extradition hearing

9 (1) In England and Wales, at the extradition hearing the appropriate judge has the same powers (as nearly as may be) as a magistrates' court would have if the proceedings were the summary trial of an information against the person in respect of whom the Part 1 warrant was issued.
(2) In Scotland, at the extradition hearing the appropriate judge has the same powers (as nearly as may be) as if the proceedings were summary proceedings

in respect of an offence alleged to have been committed by the person in respect of whom the Part 1 warrant was issued.

(3) In Northern Ireland, at the extradition hearing the appropriate judge has the same powers (as nearly as may be) as a magistrates' court would have if the proceedings were the hearing and determination of a complaint against the person in respect of whom the Part 1 warrant was issued.

(4) If the judge adjourns the extradition hearing he must remand the person in custody or on bail.

(5) If the person is remanded in custody, the appropriate judge may later grant bail.

Initial stage of extradition hearing

10 (1) This section applies if a person in respect of whom a Part 1 warrant is issued appears or is brought before the appropriate judge for the extradition hearing.

(2) The judge must decide whether the offence specified in the Part 1 warrant is an extradition offence.

(3) If the judge decides the question in subsection (2) in the negative he must order the person's discharge.

(4) If the judge decides that question in the affirmative he must proceed under section 11.

Bars to extradition

11 (1) If the judge is required to proceed under this section he must decide whether the person's extradition to the category 1 territory is barred by reason of–
 (a) the rule against double jeopardy;
 (b) extraneous considerations;
 (c) the passage of time;
 (d) the person's age;
 (e) hostage-taking considerations;
 (f) speciality;
 (g) the person's earlier extradition to the United Kingdom from another category 1 territory;
 (h) the person's earlier extradition to the United Kingdom from a non-category 1 territory;
 (i) the person's earlier transfer to the United Kingdom by the International Criminal Court;

(2) Sections 12 to 19A apply for the interpretation of subsection (1).

(3) If the judge decides any of the questions in subsection (1) in the affirmative he must order the person's discharge.

(4) If the judge decides those questions in the negative and the person is alleged to be unlawfully at large after conviction of the extradition offence, the judge must proceed under section 20.

(5) If the judge decides those questions in the negative and the person is accused of the commission of the extradition offence but is not alleged to be unlawfully at large after conviction of it, the judge must proceed under section 21.

Rule against double jeopardy

12 A person's extradition to a category 1 territory is barred by reason of the rule against double jeopardy if (and only if) it appears that he would be entitled to

be discharged under any rule of law relating to previous acquittal or conviction on the assumption–
(a) that the conduct constituting the extradition offence constituted an offence in the part of the United Kingdom where the judge exercises jurisdiction;
(b) that the person were charged with the extradition offence in that part of the United Kingdom.

Extraneous considerations

13 A person's extradition to a category 1 territory is barred by reason of extraneous considerations if (and only if) it appears that–
(a) the Part 1 warrant issued in respect of him (though purporting to be issued on account of the extradition offence) is in fact issued for the purpose of prosecuting or punishing him on account of his race, religion, nationality, gender, sexual orientation or political opinions, or
(b) if extradited he might be prejudiced at his trial or punished, detained or restricted in his personal liberty by reason of his race, religion, nationality, gender, sexual orientation or political opinions.

Passage of time

14 A person's extradition to a category 1 territory is barred by reason of the passage of time if (and only if) it appears that it would be unjust or oppressive to extradite him by reason of the passage of time since he is alleged to have–
(a) committed the extradition offence (where he is accused of its commission), or
(b) become unlawfully at large (where he is alleged to have been convicted of it).

Age

15 A person's extradition to a category 1 territory is barred by reason of his age if (and only if) it would be conclusively presumed because of his age that he could not be guilty of the extradition offence on the assumption–
(a) that the conduct constituting the extradition offence constituted an offence in the part of the United Kingdom where the judge exercises jurisdiction;
(b) that the person carried out the conduct when the extradition offence was committed (or alleged to be committed);
(c) that the person carried out the conduct in the part of the United Kingdom where the judge exercises jurisdiction.

Hostage-taking considerations

16 (1) A person's extradition to a category 1 territory is barred by reason of hostage-taking considerations if (and only if) the territory is a party to the Hostage-taking Convention and it appears that–
(a) if extradited he might be prejudiced at his trial because communication between him and the appropriate authorities would not be possible, and
(b) the act or omission constituting the extradition offence also constitutes an offence under section 1 of the Taking of Hostages Act 1982 or an attempt to commit such an offence.
(2) The appropriate authorities are the authorities of the territory which are entitled to exercise rights of protection in relation to him.
(3) A certificate issued by the Secretary of State that a territory is a party to the

Hostage-taking Convention is conclusive evidence of that fact for the purposes of subsection (1).
  (4) The Hostage-taking Convention is the International Convention against the Taking of Hostages opened for signature at New York on 18 December 1979.

Speciality

17 (1) A person's extradition to a category 1 territory is barred by reason of speciality if (and only if) there are no speciality arrangements with the category 1 territory.
  (2) There are speciality arrangements with a category 1 territory if, under the law of that territory or arrangements made between it and the United Kingdom, a person who is extradited to the territory from the United Kingdom may be dealt with in the territory for an offence committed before his extradition only if–
    (a) the offence is one falling within subsection (3), or
    (b) the condition in subsection (4) is satisfied.
  (3) The offences are–
    (a) the offence in respect of which the person is extradited;
    (b) an extradition offence disclosed by the same facts as that offence;
    (c) an extradition offence in respect of which the appropriate judge gives his consent under section 55 to the person being dealt with;
    (d) an offence which is not punishable with imprisonment or another form of detention;
    (e) an offence in respect of which the person will not be detained in connection with his trial, sentence or appeal;
    (f) an offence in respect of which the person waives the right that he would have (but for this paragraph) not to be dealt with for the offence.
  (4) The condition is that the person is given an opportunity to leave the category 1 territory and–
    (a) he does not do so before the end of the permitted period, or
    (b) if he does so before the end of the permitted period, he returns there.
  (5) The permitted period is 45 days starting with the day on which the person arrives in the category 1 territory.
  (6) Arrangements made with a category 1 territory which is a Commonwealth country or a British overseas territory may be made for a particular case or more generally.
  (7) A certificate issued by or under the authority of the Secretary of State confirming the existence of arrangements with a category 1 territory which is a Commonwealth country or a British overseas territory and stating the terms of the arrangements is conclusive evidence of those matters.

Earlier extradition to United Kingdom from category 1 territory

18 A person's extradition to a category 1 territory is barred by reason of his earlier extradition to the United Kingdom from another category 1 territory if (and only if)–
    (a) the person was extradited to the United Kingdom from another category 1 territory (the extraditing territory);
    (b) under arrangements between the United Kingdom and the extraditing territory, that territory's consent is required to the person's extradition

from the United Kingdom to the category 1 territory in respect of the extradition offence under consideration;
(c) that consent has not been given on behalf of the extraditing territory.

Earlier extradition to United Kingdom from non-category 1 territory
19 A person's extradition to a category 1 territory is barred by reason of his earlier extradition to the United Kingdom from a non-category 1 territory if (and only if)–
   (a) the person was extradited to the United Kingdom from a territory that is not a category 1 territory (the extraditing territory);
   (b) under arrangements between the United Kingdom and the extraditing territory, that territory's consent is required to the person's being dealt with in the United Kingdom in respect of the extradition offence under consideration;
   (c) consent has not been given on behalf of the extraditing territory to the person's extradition from the United Kingdom to the category 1 territory in respect of the extradition offence under consideration.

Earlier transfer to United Kingdom by International Criminal Court
19A(1) A person's extradition to a category 1 territory is barred by reason of his earlier transfer by the International Criminal Court if (and only if)–
   (a) the person was transferred to the United Kingdom to serve a sentence imposed by the Court;
   (b) under arrangements between the United Kingdom and the Court, the consent of the Presidency of the Court is required to the person's extradition from the United Kingdom to the category 1 territory in respect of the extradition offence under consideration;
   (c) that consent has not been given.
   (2) Subsection (1) does not apply if the person has served the sentence imposed by the Court and has subsequently–
   (a) remained voluntarily in the United Kingdom for more than 30 days, or
   (b) left the United Kingdom and returned to it.

Case where person has been convicted
20 (1) If the judge is required to proceed under this section (by virtue of section 11) he must decide whether the person was convicted in his presence.
   (2) If the judge decides the question in subsection (1) in the affirmative he must proceed under section 21.
   (3) If the judge decides that question in the negative he must decide whether the person deliberately absented himself from his trial.
   (4) If the judge decides the question in subsection (3) in the affirmative he must proceed under section 21.
   (5) If the judge decides that question in the negative he must decide whether the person would be entitled to a retrial or (on appeal) to a review amounting to a retrial.
   (6) If the judge decides the question in subsection (5) in the affirmative he must proceed under section 21.
   (7) If the judge decides that question in the negative he must order the person's discharge.
   (8) The judge must not decide the question in subsection (5) in the affirmative

unless, in any proceedings that it is alleged would constitute a retrial or a review amounting to a retrial, the person would have these rights–
(a) the right to defend himself in person or through legal assistance of his own choosing or, if he had not sufficient means to pay for legal assistance, to be given it free when the interests of justice so required;
(b) the right to examine or have examined witnesses against him and to obtain the attendance and examination of witnesses on his behalf under the same conditions as witnesses against him.

Human rights
21 (1) If the judge is required to proceed under this section (by virtue of section 11 or 20) he must decide whether the person's extradition would be compatible with the Convention rights within the meaning of the Human Rights Act 1998.
(2) If the judge decides the question in subsection (1) in the negative he must order the person's discharge.
(3) If the judge decides that question in the affirmative he must order the person to be extradited to the category 1 territory in which the warrant was issued.
(4) If the judge makes an order under subsection (3) he must remand the person in custody or on bail to wait for his extradition to the category 1 territory.
(5) If the person is remanded in custody, the appropriate judge may later grant bail.

Matters arising before end of extradition hearing
Person charged with offence in United Kingdom
22 (1) This section applies if at any time in the extradition hearing the judge is informed that the person in respect of whom the Part 1 warrant is issued is charged with an offence in the United Kingdom.
(2) The judge must adjourn the extradition hearing until one of these occurs–
   (a) the charge is disposed of;
   (b) the charge is withdrawn;
   (c) proceedings in respect of the charge are discontinued;
   (d) an order is made for the charge to lie on the file, or in relation to Scotland, the diet is deserted *pro loco et tempore*.
(3) If a sentence of imprisonment or another form of detention is imposed in respect of the offence charged, the judge may adjourn the extradition hearing until the person is released from detention pursuant to the sentence (whether on licence or otherwise).
(4) If before he adjourns the extradition hearing under subsection (2) the judge has decided under section 11 whether the person's extradition is barred by reason of the rule against double jeopardy, the judge must decide that question again after the resumption of the hearing.

Person serving sentence in United Kingdom
23 (1) This section applies if at any time in the extradition hearing the judge is informed that the person in respect of whom the Part 1 warrant is issued is in custody serving a sentence of imprisonment or another form of detention in the United Kingdom.
(2) The judge may adjourn the extradition hearing until the person is released from detention pursuant to the sentence (whether on licence or otherwise).

(3) In a case where an extradition hearing is adjourned under subsection (2)–
  (a) section 131 of the Magistrates' Courts Act 1980 (remand of accused already in custody) has effect as if a reference to 28 clear days in subsection (1) or (2) of that section were a reference to six months;
  (b) Article 47(2) of the Magistrates' Courts (Northern Ireland) Order 1981 (SI No 1675 (NI 26)) (period of remand in custody) has effect as if a reference to 28 days in–
  (i) paragraph (a)(iii), or
  (ii) the words after paragraph (b),
  were a reference to six months.

Extradition request
24 (1) This section applies if at any time in the extradition hearing the judge is informed that–
  (a) a certificate has been issued under section 70 in respect of a request for the person's extradition;
  (b) the request has not been disposed of;
  (c) an order has been made under section 179(2) for further proceedings on the warrant to be deferred until the request has been disposed of.
(2) The judge must remand the person in custody or on bail.
(3) If the person is remanded in custody, the appropriate judge may later grant bail.

Physical or mental condition
25 (1) This section applies if at any time in the extradition hearing it appears to the judge that the condition in subsection (2) is satisfied.
(2) The condition is that the physical or mental condition of the person in respect of whom the Part 1 warrant is issued is such that it would be unjust or oppressive to extradite him.
(3) The judge must–
  (a) order the person's discharge, or
  (b) adjourn the extradition hearing until it appears to him that the condition in subsection (2) is no longer satisfied.
...

Interpretation

Extradition offences: person not sentenced for offence
64 (1) This section applies in relation to conduct of a person if–
  (a) he is accused in a category 1 territory of the commission of an offence constituted by the conduct, or
  (b) he is alleged to be unlawfully at large after conviction by a court in a category 1 territory of an offence constituted by the conduct and he has not been sentenced for the offence.
(2) The conduct constitutes an extradition offence in relation to the category 1 territory if these conditions are satisfied–
  (a) the conduct occurs in the category 1 territory and no part of it occurs in the United Kingdom;
  (b) a certificate issued by an appropriate authority of the category 1 territory shows that the conduct falls within the European framework list;
  (c) the certificate shows that the conduct is punishable under the law of the

category 1 territory with imprisonment or another form of detention for a term of 3 years or a greater punishment.
(3) The conduct also constitutes an extradition offence in relation to the category 1 territory if these conditions are satisfied—
   (a) the conduct occurs in the category 1 territory;
   (b) the conduct would constitute an offence under the law of the relevant part of the United Kingdom if it occurred in that part of the United Kingdom;
   (c) the conduct is punishable under the law of the category 1 territory with imprisonment or another form of detention for a term of 12 months or a greater punishment (however it is described in that law).
(4) The conduct also constitutes an extradition offence in relation to the category 1 territory if these conditions are satisfied—
   (a) the conduct occurs outside the category 1 territory;
   (b) the conduct is punishable under the law of the category 1 territory with imprisonment or another form of detention for a term of 12 months or a greater punishment (however it is described in that law);
   (c) in corresponding circumstances equivalent conduct would constitute an extra-territorial offence under the law of the relevant part of the United Kingdom punishable with imprisonment or another form of detention for a term of 12 months or a greater punishment.
(5) The conduct also constitutes an extradition offence in relation to the category 1 territory if these conditions are satisfied—
   (a) the conduct occurs outside the category 1 territory and no part of it occurs in the United Kingdom;
   (b) the conduct would constitute an offence under the law of the relevant part of the United Kingdom punishable with imprisonment or another form of detention for a term of 12 months or a greater punishment if it occurred in that part of the United Kingdom;
   (c) the conduct is so punishable under the law of the category 1 territory (however it is described in that law).
(6) The conduct also constitutes an extradition offence in relation to the category 1 territory if these conditions are satisfied—
   (a) the conduct occurs outside the category 1 territory and no part of it occurs in the United Kingdom;
   (b) the conduct is punishable under the law of the category 1 territory with imprisonment or another form of detention for a term of 12 months or a greater punishment (however it is described in that law);
   (c) the conduct constitutes or if committed in the United Kingdom would constitute an offence mentioned in subsection (7).
(7) The offences are—
   (a) an offence under section 51 or 58 of the International Criminal Court Act 2001 (genocide, crimes against humanity and war crimes);
   (b) an offence under section 52 or 59 of that Act (conduct ancillary to genocide etc committed outside the jurisdiction);
   (c) an ancillary offence, as defined in section 55 or 62 of that Act, in relation to an offence falling within paragraph (a) or (b);
   (d) an offence under section 1 of the International Criminal Court (Scotland) Act 2001 (genocide, crimes against humanity and war crimes);

(e) an offence under section 2 of that Act (conduct ancillary to genocide etc committed outside the jurisdiction);
(f) an ancillary offence, as defined in section 7 of that Act, in relation to an offence falling within paragraph (d) or (e).

(8) For the purposes of subsections (3)(b), (4)(c) and (5)(b)–
  (a) if the conduct relates to a tax or duty, it is immaterial that the law of the relevant part of the United Kingdom does not impose the same kind of tax or duty or does not contain rules of the same kind as those of the law of the category 1 territory;
  (b) if the conduct relates to customs or exchange, it is immaterial that the law of the relevant part of the United Kingdom does not contain rules of the same kind as those of the law of the category 1 territory.

(9) This section applies for the purposes of this Part.

Extradition offences: person sentenced for offence

65 (1) This section applies in relation to conduct of a person if–
  (a) he is alleged to be unlawfully at large after conviction by a court in a category 1 territory of an offence constituted by the conduct, and
  (b) he has been sentenced for the offence.

(2) The conduct constitutes an extradition offence in relation to the category 1 territory if these conditions are satisfied–
  (a) the conduct occurs in the category 1 territory and no part of it occurs in the United Kingdom;
  (b) a certificate issued by an appropriate authority of the category 1 territory shows that the conduct falls within the European framework list;
  (c) the certificate shows that a sentence of imprisonment or another form of detention for a term of 12 months or a greater punishment has been imposed in the category 1 territory in respect of the conduct.

(3) The conduct also constitutes an extradition offence in relation to the category 1 territory if these conditions are satisfied–
  (a) the conduct occurs in the category 1 territory;
  (b) the conduct would constitute an offence under the law of the relevant part of the United Kingdom if it occurred in that part of the United Kingdom;
  (c) a sentence of imprisonment or another form of detention for a term of 4 months or a greater punishment has been imposed in the category 1 territory in respect of the conduct.

(4) The conduct also constitutes an extradition offence in relation to the category 1 territory if these conditions are satisfied–
  (a) the conduct occurs outside the category 1 territory;
  (b) a sentence of imprisonment or another form of detention for a term of 4 months or a greater punishment has been imposed in the category 1 territory in respect of the conduct;
  (c) in corresponding circumstances equivalent conduct would constitute an extra-territorial offence under the law of the relevant part of the United Kingdom punishable with imprisonment or another form of detention for a term of 12 months or a greater punishment.

(5) The conduct also constitutes an extradition offence in relation to the category 1 territory if these conditions are satisfied–

(a) the conduct occurs outside the category 1 territory and no part of it occurs in the United Kingdom;
(b) the conduct would constitute an offence under the law of the relevant part of the United Kingdom punishable with imprisonment or another form of detention for a term of 12 months or a greater punishment if it occurred in that part of the United Kingdom;
(c) a sentence of imprisonment or another form of detention for a term of 4 months or a greater punishment has been imposed in the category 1 territory in respect of the conduct.
(6) The conduct also constitutes an extradition offence in relation to the category 1 territory if these conditions are satisfied–
(a) the conduct occurs outside the category 1 territory and no part of it occurs in the United Kingdom;
(b) a sentence of imprisonment or another form of detention for a term of 4 months or a greater punishment has been imposed in the category 1 territory in respect of the conduct;
(c) the conduct constitutes or if committed in the United Kingdom would constitute an offence mentioned in subsection (7).
(7) The offences are–
(a) an offence under section 51 or 58 of the International Criminal Court Act 2001 (c 17) (genocide, crimes against humanity and war crimes);
(b) an offence under section 52 or 59 of that Act (conduct ancillary to genocide etc committed outside the jurisdiction);
(c) an ancillary offence, as defined in section 55 or 62 of that Act, in relation to an offence falling within paragraph (a) or (b);
(d) an offence under section 1 of the International Criminal Court (Scotland) Act 2001 (asp 13) (genocide, crimes against humanity and war crimes);
(e) an offence under section 2 of that Act (conduct ancillary to genocide etc committed outside the jurisdiction);
(f) an ancillary offence, as defined in section 7 of that Act, in relation to an offence falling within paragraph (d) or (e).
(8) For the purposes of subsections (3)(b), (4)(c) and (5)(b)–
(a) if the conduct relates to a tax or duty, it is immaterial that the law of the relevant part of the United Kingdom does not impose the same kind of tax or duty or does not contain rules of the same kind as those of the law of the category 1 territory;
(b) if the conduct relates to customs or exchange, it is immaterial that the law of the relevant part of the United Kingdom does not contain rules of the same kind as those of the law of the category 1 territory.
(9) This section applies for the purposes of this Part.
...

Extradition request and certificate

70 (1) The Secretary of State must (subject to subsection (2)) issue a certificate under this section if he receives a valid request for the extradition of a person to a category 2 territory.
(2) The Secretary of State may refuse to issue a certificate under this section if–
(a) he has power under section 126 to order that proceedings on the request be deferred,

(b) the person whose extradition is requested has been recorded by the Secretary of State as a refugee within the meaning of the Refugee Convention, or

(c) the person whose extradition is requested has been granted leave to enter or remain in the United Kingdom on the ground that it would be a breach of Article 2 or 3 of the Human Rights Convention to remove him to the territory to which extradition is requested.

(2A) In subsection (2)–

'Refugee Convention' has the meaning given by section 167(1) of the Immigration and Asylum Act 1999;

'Human Rights Convention' has the meaning given to 'the Convention' by section 21(1) of the Human Rights Act 1998.

(3) A request for a person's extradition is valid if–
   (a) it contains the statement referred to in subsection (4) or the statement referred to in subsection (4A), and
   (b) it is made in the approved way.

(4) The statement is one that–
   (a) the person is accused in the category 2 territory of the commission of an offence specified in the request, and
   (b) the request is made with a view to his arrest and extradition to the category 2 territory for the purpose of being prosecuted for the offence.

(4A) The statement is one that–
   (a) the person has been convicted of an offence specified in the request by a court in the category 2 territory, and
   (b) the request is made with a view to his arrest and extradition to the category 2 territory for the purpose of being sentenced for the offence or of serving a sentence of imprisonment or another form of detention imposed in respect of the offence.

(5) A request for extradition to a category 2 territory which is a British overseas territory is made in the approved way if it is made by or on behalf of the person administering the territory.

(6) A request for extradition to a category 2 territory which is the Hong Kong Special Administrative Region of the People's Republic of China is made in the approved way if it is made by or on behalf of the government of the Region.

(7) A request for extradition to any other category 2 territory is made in the approved way if it is made–
   (a) by an authority of the territory which the Secretary of State believes has the function of making requests for extradition in that territory, or
   (b) by a person recognised by the Secretary of State as a diplomatic or consular representative of the territory.

(8) A certificate under this section must–
   (a) certify that the request is made in the approved way[, and
   (b) identify the order by which the territory in question is designated as a category 2 territory.

(9) If a certificate is issued under this section the Secretary of State must send the request and the certificate to the appropriate judge.

Arrest
Arrest warrant following extradition request
71 (1) This section applies if the Secretary of State sends documents to the appropriate judge under section 70.
  (2) The judge may issue a warrant for the arrest of the person whose extradition is requested if the judge has reasonable grounds for believing that–
    (a) the offence in respect of which extradition is requested is an extradition offence, and
    (b) there is evidence falling within subsection (3).
  (3) The evidence is–
    (a) evidence that would justify the issue of a warrant for the arrest of a person accused of the offence within the judge's jurisdiction, if the person whose extradition is requested is accused of the commission of the offence;
    (b) evidence that would justify the issue of a warrant for the arrest of a person unlawfully at large after conviction of the offence within the judge's jurisdiction, if the person whose extradition is requested is alleged to be unlawfully at large after conviction of the offence.
  (4) But if the category 2 territory to which extradition is requested is designated for the purposes of this section by order made by the Secretary of State, subsections (2) and (3) have effect as if 'evidence' read 'information'.
  (5) A warrant issued under this section may–
    (a) be executed by any person to whom it is directed or by any constable or customs officer;
    (b) be executed even if neither the warrant nor a copy of it is in the possession of the person executing it at the time of the arrest.
  (6) If a warrant issued under this section–
    (a) is directed to a service policeman, and
    (b) is in respect of a person subject to service law or a civilian subject to service discipline,
    it may be executed anywhere.
  (7) In any other case, a warrant issued under this section may be executed in any part of the United Kingdom.

Person arrested under section 71
72 (1) This section applies if a person is arrested under a warrant issued under section 71.
  (2) A copy of the warrant must be given to the person as soon as practicable after his arrest.
  (3) The person must be brought as soon as practicable before the appropriate judge.
  (4) But subsection (3) does not apply if–
    (a) the person is granted bail by a constable following his arrest, or
    (b) the Secretary of State decides under section 126 that the request for the person's extradition is not to be proceeded with.
  (5) If subsection (2) is not complied with and the person applies to the judge to be discharged, the judge may order his discharge.
  (6) If subsection (3) is not complied with and the person applies to the judge to be discharged, the judge must order his discharge.

(7) When the person first appears or is brought before the appropriate judge, the judge must–
   (a) inform him of the contents of the request for his extradition;
   (b) give him the required information about consent;
   (c) remand him in custody or on bail.
(8) The required information about consent is–
   (a) that the person may consent to his extradition to the category 2 territory to which his extradition is requested;
   (b) an explanation of the effect of consent and the procedure that will apply if he gives consent;
   (c) that consent must be given in writing and is irrevocable.
(9) If the person is remanded in custody, the appropriate judge may later grant bail.
(10) Subsection (4)(a) applies to Scotland with the omission of the words 'by a constable'.

Provisional warrant

73 (1) This section applies if a justice of the peace is satisfied on information in writing and on oath that a person within subsection (2)–
   (a) is or is believed to be in the United Kingdom, or
   (b) is or is believed to be on his way to the United Kingdom.
(2) A person is within this subsection if–
   (a) he is accused in a category 2 territory of the commission of an offence, or
   (b) he is alleged to be unlawfully at large after conviction of an offence by a court in a category 2 territory.
(3) The justice may issue a warrant for the arrest of the person (a provisional warrant) if he has reasonable grounds for believing that–
   (a) the offence of which the person is accused or has been convicted is an extradition offence, and
   (b) there is written evidence falling within subsection (4).
(4) The evidence is–
   (a) evidence that would justify the issue of a warrant for the arrest of a person accused of the offence within the justice's jurisdiction, if the person in respect of whom the warrant is sought is accused of the commission of the offence;
   (b) evidence that would justify the issue of a warrant for the arrest of a person unlawfully at large after conviction of the offence within the justice's jurisdiction, if the person in respect of whom the warrant is sought is alleged to be unlawfully at large after conviction of the offence.
(5) But if the category 2 territory is designated for the purposes of this section by order made by the Secretary of State, subsections (3) and (4) have effect as if 'evidence' read 'information'.
(6) A provisional warrant may–
   (a) be executed by any person to whom it is directed or by any constable or customs officer;
   (b) be executed even if neither the warrant nor a copy of it is in the possession of the person executing it at the time of the arrest.
(7) If a warrant issued under this section–
   (a) is directed to a service policeman, and

(b) is in respect of a person subject to service law or a civilian subject to service discipline,

it may be executed anywhere.
(8) In any other case, a warrant issued under this section may be executed in any part of the United Kingdom.
(9) ...
(10) The preceding provisions of this section apply to Scotland with these modifications–
- (a) in subsection (1) for 'justice of the peace is satisfied on information in writing and on oath' substitute 'sheriff is satisfied, on an application by a procurator fiscal,';
- (b) in subsection (3) for 'justice' substitute 'sheriff';
- (c) in subsection (4) for 'justice's', in paragraphs (a) and (b), substitute 'sheriff's'.
(11) Subsection (1) applies to Northern Ireland with the substitution of 'a complaint' for 'information'.

Person arrested under provisional warrant

74 (1) This section applies if a person is arrested under a provisional warrant.
(2) A copy of the warrant must be given to the person as soon as practicable after his arrest.
(3) The person must be brought as soon as practicable before the appropriate judge.
(4) But subsection (3) does not apply if–
- (a) the person is granted bail by a constable following his arrest, or
- (b) in a case where the Secretary of State has received a valid request for the person's extradition, the Secretary of State decides under section 126 that the request is not to be proceeded with.

(5) If subsection (2) is not complied with and the person applies to the judge to be discharged, the judge may order his discharge.
(6) If subsection (3) is not complied with and the person applies to the judge to be discharged, the judge must order his discharge.
(7) When the person first appears or is brought before the appropriate judge, the judge must–
- (a) inform him that he is accused of the commission of an offence in a category 2 territory or that he is alleged to be unlawfully at large after conviction of an offence by a court in a category 2 territory;
- (b) give him the required information about consent;
- (c) remand him in custody or on bail.

(8) The required information about consent is–
- (a) that the person may consent to his extradition to the category 2 territory in which he is accused of the commission of an offence or is alleged to have been convicted of an offence;
- (b) an explanation of the effect of consent and the procedure that will apply if he gives consent;
- (c) that consent must be given in writing and is irrevocable.

(9) If the person is remanded in custody, the appropriate judge may later grant bail.

(10) The judge must order the person's discharge if the documents referred to in section 70(9) are not received by the judge within the required period.
(11) The required period is–
   (a) 45 days starting with the day on which the person was arrested, or
   (b) if the category 2 territory is designated by order made by the Secretary of State for the purposes of this section, any longer period permitted by the order.
(12) Subsection (4)(a) applies to Scotland with the omission of the words 'by a constable'.

The extradition hearing

Date of extradition hearing: arrest under section 71

75 (1) When a person arrested under a warrant issued under section 71 first appears or is brought before the appropriate judge, the judge must fix a date on which the extradition hearing is to begin.
(2) The date fixed under subsection (1) must not be later than the end of the permitted period, which is 2 months starting with the date on which the person first appears or is brought before the judge.
(3) If before the date fixed under subsection (1) (or this subsection) a party to the proceedings applies to the judge for a later date to be fixed and the judge believes it to be in the interests of justice to do so, he may fix a later date; and this subsection may apply more than once.
(4) If the extradition hearing does not begin on or before the date fixed under this section and the person applies to the judge to be discharged, the judge must order his discharge.

Interpretation

Extradition offences: person not sentenced for offence

137 (1) This section applies in relation to conduct of a person if–
   (a) he is accused in a category 2 territory of the commission of an offence constituted by the conduct, or
   (b) he is alleged to be unlawfully at large after conviction by a court in a category 2 territory of an offence constituted by the conduct and he has not been sentenced for the offence.
(2) The conduct constitutes an extradition offence in relation to the category 2 territory if these conditions are satisfied–
   (a) the conduct occurs in the category 2 territory;
   (b) the conduct would constitute an offence under the law of the relevant part of the United Kingdom punishable with imprisonment or another form of detention for a term of 12 months or a greater punishment if it occurred in that part of the United Kingdom;
   (c) the conduct is so punishable under the law of the category 2 territory (however it is described in that law).
(3) The conduct also constitutes an extradition offence in relation to the category 2 territory if these conditions are satisfied–
   (a) the conduct occurs outside the category 2 territory;
   (b) the conduct is punishable under the law of the category 2 territory with imprisonment or another form of detention for a term of 12 months or a greater punishment (however it is described in that law);

(c) in corresponding circumstances equivalent conduct would constitute an extra-territorial offence under the law of the relevant part of the United Kingdom punishable with imprisonment or another form of detention for a term of 12 months or a greater punishment.

(4) The conduct also constitutes an extradition offence in relation to the category 2 territory if these conditions are satisfied–
  (a) the conduct occurs outside the category 2 territory and no part of it occurs in the United Kingdom;
  (b) the conduct would constitute an offence under the law of the relevant part of the United Kingdom punishable with imprisonment or another form of detention for a term of 12 months or a greater punishment if it occurred in that part of the United Kingdom;
  (c) the conduct is so punishable under the law of the category 2 territory (however it is described in that law).

(5) The conduct also constitutes an extradition offence in relation to the category 2 territory if these conditions are satisfied–
  (a) the conduct occurs outside the category 2 territory and no part of it occurs in the United Kingdom;
  (b) the conduct is punishable under the law of the category 2 territory with imprisonment for a term of 12 months or another form of detention or a greater punishment (however it is described in that law);
  (c) the conduct constitutes or if committed in the United Kingdom would constitute an offence mentioned in subsection (6).

(6) The offences are–
  (a) an offence under section 51 or 58 of the International Criminal Court Act 2001 (genocide, crimes against humanity and war crimes);
  (b) an offence under section 52 or 59 of that Act (conduct ancillary to genocide etc committed outside the jurisdiction);
  (c) an ancillary offence, as defined in section 55 or 62 of that Act, in relation to an offence falling within paragraph (a) or (b);
  (d) an offence under section 1 of the International Criminal Court (Scotland) Act 2001 (asp 13) (genocide, crimes against humanity and war crimes);
  (e) an offence under section 2 of that Act (conduct ancillary to genocide etc committed outside the jurisdiction);
  (f) an ancillary offence, as defined in section 7 of that Act, in relation to an offence falling within paragraph (d) or (e).

(7) If the conduct constitutes an offence under the military law of the category 2 territory but does not constitute an offence under the general criminal law of the relevant part of the United Kingdom it does not constitute an extradition offence; and subsections (1) to (6) have effect subject to this.

(8) The relevant part of the United Kingdom is the part of the United Kingdom in which–
  (a) the extradition hearing took place, if the question of whether conduct constitutes an extradition offence is to be decided by the Secretary of State;
  (b) proceedings in which it is necessary to decide that question are taking place, in any other case.

(9) Subsections (1) to (7) apply for the purposes of this Part.

Extradition offences: person sentenced for offence

138 (1) This section applies in relation to conduct of a person if–
 (a) he is alleged to be unlawfully at large after conviction by a court in a category 2 territory of an offence constituted by the conduct, and
 (b) he has been sentenced for the offence.
(2) The conduct constitutes an extradition offence in relation to the category 2 territory if these conditions are satisfied–
 (a) the conduct occurs in the category 2 territory;
 (b) the conduct would constitute an offence under the law of the relevant part of the United Kingdom punishable with imprisonment or another form of detention for a term of 12 months or a greater punishment if it occurred in that part of the United Kingdom;
 (c) a sentence of imprisonment or another form of detention for a term of 4 months or a greater punishment has been imposed in the category 2 territory in respect of the conduct.
(3) The conduct also constitutes an extradition offence in relation to the category 2 territory if these conditions are satisfied–
 (a) the conduct occurs outside the category 2 territory;
 (b) a sentence of imprisonment or another form of detention for a term of 4 months or a greater punishment has been imposed in the category 2 territory in respect of the conduct;
 (c) in corresponding circumstances equivalent conduct would constitute an extra-territorial offence under the law of the relevant part of the United Kingdom punishable with imprisonment or another form of detention for a term of 12 months or a greater punishment.
(4) The conduct also constitutes an extradition offence in relation to the category 2 territory if these conditions are satisfied–
 (a) the conduct occurs outside the category 2 territory and no part of it occurs in the United Kingdom;
 (b) the conduct would constitute an offence under the law of the relevant part of the United Kingdom punishable with imprisonment or another form of detention for a term of 12 months or a greater punishment if it occurred in that part of the United Kingdom;
 (c) a sentence of imprisonment or another form of detention for a term of 4 months or a greater punishment has been imposed in the category 2 territory in respect of the conduct.
(5) The conduct also constitutes an extradition offence in relation to the category 2 territory if these conditions are satisfied–
 (a) the conduct occurs outside the category 2 territory and no part of it occurs in the United Kingdom;
 (b) a sentence of imprisonment or another form of detention for a term of 4 months or a greater punishment has been imposed in the category 2 territory in respect of the conduct;
 (c) the conduct constitutes or if committed in the United Kingdom would constitute an offence mentioned in subsection (6).
(6) The offences are–
 (a) an offence under section 51 or 58 of the International Criminal Court Act 2001 (genocide, crimes against humanity and war crimes);

(b) an offence under section 52 or 59 of that Act (conduct ancillary to genocide etc committed outside the jurisdiction);
(c) an ancillary offence, as defined in section 55 or 62 of that Act, in relation to an offence falling within paragraph (a) or (b);
(d) an offence under section 1 of the International Criminal Court (Scotland) Act 2001 (genocide, crimes against humanity and war crimes);
(e) an offence under section 2 of that Act (conduct ancillary to genocide etc committed outside the jurisdiction);
(f) an ancillary offence, as defined in section 7 of that Act, in relation to an offence falling within paragraph (d) or (e).

(7) If the conduct constitutes an offence under the military law of the category 2 territory but does not constitute an offence under the general criminal law of the relevant part of the United Kingdom it does not constitute an extradition offence; and subsections (1) to (6) have effect subject to this.

(8) The relevant part of the United Kingdom is the part of the United Kingdom in which–
(a) the extradition hearing took place, if the question of whether conduct constitutes an extradition offence is to be decided by the Secretary of State;
(b) proceedings in which it is necessary to decide that question are taking place, in any other case.

(9) Subsections (1) to (7) apply for the purposes of this Part.

APPENDIX C

EAW validity checklist

Date EAW issued	
Date EAW certified	
Is it an accusation or conviction warrant? [Box B] Is the warrant as a whole unclear?	
Date of offence [Box E]	
Place of offence [Box E]	
Description of offence [Box E] Is the description sufficiently particularised?	
Accusation: maximum sentence [Box C] Conviction: sentence imposed [Box C] Is the sentence sufficiently particularised?	
Extradition offences? [Box E] a) Would the conduct constitute an offence in the UK? If so, is it punishable in requesting state by at least 12 months (accusation) or did requested person receive sentence of at least 4 months (conviction)? b) If not an offence in UK, is it a framework offence? If so, is it punishable in requesting state by at least 3 years (accusation) or did requested person receive sentence of at least 12 months (conviction)?	
Conviction: Was the requested person present at trial? [Box D]	

APPENDIX D

EAW first appearance checklist

Check identity	
Consider s4	
Has the requested person been given a copy of the EAW? If not, judge may discharge	
Has the requested person been brought as soon as practicable before the appropriate judge? If not, judge must discharge	
Explain extradition procedure – court not interested in whether/by whom offence was committed, but whether procedural requirements met; timescale	
Explain consent and specialty	
Is the requested person serving a sentence in the UK or subject to a domestic charge?	
Are there any issues to raise?	
Consider bars	
Conviction in absence?	
Human rights	
Physical/mental health	
Why does the requested person think s/he shouldn't be extradited?	
In appropriate cases, fill out the legal aid form	
Explain appeal process	

APPENDIX E

Bail checklist

Circumstances of arrest: where was the requested person arrested (ie home? Work?) Does s/he accept any statements said to have been made by him/her?	
When did the requested person come to the UK and why?	
Has the requested person been back to the requesting state?	
Was the requested person aware of criminal proceedings and if so, was s/he present and why did s/he leave?	
Does the requested person have family? Where are the family based and what are their circumstances? Are they dependent?	
Is the requested person employed? If so, what are his or her hours of work? How far is the place of work from home?	
What is the requested person's housing situation?	
Does the requested person have community ties?	
Are details on police national computer print out correct? Is there any explanation for failing to attend on previous occasions?	
Has the requested person instructed lawyers in requesting state?	
What is his or her immigration status?	

Where are his or her identity documents? If not in the requested person's property, can someone else find them to surrender them to the court/police?	
Does the requested person know whether a surety or security may be available? If so, obtain telephone numbers.	
Where is the nearest police station to the requested person's home address located? Would a reporting condition at any particular time be problematic?	
If a curfew were imposed, what hours would be practicable for the requested person?	

APPENDIX F

Case management form

It is now a standard direction in extradition cases at Westminster Magistrates' Court that you provide the following details that may be relevant in these proceedings. The information you provide must be accurate as it may be checked, and it may be referred to at later hearings.

About you   :   Please print your full name and date of birth :

....

1. Are you the person requested in the warrant? Y/N

2. Have you any serious physical or mental health problems that may be relevant to these proceedings   Y/N
   (if so, please describe them).

3. Are you currently working?
   (if so, please state whether employed or self employed)

About your family

1. Please give names and dates of birth (or ages) of any family member dependent on you in the United Kingdom.

2. Do any of your UK dependents have **serious** physical or mental health problems t relevant to these proceedings ? Y/N .   If so please describe them :

3. If your extradition is ordered will any other person be able to care for your dependent(s) ? Y/N   If not, why not ?

Your connection with the United Kingdom

1. Do you live here? Y/N : If so , since when ?

Your connection with the Requesting State

1. Are you a citizen of the requesting state ? **Y/N**

2. If not, have you been there? **Y/N** : if so when were you last there ?

3. If you have now been arrested on a conviction warrant, were you present at the conviction hearing ? **Y/N**

4. When did you first know of these proceedings ?

5. Have you been granted asylum from the requesting state ? **Y/N** : If Yes, when ?

6. What hardship do you believe you would suffer in the requesting state, if returned?

7. Is there any other good reason why you should not be extradited ?

SIGNED BY REQUESTED PERSON ....

DATE ....

INFORMATION FROM LAWYER :

Name..
  (please print)

Name of firm of solicitors

....
  (please print)

Have you had sufficient time to advise your client on potential challenges ? **Y/N** If not, please explain :

What potential issues have been identified for these proceedings ?

APPENDIX G

Application notice – Form N161

Appellant's notice
(All appeals except small claims track appeals)

	Click here to reset form	Click here to print form
	For Court use only	
Appeal Court Ref. No.		
Date filed		

Notes for guidance are available which will help you complete this form. Please read them carefully before you complete each section.

SEAL

Section 1 Details of the claim or case you are appealing against

Claim or Case no.

Name(s) of the ☐ Claimant(s) ☐ Applicant(s) ☐ Petitioner(s)

Name(s) of the ☐ Defendant(s) ☐ Respondent(s)

Details of the party appealing ('The Appellant')
Name

Address (including postcode)

Tel No.
Fax
E-mail

Details of the Respondent to the appeal
Name

Address (including postcode)

Tel No.
Fax
E-mail

Details of additional parties (if any) are attached ☐ Yes ☐ No

N161 Appellant's notice (04.12) © Crown copyright 2012

Section 2 Details of the appeal

From which court is the appeal being brought?

☐ The County Court at

☐ High Court

    ☐ Queen's Bench Division

    ☐ Chancery Division

    ☐ Family Division

☐ Other (please specify)

What is the name of the Judge whose decision you want to appeal?

What is the status of the Judge whose decision you want to appeal?

☐ District Judge or Deputy   ☐ Circuit Judge or Recorder   ☐ Tribunal Judge

☐ Master or Deputy   ☐ High Court Judge or Deputy

What is the date of the decision you wish to appeal against?

To which track, if any, was the claim or case allocated?

☐ Fast track

☐ Multi track

☐ Not allocated to a track

Nature of the decision you wish to appeal

☐ Case management decision   ☐ Grant or refusal of interim relief

☐ Final decision   ☐ A previous appeal decision

Application notice – Form N161 225

Section 3 Legal representation

Are you legally represented?   ☐ Yes ☐ No
If 'Yes', please give details of your solicitor below

Name of the firm of solicitors representing you

The address (including postcode) of the firm of solicitors representing you

Tel No.	
Fax	
E-mail	
DX	
Ref.	

Are you, the Appellant, in receipt of a Legal Aid Certificate or a Community Legal Service Fund (CLSF) certificate?   ☐ Yes ☐ No

Is the respondent legally represented?   ☐ Yes ☐ No
If 'Yes', please give details of the respondent's solicitor below

Name and address (including postcode) of the firm of solicitors representing the respondent

Tel No.	
Fax	
E-mail	
DX	
Ref.	

Section 4 Permission to appeal

Do you need permission to appeal?   ☐ Yes ☐ No

Has permission to appeal been granted?

☐ **Yes** (Complete Box A)   ☐ **No** (Complete Box B)

Box A

Date of order granting permission

Name of Judge granting permission

Box B

I

the Appellant('s solicitor) seek permission to appeal.

If permission to appeal has been granted **in part** by the lower court, do you seek permission to appeal in respect of the grounds refused by the lower court?   ☐ Yes ☐ No

Section 5 Other information required for the appeal

Please set out the order (or part of the order) you wish to appeal against

Have you lodged this notice with the court in time?
(There are different types of appeal -
see Guidance Notes N161A)

☐ Yes ☐ No

If **'No'** you must complete
Part B of Section 9

Section 6 Grounds of appeal

Please state, in numbered paragraphs, **on a separate sheet** attached to this notice and entitled 'Grounds of Appeal' (also in the top right hand corner add your claim or case number and full name), why you are saying that the Judge who made the order you are appealing was wrong.

☐ I confirm that the grounds of appeal are attached to this notice.

Section 7 Arguments in support of grounds for appeal

☐ I confirm that the arguments (known as a 'Skeleton Argument') in support of the 'Grounds of Appeal' are set out **on a separate sheet** and attached to this notice.

OR

☐ I confirm that the arguments (known as a 'Skeleton Argument') in support of the 'Grounds of Appeal' will follow within 14 days of filing this Appellant's Notice

Section 8 What are you asking the Appeal Court to do?

I am asking the appeal court to:-
(please tick the appropriate box)

☐ set aside the order which I am appealing

☐ vary the order which I am appealing and substitute the following order. Set out in the following space the order you are asking for:-

☐ order a new trial

Section 9 Other applications

Complete this section **only** if you are making any additional applications.

Part A
☐ I apply for a stay of execution. (You must set out in Section 10 your reasons for seeking a stay of execution and evidence in support of your application.)

Part B
☐ I apply for an extension of time for filing my appeal notice. (You must set out in Section 10 the reasons for the delay and what steps you have taken since the decision you are appealing.)

Part C
☐ I apply for an order that:

(You must set out in Section 10 your reasons and your evidence in support of your application.)

Section 10 Evidence in support

In support of my application(s) in Section 9, I wish to rely upon the following reasons and evidence:

Statement of Truth – This must be completed in support of the evidence in Section 10
I believe (The appellant believes) that the facts stated in this section are true.

Full name

Name of appellant's solicitor's firm

signed _____   position or office held _____
    Appellant ('s solicitor)   (if signing on behalf of firm or company)

Section 11 Supporting documents

To support your appeal you should file with this notice all relevant documents listed below. To show which documents you are filing, please tick the appropriate boxes.

If you do not have a document that you intend to use to support your appeal complete the box over the page.

☐ two additional copies of your appellant's notice for the appeal court;

☐ one copy of your appellant's notice for each of the respondents;

☐ one copy of your grounds for appeal for each of the respondents;

☐ one copy of your skeleton argument for each copy of the appellant's notice that is filed;

☐ a sealed *(stamped by the court)* copy of the order being appealed;

☐ a copy of any order giving or refusing permission to appeal, together with a copy of the judge's reasons for allowing or refusing permission to appeal;

☐ any witness statements or affidavits in support of any application included in the appellant's notice;

☐ a copy of the order allocating the case to a track *(if any)*; and

☐ a copy of the legal aid or CLSF certificate *(if legally represented)*.

A bundle of documents for the appeal hearing containing copies of all the papers listed below:-

☐ a sealed copy *(stamped by the court)* of your appellant's notice;

☐ a sealed copy *(stamped by the court)* of the order being appealed;

☐ a copy of any order giving or refusing permission to appeal, together with a copy of the judge's reasons for allowing or refusing permission to appeal;

☐ any affidavit or witness statement filed in support of any application included in the appellant's notice;

☐ a copy of the grounds for appeal;

☐ a copy of the skeleton argument;

☐ a transcript or note of judgment, and in cases where permission to appeal was given by the lower court or is not required those parts of any transcript of evidence which are directly relevant to any question at issue on the appeal;

☐ the claim form and statements of case (where relevant to the subject of the appeal);

☐ any application notice (or case management documentation) relevant to the subject of the appeal;

☐ in cases where the decision appealed was itself made on appeal (eg from district judge to circuit judge), the first order, the reasons given and the appellant's notice used to appeal from that order;

☐ in the case of judicial review or a statutory appeal, the original decision which was the subject of the application to the lower court;

☐ in cases where the appeal is from a Tribunal, a copy of the Tribunal's reasons for the decision, a copy of the decision reviewed by the Tribunal and the reasons for the original decision and any document filed with the Tribunal setting out the grounds of appeal from that decision;

☐ any other documents which are necessary to enable the appeal court to reach a decision; and

☐ such other documents as the court may direct.

Reasons why you have not supplied a document and date when you expect it to be available:-

Title of document and reason not supplied	Date when it will be supplied

Section 12 The notice of appeal must be signed here

Signed _____ Appellant('s Solicitor)

[Click here to reset form] [Click here to print form]

Index

EAW = European Arrest Warrant (EAW)
SSHD = Secretary of State for the Home Department (SSHD)
SOCA = Serious Organised Crime Agency (SOCA)

absence, conviction in 6.4, 6.59–6.63
  awareness of proceedings 5.14
  bars/challenges to extradition 4.51
  burden of proof 6.60
  EAW requests 3.12, 6.62
  fugitives 6.59–6.60
  initial hearings 8.42
  instructions 9.20
  retrials 3.12, 4.51, 6.59, 6.61–6.63, 9.20
absence, sentences in 12.2
abuse of process 4.52, 6.4, 6.70–6.74, 7.15
access to legal advice 2.4, 4.15, 5.9, 8.13
accusation cases
  awareness of proceedings 5.14
  bail 8.52–8.56
  clarity as to purpose of warrant, lack of 3.25–3.26
  compromising the extradition request 12.2
  deficient particulars 3.23, 3.27–3.34, 3.38
  extradition offences 3.39–3.40, 4.53, 4.57–4.59
  first hearings 4.27, 4.39
  hybrid warrants 3.8

  passage of time as bar 6.27, 6.37, 6.43, 9.16
  threshold of punishment 3.14, 3.40, 4.57–4.59
active pursuit of requested persons 4.13
ad hoc arrangements 1.17, 4.4
adjournments
  applications 10.8–10.11, 10.14, 11.47–11.49
  asylum seekers 6.75
  bars/challenges to extradition 8.41
  charges in UK, persons facing 5.6, 8.34
  compromising the extradition request 12.5
  day of hearing 10.8–10.11
  directions 10.9–10.10
  discretion 8.35
  estimates of time 10.15
  experts' reports 7.27
  fees 11.47
  first hearings after provisional arrest 4.28–4.30
  fixing hearing dates 4.38
  forms 11.48
  health 6.64
  immigration status 6.75
  imprisonment in UK, persons subject to 4.29–4.30, 5.6, 8.35
  initial hearings 8.34–8.35, 8.41
  judicial review 10.11
  legal aid 5.19
  notice 10.8–10.10, 11.48
  papers, hearings on the 11.49

adjournments *continued*
  reasons 10.10
  refusal 10.11
  service 11.48
  time limits 4.38, 8.35, 10.9, 10.15
  vacating hearing dates 11.47
  witness statements 11.48
Administrative Court 1.27–1.28, 11.5–11.33, 11.40, 11.44–11.46, 12.18
Administrative Court Office (ACO) 11.6–11.8, 11.30, 11.38, 11.46, 11.48, 11.55–11.56, 11.62–11.64
age bar 6.3, 6.45–6.46
appeals 11.1–11.116 *see also* **Supreme Court**
  adjournment applications 11.47–11.49
  Administrative Court 1.27–1.28, 11.5, 11.11–11.33, 11.44–11.46
  appropriate judge, production before the 8.32–8.33
  bundles 11.15–11.16, 11.20, 11.22–11.23, 11.26, 11.50–11.51
  case management and directions 11.39–11.46
  certify a point of law, making applications to 11.95–11.100
  conditions for allowing appeals 11.75–11.77, 11.80–11.81, 11.88, 11.90
  court's powers 11.75–11.77, 11.80–11.82
  designated Category 1 territories 1.15
  discharge 10.44, 11.1–11.2, 11.77–11.79, 11.82–11.85, 11.89
  documents 11.15–1.16, 11.20–11.23, 11.26, 11.34, 11.38, 11.46, 11.50–11.51
  EAW requests 11.2, 11.11–11.27, 11.75–11.77
  estimates of time 11.24
  extension of time 8.65, 11.4, 11.19, 11.31, 11.35–11.38

extradition orders 4.75, 8.61, 11.1–11.2, 11.11, 11.77, 11.86–11.90, 11.101–11.103, 11.106
fax, lodging by 11.38
fees 11.22–11.23, 11.52
fixing hearing dates 11.24–11.25
forms 11.15, 11.18–11.20, 11.59
grounds 11.21, 11.30
initial hearings 8.32–8.33, 8.65
interim measures, application to ECtHR for 11.108–11.116
judgments 10.42–10.43
legal aid 11.6–11.10, 11.17
lodging appeals 11.22–11.27, 11.30, 11.38–11.39
new evidence, introduction of 11.68–11.76
notice 11.12–11.14, 11.23, 11.30–11.32, 11.45
Part 2 requests 1.14–1.17, 11.2, 11.28–11.31, 11.39–11.43, 11.80–11.82.11.86–11.90
preparation 11.15–11.21
quashing orders 11.77, 11.82, 11.89
removal 8.65, 11.11, 11.106–11.107
reopening appeals 11.103–11.105
service 11.12, 11.22–11.27
skeleton arguments 11.32, 11.45
specialty rights 5.8
SSHD 1.8–1.9, 11.2, 11.28–11.30, 11.33–11.34, 11.86–11.90
summaries 10.42
supervening events 11.101–11.105
time limits 8.61, 8.65, 11.4, 11.32, 11.35–11.38, 11.45
  EAW requests 11.11–11.13, 11.19, 11.27, 11.106
  extension of time 8.65, 11.4, 11.19, 11.31, 11.35–11.38
  judgments 10.43
  Part 2 requests 11.28, 11.30
  removal 8.65
  unless orders 11.45
urgent appeals 11.38
warned list 11.25

Index 233

withdrawal of representation 11.53–11.67
withdrawing the appeal 11.52
appropriate judge, production before 8.14–8.23
appeals 8.32–8.33, 11.79, 11.83–11.84
appointment 1.26
arrest 2.5, 4.22–4.25
as soon as practicable requirement 2.5, 4.22–4.25, 5.3–5.4, 8.14–8.20
challenges 8.22–8.23
delay 4.23
error 8.17
factors taken into consideration 8.19–8.20
habeas corpus 8.16–8.17
initial hearings 8.7, 8.10, 8.14–8.23, 8.32–8.33
list of judges 1.26
remission back to judges 11.79, 11.83–11.84
submissions 8.22–8.23
time limits 8.4–8.5
transport, arranging 4.24
Westminster Magistrates' Court 4.19, 4.22–4.25, 8.17–8.18
arrest *see also* **arrest, police powers of; European Arrest Warrant (EAW) requests**
access to legal advice 2.4, 4.15
active pursuit of requested person 4.13
appropriate judge, production before the 4.20–4.25
as soon as practicable requirement 2.5, 4.20–4.21
bail 2.5, 4.25
caution, terms of 4.14
code of practice 2.2
competing requests 4.14
date of arrest 11.19
duty solicitors 4.15
first hearings after provisional arrest 4.27–4.34
high-profile cases 4.13
identity 2.2–2.3, 4.26, 5.5, 8.26
informed of arrest, right to have someone 2.4
interpreter, right to an 2.4
Part 2 requests 4.9, 4.12–4.16, 4.19–4.21
place of arrest 4.24
police 2.2–2.4, 4.15
searches and seizure and retention of material 2.2
serious cases 4.13
statements 2.9, 8.10, 8.12, 8.26
as soon as practicable requirement
appropriate judge, production before 2.5, 4.22–4.25, 5.3–5.4, 8.14–8.20
arrest 2.5, 4.20–4.21, 8.11
bail 4.21
delay, causes of 5.4
discharge 4.20, 5.4
error 8.17
factors to be taken into consideration 8.19–8.20
initial hearings 8.10, 8.14–8.23, 8.32–8.33
service of EAW 8.11
asylum seekers 5.15, 6.75
attending the client 5.1–5.19 *see also* **instructions**
audience, rights of 11.43
autrefois convict 6.7

background and personal circumstances 5.12–5.13, 9.11, 9.19, 9.28
bail
arrest 2.5, 4.15, 4.21, 4.25
attending the client 5.5, 5.6, 5.12–5.13
conditions 8.53, 10.43–10.44
consent 8.34
court, attending 10.20
EAW requests 3.2–3.18, 3.39
first hearings 4.35, 4.39
geographical restrictions 8.53
identity, disputes as to 5.5
initial hearings 8.34, 8.51–8.56
international travel documents, condition not to apply for 8.53

bail *continued*
'iron letters' 12.6
legal aid 5.19
Part 2 requests 4.6–4.7, 4.15, 4.21
personal circumstances 5.12–5.13
remand 8.55–8.56
security 2.11, 8.51–8.54, 12.6
travel documents, surrender or retention of 8.53
voluntary returns 5.17
Baker Review 1.7–1.8
barristers *see* **counsel**
bars/challenges to requests 6.1–6.77 *see also* **absence, conviction in; European Convention on Human Rights; passage of time as bar**
abuse of process 4.52, 6.4, 6.70–6.74
age 6.3, 6.45–6.46
attending the client 5.16–5.17
death penalty 4.72–4.73, 6.3, 6.58
documentation requirements, non-compliance with 4.50
double jeopardy 5.16, 6.3, 6.5–6.9
earlier extradition from territory 6.3, 6.53–6.54
EAW requests 6.46, 6.75, 7.2–7.7
extraneous considerations 5.16, 6.3, 6.10–6.22
extradition offences, conduct not amounting to 4.50
forum 1.8–1.9, 6.3, 6.55–6.57
Framework Decision 12.8
health issues 5.16, 6.4, 6.64–6.69, 8.42, 9.11, 9.21
hostage-taking considerations 6.3, 6.47–6.48
immigration status 5.15, 6.75–6.77
initial hearings 8.34, 8.51–8.56
instructions 9.13
International Criminal Court, earlier extradition by 6.3
issues to be taken 5.16–5.17
list of grounds 4.48, 5.16
Part 2 requests 4.6, 4.48–4.52, 6.1–6.77

particulars of offences, warrants do not contain 4.49
personal circumstances 5.12
prison conditions 9.13
specialty 6.3, 6.49–6.52
statements of issues 9.22
statutory bars 6.1–6.77
transfer of prisoners 12.8
voluntary returns 5.17
Belmarsh Prison 8.55
bundles
appeals 11.15–11.16, 11.20, 11.22–11.23, 11.26, 11.50–11.51
case management 9.8
contents 11.15, 11.29
copies 11.23, 11.50
electronic service 9.39
expert evidence 10.29
format and contents 9.38
hearings 10.12–10.13, 10.33, 10.36
judge at WMC, assignment of 9.39
number 11.16
Part 2 requests 11.29
preparation 9.38–9.39, 11.50–11.51
service 9.38–9.39, 11.26, 11.51
burden of proof
absence, conviction in 6.60
abuse of process 6.73
extraneous considerations 6.15–6.16
hearings 10.5, 10.17
fair hearing, right to a 7.17–7.18
identity 4.45, 5.3, 8.25
life, right to 7.10
passage of time as bar 6.26, 6.29
standard of proof 10.17
torture or inhuman or degrading treatment 7.10

candour, duty of 10.6
case management and directions 9.7–9.10
adjournments 10.9–10.10
Administrative Court 11.44–11.46
appeals 11.39, 11.44–11.46

case management 9.7–9.10
  compliance 9.10, 11.44–11.46
  conferences 11.39–11.43, 11.67
  documents 9.7–9.9, 11.40
  estimates of time 8.46, 11.41
  evidence, proof of 8.47, 9.24
  extension of time 8.50, 9.10
  first hearings 4.42
  fixing hearing dates 8.45–8.47, 11.41–11.42
  forms 2.11, 4.42, 8.43–8.50
  judges, allocation of 8.45
  legal aid 8.47, 11.67
  masters or deputy masters of Administrative Court 11.40
  new issues, notification of 8.44
  Part 2 requests 11.39–11.43
  resisting extradition 8.43–8.50
  review hearings 9.9
  service of documents 9.9
  skeleton arguments 8.47–8.48
  time limits 8.46, 11.39, 11.41
  wasted costs 9.10
case reference numbers 11.46
caution, terms of 4.14
cells, interaction with clients in 2.10, 5.1
central funds, costs paid out of 12.12
certification
  ad hoc arrangements 4.4
  counsel 9.40–9.41
  EAW requests 8.2–8.6
  general public importance, certification of point of law of 1.29, 11.91–11.100, 11.106
  legal aid 12.13, 12.19, 12.20
  SSHD 1.23, 4.17–4.19, 4.36
  SOCA 3.2–3.3, 3.20–3.21, 8.5, 8.12
challenging the EAW 3.19–3.38, 8.23
change of circumstances 6.33, 6.41, 6.44
charges in UK, persons facing 4.25, 4.28–4.30, 4.68, 5.6, 8.34, 8.36
children, interests of 7.24–7.26
circumstances of offence, information on 3.13

Civil Procedure Rules (CPR) 11.5, 11.104
collateral purposes, requests made for 6.74
competing requests 4.15, 4.21, 4.77–4.81, 8.63–8.64
compromising the extradition request 5.17, 12.2–12.5
consent 4.28–4.30, 4.39, 4.71, 5.8–5.10, 6.52, 8.34–8.40, 9.14, 11.52
contested extradition hearings 10.1–10.44 *see also* **preparation for contested hearings**
  adjournment applications 10.8–10.11, 10.14
  bundles 10.12–10.13, 10.33, 10.36
  documents 10.2–10.4, 10.12–10.13
  evidence, adducing other 10.32–10.33
  evidence in chief from client 10.19–10.27
  expert evidence 10.28–10.31
  further information, requests for 10.6–10.7
  housekeeping 10.12–10.15
  judgments 10.38–10.44
  order of proceedings 10.13–10.14, 10.16–10.18
  submissions 10.34–10.37
controversy 1.5–1.10
conviction cases *see also* **absence, conviction in**
  bail 8.52–8.56
  clarity as to purpose of warrant, lack of 3.25
  compromising the extradition request 12.2
  deficient particulars 3.23, 3.25, 3.27–3.34, 3.38
  EAW requests 3.5, 3.8, 3.12, 3.14, 3.23, 3.27–3.34
  extradition offences 3.39–3.40, 4.53, 4.57–4.59
  first hearings 4.27, 4.39
  hybrid warrants 3.8
  multiple offences 3.38
  passage of time as bar 6.28, 6.37–6.40, 6.43, 9.16

conviction cases *continued*
  sentence, deficient particulars of 3.38
  threshold of punishment 3.14, 3.40, 4.57–4.59
costs
  bill of costs 12.18
  central funds, costs paid out of 12.12
  leading and junior counsel, costs of 11.60, 11.65–11.66
  Senior Court Costs Office 12.18–12.19
  solicitor's responsibility 9.33
  taxation 11.61, 12.13, 12.18
  wasted costs 9.10
counsel
  leading counsel and junior counsel, costs of 11.9, 11.60, 11.65–11.66
  legal aid 9.40–9.41
  Queen's Counsel 9.40, 11.65
  Westminster Magistrates' Court, applications to 9.41
credibility 5.5, 9.26
Crimes and Courts Bill 1.9–1.10, 6.55
Criminal Procedure Rules (CPR) 2.16, 9.31
cross-border conduct 3.44–3.45, 6.8
Cross-Border Transfer Section of NOMs 12.11
cross-examination 9.25–9.26, 10.27
Crown Prosecution Service (CPS) 1.20–1.22, 2.9, 4.31, 8.44, 9.36, 10.6-10.7, 10.44
curfews 5.11, 8.53
custody *see* **detention, persons in; prisoners**

death penalty bar 4.72–4.73, 6.3, 6.58
defence lawyers *see* **duty solicitors at Westminster Magistrates' Court**
deferrals 4.69–4.70, 4.77–4.80, 8.63–8.64
deficient particulars 3.23, 3.25, 3.27–3.38
definition of extradition 1.11
delay *see* **passage of time as bar**

designated territories 1.15, 4.4, 4.33, 4.61
detention, persons in 4.15, 4.21, 7.9, 9.2–9.3, 10.20 *see also habeas corpus*; **imprisonment, sentences of; prisoners**
diplomatic or consular representatives 4.18
directions *see* **case management and directions**
disclosure 9.36, 10.6–10.7
distinctive marks 8.28
documents *see also* **bundles**
  appeals 11.15–1.16, 11.20–11.23, 11.26, 11.34, 11.38, 11.46, 11.50–11.51
  arrest 4.20–4.21
  authentication 10.2–10.3
  bail 8.51
  case management and directions 9.7–9.9, 11.40
  discharge 4.20, 4.34
  EAW requests 5.19, 10.2, 11.23, 11.26
  evidence in chief 10.21, 10.23–10.25
  extensions of time 4.33
  hearings 10.2–10.4, 10.12–10.13
  identity 2.2–2.3, 2.11, 3.19, 5.5, 5.12, 8.26, 8.54
  instructions 9.11
  legal aid 5.18
  list of documents 4.37
  sealing 10.3, 11.23, 11.26, 11.30, 11.34
  seizure 8.26
  service 4.32–4.38, 4.44, 9.7, 9.9, 9.38–9.39, 11.17, 11.27, 11.51
double jeopardy 5.16, 6.3, 6.5–6.9, 9.14
dual criminality test 3.8, 3.39, 3.22, 3.42–3.43, 3.45, 4.53, 9.14
duty solicitors at Westminster Magistrates' Court
  arrest 4.15
  arrival of arrested persons 2.11
  assistance, obtaining 2.11
  bail 2.11
  cells, attendance at 2.10

Crown Prosecution Service,
  availability of 2.9
EAW requests 2.9
essential materials 2.17
explanation of outcome to clients
  2.15, 7.28
gaolers, making yourself known
  to 2.10
hearings, importance of covering
  all matters before 2.15
hours of work 2.9
information 2.10–2.11
interpreters 2.6, 2.10–2.12, 9.6
legal aid forms 2.11, 2.14
number of cases 2.11
Part 2 requests 4.5–4.6, 4.10
referral time 2.11, 4.16, 8.18
requested persons, information
  from 2.11
rota 1.4
second opinions on advice 11.59
time constraints 5.1
Westminster Magistrates' Court
  2.7–2.8
withdrawing representation
  11.53–11.67

earlier extradition from territory
  4.72–4.73, 6.3, 6.53–6.54
Eastern Europe 9.2 *see also* **Poland**
employment, persons in 5.19
error 3.1, 3.3, 4.21, 8.17, 10.40
estimates of time 8.46, 10.15, 11.24,
  11.41
**European Arrest Warrant (EAW)
  requests** 3.1–3.46 *see also*
  **Framework Decision on
  European Arrest Warrant; validity
  of EAW, challenging the**
  absence, conviction in 3.12, 6.62
  abuse of process 6.71, 6.74
  appeals 11.2, 11.11–11.27, 11.75–
    11.77
  attending the client 5.2, 5.4
  bail 2.5
  bars/challenges to extradition
    6.46, 6.75, 7.2–7.7
  boxes 3.2–3.18, 3.39
  certification 3.2–3.3, 8.2–8.6

  challenging the EAW 3.19–3.38,
    8.23
  circumstances of offence,
    information on 3.13
  competing requests 4.79–4.81,
    8.63–8.64
  confidence, high level of 7.3–7.4
  confiscation orders 3.16
  contents 3.3–3.18
  designated authority for receipt
    1.22
  documentation 5.19, 10.2
  dual criminality test 3.14
  duty solicitors 2.9
  earlier extradition from territory
    6.54
  errors 3.1, 3.3
  evidence, return of 3.16
  execution 3.3
  extradition offences 3.39–3.46
  extradition orders 10.43
  extraterritoriality 3.15
  Framework offences list 3.10,
    3.14, 3.39
  hybrid warrants 3.8
  identity, information on 3.4, 3.6
  information 3.3–3.18
  initial hearings 8.1–8.65
  knowledge of proceedings,
    statements of requested
    persons' 3.15
  legal aid 5.19
  life sentences with no review,
    refusal to execute in cases
    where 3.17
  locate requested person, attempts
    to 3.15
  model form 3.1
  mutual trust and recognition
    6.71, 7.3
  number of requests 1.3, 1.5
  overuse 1.5, 1.7
  Part 2 requests 4.1
  problems, identification of
    potential 3.15
  proportionality 1.7
  refusal to execute 3.17
  remaining sentence to be served,
    statements of 3.11

European Arrest Warrant *continued*
  retrial, right to a 3.12
  seizure 3.16
  sentences 3.8–3.11, 3.14
  service 5.4, 8.10, 8.11–8.13, 8.32–8.33
  signing and dating 3.3
  SOCA 1.22
  specialty rights 6.50–6.51
  statements of decisions on which warrant based 3.7–3.8
  statements of purpose 3.3–3.5
  surrender, system of 1.18
  threshold of punishment 3.10–3.11, 3.14
  time limits 3.15
  trivial offences 1.5
  validity 3.1, 3.3, 3.13, 3.19–3.38, 8.42
  withdrawal 5.17
European Convention on Extradition 1957 6.51
European Convention on Human Rights 1.1, 5.16, 6.4, 7.1–7.27 *see also* **particular rights**
  appeals 1.8–1.9, 11.101
  asylum seekers 6.75
  compliance, presumption of 7.5–7.8
  Crime and Courts Bill 1.9–1.10, 11.102
  EAW requests 7.2–7.7
  extraneous considerations 6.14, 6.18
  good faith, assumption of 7.8
  Human Rights Act 1998 4.52, 7.1
  immigration status 6.75
  instructions 9.19
  initial hearings 8.42
  Part 2 requests 4.6, 4.52, 7.2, 7.8
  personal circumstances 9.19
  Rule 39 interim measures against removal 11.108–11.116
  SSHD 1.8–1.10, 11.101–11.102
evidence *see also* **expert evidence**
  appeals 11.68–11.76
  compromising the extradition request 12.5
  disclosure 9.36, 10.6–10.7
  double jeopardy 6.9, 9.14
  EAW requests 3.16
  European Convention on Human Rights 7.8
  evidence in chief from client 10.19–10.27
  extraneous considerations 6.16–6.22
  failure to mention facts and credibility 9.26
  fair hearing, right to a 7.8
  good faith 7.8
  hearings 10.32–10.33
  identity 2.2–2.3
  life, right to 7.11
  medical evidence 6.67, 6.69, 9.21
  new evidence, introduction of 11.68–11.76
  objective evidence 9.34
  other evidence, adducing 10.19–10.27
  passage of time as bar 6.35, 9.16
  prima facie case 4.61–4.65
  prison conditions 7.12, 9.13
  proof of evidence 8.47, 9.24–9.26
  representation orders 11.63–11.65
  service 8.47
  third parties, consent to obtaining evidence from 9.14
  torture, admissibility of evidence obtained by 7.11, 7.19
  witnesses 7.20, 9.27, 9.32, 10.19, 10.33, 11.48, 11.70
exceptional circumstances 7.7, 11.35–11.36, 11.104, 12.14
  appeals 11.4, 11.104
  European Convention on Human Rights 7.7
  expert evidence 9.29
  extension of time 11.4, 11.35–11.36
  interpreters 9.6
  legal aid 9.6, 9.29, 12.14
  passage of time 6.25
  private and family life, right to respect for 7.23
  Rule 39 interim measures 11.108
expert evidence

Index 239

adjournments 7.27
attendance at court 9.33
bundles 10.29
clarity as to purpose of warrant, lack of 3.25
costs, solicitor's responsibility for 9.33
exceptional circumstances funding 9.29
fair hearing, right to a 7.16–7.17, 7.20
further information 9.35, 10.31
governmental, international and non-governmental organizations 7.11, 9.34
guidance 7.26–7.27
hearings 9.28–9.33, 10.28–10.31
legal aid 9.29–9.30, 9.32–9.33, 11.10, 11.60, 11.64
letters of instruction 9.31–9.32
life, right to 7.11
objectivity 9.31, 9.34
oral evidence 10.19
personal circumstances 9.28
private and family life, right to respect for 7.26–7.27, 9.28
qualifications and experience 10.30
reliant on requested person, effect on those 9.17
reports 9.31–9.33, 10.29, 10.31
retrials 6.62, 9.20
service 10.28
situation in requesting state 9.28
time limits 9.32
torture or inhuman or degrading treatment 7.11
extensions of time
appeals 8.65, 11.4, 11.19, 11.31, 11.35–11.38
case management and directions 8.50, 9.10
exceptional circumstances 11.4, 11.35–11.36
forms, completion of 8.50
provisional requests 8.5
removal 5.18, 8.39
SSHD 4.71
unrepresented persons 11.36

Extradition Act 2003 1.12–1.17
ad hoc arrangements 1.17, 4.4
attending the client 5.4–5.5
bars/challenges to extradition 6.1–6.77
Crime and Courts Bill 1.9–1.10, 11.102
entry into force 1.12
EAW (Part 1) cases 1.13–1.17
Extradition Act 1989, claims under 1.12
number of cases 1.2
parts 1.13
extradition offences 3.39–3.46
accusation cases 3.39–3.40, 4.53, 4.57–4.59
bars/challenges to extradition 4.50
boxes 3.39–3.40
conviction cases 3.39–3.40, 4.53, 4.57–4.59
cross-border conduct 3.44–3.45, 6.8
definition 3.39–3.41, 4.54–4.55
dual criminality test 3.39, 3.42–3.43, 4.53
EAW requests 3.34, 3.39–3.46
extraterritoriality 3.15, 4.57
flowcharts 4.60
Framework Decision 3.39
Framework Offences list 3.10, 3.14, 3.39–3.41
judgments 10.43
location of conduct 3.44–3.46, 4.54–4.59
Part 2 requests 4.53–4.65
prima facie case 4.61–4.65
reasonable grounds for belief 4.9
sentence, deficient particulars of 3.36
sentencing threshold 3.40–3.41, 4.54–4.59
tax or custom offences 4.60
extradition orders *see also* **removal**
appeals 4.75, 8.61, 11.1–11.2, 11.19, 11.77, 11.82, 11.86–11.90, 11.101–11.103
conditions 8.58–8.60
injunctions 11.101, 11.103

extradition orders *continued*
  representations 8.60
  SSHD 4.73–4.75, 11.86–11.90, 11.101–11.102
  time limits 4.75
  uncontested hearings 8.58–8.61
extraneous considerations 5.16, 6.3, 6.10–6.22, 9.15
Extradition Unit of Special Crime Division 1.20
extraterritoriality 3.15, 4.57

fair hearing, right to a 5.16, 6.62, 7.8, 7.14–7.20
false sense of security, requested person given a 6.38–6.39, 6.44, 9.16
fees 11.8, 11.10, 11.22–11.23, 11.47, 11.52, 11.55, 11.95
fingerprints 8.27
first hearings
  full requests 4.39–4.42
  provisional arrest 4.26–4.38
fixing hearing dates
  adjournments 4.38
  appeals 11.24–11.25, 11.41–11.42
  case management 8.45–8.47, 11.41–11.42
  discharge 4.40
  EAW requests 11.24–11.25
  later date, interests of justice to fix 4.41
  Part 2 requests 4.6
  time limits 4.38, 4.40
floodgates, opening the 10.37
forms
  adjournments 11.48
  appeals 11.15, 11.18–11.20, 11.59
  case management 2.11, 4.42, 8.43–8.50
  EAW requests 11.15, 11.18–11.20
  extension of time for completion 8.50
  injunctions 11.103
  legal aid 2.11, 5.19, 11.6–11.8, 12.13, 12.20
  second opinions 11.59
  self-representation 11.55
  Supreme Court 11.95

  withdrawal of representation 11.55
forum bar 1.8–1.9, 6.3, 6.55–6.57
Framework Decision on European Arrest Warrant
  absence, conviction in 3.12
  bars/challenges to extradition 12.8
  European Convention on Human Rights 7.3–7.4
  extradition offences 3.10, 3.14, 3.39–3.41
  life sentences with no review, refusal to execute in cases where 3.17
  model form 3.1
  purpose 3.1
  refusal to execute 3.17
  remand, deductions for time spent on 5.11
  specialty rights 6.51
  surrender, system of 1.18
  transfer of prisoners 12.8, 12.11
fresh evidence, introduction of 11.68–11.76
fugitives 4.7, 6.25–6.28, 6.59–6.60, 9.16
full Part 2 requests 4.2, 4.6, 4.17–4.21, 4.36–4.38
further information, requests for 3.22, 9.22, 9.35–9.36, 10.6–10.7, 10.31
further offences, prosecution of 5.10

gender, considerations of 6.10–6.22, 9.15
general public importance, certification of point of law of 1.29, 11.91–11.100, 11.106
good faith 7.8, 10.6
governmental, international and non-governmental organizations (NGOs) 7.11, 9.34

habeas corpus 8.16–8.17, 8.33
health bar 5.16, 6.4, 6.64–6.69, 8.42, 9.11, 9.21
hearings *see also* **contested extradition hearings; fixing hearing dates**

covering all matters before hearings, importance of 2.15
dates 11.47
discharge 11.78–11.79, 11.83–11.85
experts, attendance of 9.33
explanation of outcome to clients 2.15
first hearings after provisional arrest 4.27–4.34
initial hearings 8.1–8.65
oral hearings 11.105
uncontested hearings 8.58–8.61
vacating hearing dates 11.47
high-profile cases 1.1, 4.13
High Court *see* **Administrative Court**
Holloway Prison 8.55
Home Office *see* **Secretary of State for the Home Department (SSHD)**
hostage-taking considerations 6.3, 6.47–6.48
hourly rates 9.29, 12.13, 12.16
housekeeping 10.12–10.15
human rights *see* **European Convention on Human Rights; Human Rights Act 1998**
Human Rights Act 1998 4.52, 7.1
hybrid warrants 3.8

identity 8.24–8.31
arrest 2.2–2.3, 4.26, 5.5, 8.26
bail 5.5
burden of proof 4.45, 5.3, 8.25
disputes 5.5
documents 2.2–2.3, 2.11, 3.19, 5.5, 5.12, 8.26, 8.54
EAW requests 3.4, 3.6
evidence in chief 10.23
initial hearings 4.44–4.47, 8.8–8.9, 8.24–8.33
Part 2 requests 4.44–4.47
immigration status 5.15, 6.75–6.77
imprisonment, sentences of *see also* **prisoners**
compromising the extradition request 12.2
life sentences with no review, refusal to execute in cases where 3.17
suspension or deferral 12.2
UK, persons subject to imprisonment in 4.29–4.31, 4.69–4.70, 5.6, 8.35–8.37
in camera proceedings 4.10
informed of arrest, right to have someone 2.4
inhuman or degrading treatment 5.16, 7.9–7.13, 7.18
initial hearings
adjournments 8.34–8.35, 8.41
appeals 8.32–8.33, 8.65
appropriate judge, production before 8.7, 8.10, 8.14–8.23, 8.32–8.33
arrest statements, copies of 8.10, 8.12
as soon as practicable requirement 8.10–8.23, 8.32–8.33
bail 8.34, 8.51–8.56
bars/challenges to extradition 4.46, 8.41–8.56
case management forms 8.43–8.50
competing requests 8.63–8.64
consent 8.34–8.40
documents, consideration of 4.43–4.44, 4.46–4.47
EAW requests 8.1–8.65
extradition offences 4.44, 4.46–4.47
identity 4.44–4.47, 8.8–8.9, 8.24–8.33
imprisonment in UK, persons subject to 8.35–8.37
Part 2 requests 4.43–4.47
resist extradition, issues to be raised to 8.41–8.56
service of EAW 8.10, 8.11–8.13, 8.32–8.33
uncontested hearings 8.57–8.62
injunctions 11.101, 11.103
instructions 5.12–5.13, 9.11–9.21, 9.31–9.32

International Criminal Court (ICC) 6.3
International Jurisdiction Office (IJO) 1.4, 2.12, 4.16
international organizations, evidence from 7.11, 9.34
interpreters
  consent 8.38
  custody, visits to clients in 9.2
  duty solicitors 2.6, 2.10–2.12, 9.6
  evidence in chief 10.22
  exceptional cases and legal aid 9.6
  fees 9.6
  hearings 8.8, 9.4–9.6
  International Jurisdiction Office 2.12
  Language Line 2.4
  Law Society practice note 9.4
  legal aid 9.6, 11.10, 11.60
  notification 2.12
  oaths or affirmations 10.22
  quality 9.4, 2.12
  self-representation 11.56
'iron letters' 12.6
Italy, retrials in 6.62

judges see appropriate judge, production before
judgments 10.38–10.44
  amendments 10.40
  appeals 10.42–10.43
  copies for parties 10.41
  ex tempore judgments 10.42
  factual errors 10.40
  note-taking 10.41–10.42
  reserved judgments 10.38–10.39
  SSHD, sending case to 10.43
  summaries 10.42
  written rulings 10.39–10.41
judicial review 8.33, 10.11, 12.20

key organisations 1.19–1.32
knowledge of proceedings, statements of requested persons' 3.15

language 8.12 see also interpreters

lawyers see counsel; duty solicitors at Westminster Magistrates' Court; lawyers from requesting states, assistance of; solicitors
lawyers from requesting states, assistance of 5.17, 12.5–12.6, 12.11
leaving state, circumstances of 6.38, 6.41, 6.44
legal aid see also representation orders
  adjournments 5.19
  Administrative Court 11.6–11.9, 11.38, 12.18
  Administrative Court Office 11.6–11.8
  appeals 11.17, 11.38
  bail 5.19
  bill of costs 12.18
  certificates 12.13, 12.20
  counsel 9.40–9.41, 12.13, 12.19, 12.20
  delays 5.19, 11.6
  disbursements 11.8, 11.10, 12.18
  documentation 5.18
  EAW requests 5.19, 11.17
  eligibility 2.14, 5.19, 11.6
  employment, documentation on 5.19
  enhancements/uplifts of fees 12.14–12.19
  exceptional circumstances funding 9.6, 9.29, 12.14
  experts 9.29–9.33, 11.10
  fees 11.8, 11.10
  forms 2.11, 2.14, 5.19, 9.29–9.33, 11.6–11.8, 12.13, 12.20
  Funding Code 12.20
  hourly rates 9.29
  interpreters 9.6, 11.10
  judicial review 12.20
  leading counsel and junior counsel 11.9
  means testing 2.14, 11.6
  partners, forms signed by 5.19
  personal circumstances 5.12
  self-certification of wages 5.19
  sufficient benefit test 2.4
  taxation 12.13, 12.18

Index 243

time for completion 2.11
urgent cases 12.20
Westminster Magistrates' Court
  12.13–12.17
legal funding 12.12 *see also* **legal aid**
legal representation *see* duty
  solicitors at Westminster
  Magistrates' Court; lawyers from
  requesting states, assistance of
liberty and security, right to 5.16,
  7.14–7.20
life imprisonment 3.17, 7.9
life, right to 7.9–7.13
limitation periods *see* time limits
livescan checks 8.26
locate requested person, attempts to
  3.15
location of conduct 3.44–3.46, 4.54–
  4.59
lodging appeals 11.38–11.39, 11.48

medical records 6.67, 9.21
mental health bar 5.16, 6.4, 6.64–
  6.69, 8.42, 9.11, 9.21
Metropolitan Police Extradition
  Squad 1.24
multiple offences 3.38
mutual recognition 3.43, 7.3

nationality, considerations of 6.10–
  6.22, 9.15
new evidence, introduction of
  11.68–11.74
new issues, notification of 8.44,
  9.23
non-governmental organizations
  (NGOs) 7.11, 9.34
note-taking at hearings 10.41–10.42
number of requests 1.2–1.3, 1.15

oaths or affirmations 4.7, 4.9
off the record, coming off the
  11.53–11.67
oppression 6.23–6.42, 6.64–6.66,
  6.69, 9.17–9.18
order of proceedings 10.13–10.14,
  10.16–10.18
out-of-time applications *see*
  extensions of time

Part 1 requests *see* **European Arrest
  Warrant (EAW) requests**
Part 2 requests 1.13–1.17, 4.1–4.81
  ad hoc arrangements 1.17, 4.4
  appeals 11.2, 11.28–11.31, 11.39–
    11.43
  appropriate judge, production
    before the 4.19
  approved way, requests made in
    4.17–4.19
  arrest warrants 4.9, 4.12–4.16,
    4.19–4.21
  bail 4.6–4.7, 4.21
  bars/challenges to extradition
    4.6, 4.46, 6.1–6.77
  bundles 11.29
  case management conferences
    11.39–11.43
  challenges to extradition 4.6,
    4.48–4.52
  competing requests 4.21, 4.77–
    4.81
  dealing with requests 4.5–4.6
  designated Category 2 territories
    1.16, 4.3
  documents 4.20–4.21, 4.43–4.44,
    4.46–4.47
  duty solicitors at WMC 4.5–4.6,
    4.10
  EAW requests 1.14–1.17, 4.1
  European Convention on Human
    Rights 4.6
  extradition offences 4.9, 4.44,
    4.46–4.47, 4.53–4.65
  first hearings 4.26–4.42
  fixing a hearing date 4.6
  fugitives 4.7
  full requests 4.2, 4.6, 4.17–4.21,
    4.36
  identity 4.44–4.47
  initial stages of hearings 4.43–
    4.47
  procedure 4.1–4.2
  provisional requests 4.2, 4.6–4.16
  remand, deductions for time
    spent on 5.11
  sentencing threshold 3.41
  special extradition arrangements
    4.4

Part 2 requests *continued*
  SSHD 1.23, 4.17–4.19, 4.21,
    4.66–4.81, 6.50, 10.43, 11.2,
    11.28–11.30
  time limits 11.28, 11.30
  Westminster Magistrates' Court,
    production at 4.21–4.25
passage of time as bar 5.16, 6.3,
  6.23–6.44
  accusation cases 6.27, 6.37, 6.43,
    9.16
  burden of proof 6.26, 6.29
  cases, examples of 6.36–6.44
  change of circumstances 6.33,
    6.41, 6.44
  conviction cases 6.28, 6.37–6.40,
    6.43, 9.16
  culpable delay by requesting state
    6.37, 6.39, 6.44
  evidence 6.35, 9.16
  false sense of security, requested
    person given a 6.38–6.39,
    6.44, 9.16
  fugitives 6.25–6.28, 9.16
  gravity of offence 6.34–6.35
  health 6.69
  instructions 9.16–9.18
  Italy v Merico 6.40–6.42
  Kovac v Regional Court in Prague
    6.39
  La Torre v Italy 6.37
  leaving state, circumstances of
    6.38, 6.41, 6.44
  length of delay 6.34, 6.37, 6.44
  private and family life, right to
    respect for 6.35
  *R on the application of Cepkauskas
    v District Court of
    Marijampole* 6.43
  reliant on requested person, effect
    on those 6.35, 6.41–6.44, 9.17
  unjust or oppressive test 6.23–
    6.42, 9.17–9.18
  *Wenting v High Court of
    Valenciennes* 6.38
**personal circumstances and
  background** 5.12–5.13, 9.11, 9.19,
  9.28
photographs 8.29

physical or mental health bar 5.16,
  6.4, 6.64–6.69, 8.42, 9.11, 9.21
Poland 1.3, 3.11, 3.37, 6.75, 7.12,
  9.2
police 1.24, 2.2–2.4, 3.3, 4.15, 6.74,
  8.53
practical considerations 2.1–2.17
practice directions 11.5, 11.99
preparation
  appeals 11.15–11.21
  bundles, preparation of the 9.38–
    9.39, 11.50–11.51
  case management and directions
    9.7–9.10
  contested hearings 9.1–9.41
  custody, visits to clients in 9.2–
    9.3
  evidence, drafting a proof of
    9.24–9.26
  expert evidence 9.28–9.33
  instructions, taking 9.11–9.21
  interpreters 9.4–9.6
previous convictions, records of 2.9
prima facie case 4.61–4.65
prisoners *see also* **detention;
  imprisonment, sentences of**
  attending the client 5.6
  Category A 8.55
  conditions 7.9, 9.14
  early release date 5.6
  induction visits 8.56
  remand 4.39, 5.11, 8.55–8.56,
    8.62, 10.43–10.44
  transfer of prisoners 12.7–12.11
**private and family life, right to
  respect for** 3.11, 5.16, 6.35, 6.57,
  7.21–7.28, 9.28
private funding 12.12
pro bono work 12.3
**production before the appropriate
  judge** *see* **appropriate judge,
  production before**
proportionality 1.7, 3.11, 7.23
provisional requests 4.2, 4.6–4.16,
  8.2–8.6
public funding *see* **legal aid**
public interest 7.22–7.23
public opinions, considerations of
  6.10–6.22, 9.15

Index

Queen's Counsel 9.40, 11.65

race and ethnicity 6.10–6.22, 7.9, 9.15
realistic advice, giving 7.28
referral time 2.11, 4.16, 8.18
refugees to home countries, return of 5.15, 6.76
reliant on requested person, effect on those 6.35, 6.41–6.44, 7.24–7.26, 9.17
religion, considerations of 6.10–6.22, 9.15
remand 4.39, 5.11, 8.55–8.56, 8.62, 10.43–10.44
removal *see also* extradition orders
 appeals 8.65, 11.11, 11.106–11.107
 arrangements 1.23
 discharge, applications for 4.76
 extensions of time 4.75, 5.18, 8.39
 immediate removal, risk of 11.112
 injunctions 11.101, 11.103
 procedure 5.18
 Rule 39 interim measures against removal 11.112
 SSHD 1.23, 4.75–4.76
 time limits 4.75–4.76, 5.18, 8.65, 11.106–11.107
 undertakings not to remove 11.101
reopening appeals 11.103–11.105
repatriation of prisoners 12.7–12.11
representation orders 11.9–11.10, 12.3, 12.18
 appeals 11.17
 compromising the extradition request 12.3
 extension, applications for 11.60–11.67
 Supreme Court 11.94
 withdrawal of representation 11.60–11.67
representations/submissions 4.71–4.76, 8.22–8.23, 8.60, 10.34–10.37
requests from outside the EU *see* Part 2 requests
retrials 3.12, 4.51, 6.59, 6.61–6.63, 9.20

review dates 8.45
review hearings 9.9
risk of serious, irreversible harm 11.109–11.110
Romania, retrials in 6.62
Rule 39 interim measures against removal
 European Convention on Human Rights 11.108–11.116
 fax, applications sent by 11.113–11.114
 immediate removal, risk of 11.112
 real risk of serious, irreversible harm 11.109–11.110
 reasons 11.110

sealing documents 10.3, 11.23, 11.26, 11.30, 11.34
searches by police 2.2
second opinions 11.59
Secretary of State for the Home Department (SSHD)
 ad hoc arrangements 4.4
 appeals 1.8–1.9, 11.2, 11.28–11.30, 11.33–11.34, 11.86–11.90
 certification 1.23, 4.17–4.19, 4.36
 charged with offence in UK, persons who are 4.68
 competing requests 4.77–4.81
 consent 4.71
 death penalty, consideration of 4.72–4.73
 deferral of decisions 4.69–4.70
 discharge 4.67, 4.73–4.74, 4.76, 11.90
 earlier extraditions from category 1 or 2 territories, consideration of 4.72–4.73
 European Convention on Human Rights 1.8–1.10, 11.101–11.102
 extension of time limits 4.71
 extradition orders 4.73–4.75, 11.86–11.90, 11.101–11.102
 Part 2 requests 1.23, 4.17–4.19, 4.21, 4.66–4.81, 6.50, 10.43, 11.2, 11.28–11.30

Secretary of State for the Home
Department *continued*
  removal 1.23, 4.75–4.76
  representations to SSHD 4.71–4.76
  sending cases to SSHD 10.43
  sentenced to imprisonment in UK, persons who are 4.69–4.70
  special extradition arrangements 4.4
  specialty, representations on 6.50, 4.72–4.73, 6.50
  time limits 4.67, 4.71, 4.75
  Treasury Solicitor 11.34
security 2.11, 5.17, 8.51–8.54, 12.6
seeing the client *see* **attending the client**
seizure and retention of material 2.2, 3.16, 8.26
self-representation 11.55–11.56
sentencing *see also* **imprisonment, sentences of**
  accusation cases 3.38, 3.40, 4.57–4.59
  aggregate sentences 3.38
  conviction cases 3.38, 3.40, 4.57–4.59
  deficient particulars 3.24, 3.36–3.38
  indication of length 3.8–3.10
  life imprisonment 3.17, 7.9
  multiple offences 3.38
  Part 2 cases 3.41
  remand, deductions for time spent on 5.11, 8.62
  remaining sentence to be served 3.11
  suspended sentences 3.11, 3.37
  threshold 3.10–3.11, 3.14, 3.40–3.41, 4.54–4.59
Serious Organised Crime Agency (SOCA)
  certification 3.2–3.3, 3.20–3.21, 8.5, 8.12
  EAWs, designated authority for receipt of 1.22
  injunctions 11.103
  remand, deductions for time spent on 5.11, 8.62

  surrender, arrangements for 1.22
  validity of EAW requests, checking 3.19–3.21
service
  adjournments 11.48
  appeals 11.12, 11.22–11.27
  bundles 9.38–9.39, 11.17, 11.51
  case management and directions 9.9
  documents 4.32–4.38, 4.44, 9.7, 9.9, 9.38–9.39, 11.17, 11.27, 11.51
  EAW requests 5.3–5.4, 8.10–8.13, 8.32–8.33, 11.12, 11.22–22.17
  electronic service 9.39
  evidence, proof of 8.47, 9.24–9.25
  experts 10.28
  full extradition request 4.36–4.38
  further information, provision of 9.35
  initial hearings 8.10, 8.11–8.13, 8.32–8.33
  SOCA certificate 8.12
  submissions 8.22–8.23
  time limits 4.38, 8.47, 11.27
  witness statements 9.27
sexual orientation, considerations of 6.10–6.22, 9.15
skeleton arguments 8.47–8.48, 9.37, 10.12–10.13, 10.34, 11.32, 11.45
solicitors *see also* **duty solicitors at Westminster Magistrates' Court**
  costs, responsibility for 9.33
  firm of private solicitors by requesting state 1.21
  solicitor-shopping 11.59
special extradition arrangements 4.4
specialty rights 3.9, 4.72–4.73, 5.7–5.10, 6.49–6.52, 8.39
SSHD *see* **Secretary of State for the Home Department (SSHD)**
standard of proof 10.5, 10.17
statements
  accused or convicted, that person is 4.17
  arrest, of 2.9, 8.10, 8.12, 8.26
  issues, of 9.22–9.23
  purpose, of 3.3–3.5

truth, of 11.63
witnesses 7.20, 9.27, 9.32, 10.33, 11.48, 11.70
submissions/representations 4.71–4.76, 8.22–8.23, 8.60, 10.34–10.37
suicide, risk of 6.66–6.68, 9.21, 11.32
supervening events and appeals 11.101–11.105
Supreme Court 11.91–11.100
  applications 11.95–11.100
  fees 11.95
  forms 11.95
  general public importance, certification of point of law of 1.29, 11.91–11.100, 11.106
  number of judges 1.30
  leave to appeal 1.29, 11.91, 11.93–11.94, 11.96–11.97
  number of cases 1.2
  powers on appeal 11.100
  President 1.29
  refusal of leave, appeals against 11.93
  representation orders 11.94
  rules and practice directions 11.99
  time limits 11.92, 11.96–11.98, 11.106
surrender, arrangements for 1.22
suspended sentences 3.11, 3.37

tax or custom offences 3.46, 4.60
telephone advice 2.4
temporary surrender 4.31, 8.37
threshold of punishment 3.10–3.11, 3.14
time limits see also **extensions of time**
  adjournments 4.38, 8.35, 10.9, 10.15
  appeals 8.61, 8.65, 11.4, 11.32, 11.35–11.38, 11.45
    EAW requests 11.11–11.13, 11.19, 11.27, 11.106
    judgments 10.43
    Part 2 requests 11.28, 11.30
    removal 8.65
    Supreme Court 11.92, 11.96–11.98, 11.106

appropriate judge, production before the 8.4–8.5
arrest, date of 11.19
case management conferences 11.39
discharge 4.67
EAW requests 3.15, 11.11–11.13, 11.19, 11.27, 11.106
experts 9.32
extradition orders 4.75
fixed hearing dates 4.40
removal 4.75, 5.18, 8.61, 8.65, 11.106–11.107
representations 4.71
service 4.38, 8.47, 11.27
skeleton arguments 11.32
SSHD 4.67, 4.71, 4.75
suicide, risk of 11.32
Supreme Court 11.92, 11.96–11.98, 11.106
unless orders 11.45
unrepresented persons 11.36
torture or inhuman or degrading treatment 5.16, 7.9–7.13
  evidence 7.11, 7.19
  expert witnesses 7.11
  factual issues 7.12–7.13
  life imprisonment with parole 7.9
  non-state actors, risk from 7.9–7.10
  prison conditions 7.9, 9.13
  race and ethnicity 7.9
transfer of prisoners 12.7–12.11
  bars to extradition 12.8
  Cross-Border Transfer Section of NOMs 12.11
  international arrangements 12.9–12.10
  judicial cooperation 12.8
  lawyers in negotiating states, assistance of 12.11
transit, persons in 4.11, 4.13
transport, arranging 4.24
travel documents 8.53
Treasury Solicitor 11.34
trivial offences 1.5

uncontested extradition hearings 8.57–8.62

United States 1.1, 1.5, 7.8
unjust or oppressive test 6.23–6.42, 6.64–6.66, 6.69, 9.17–9.18
unlawfully at large, persons who are 4.7, 6.25–6.28, 6.59–6.60, 9.16
unless orders 11.45
unrepresented persons 11.14, 11.36, 11.53
urgent cases 11.38, 11.108–11.116, 12.20

vacating hearing dates 11.47
validity of EAW, challenging the 3.19–3.38
  accusation/conviction, deficient particulars of 3.23, 3.27–3.34
  checking 3.19–3.21
  clarity as to purpose of warrant, lack of 3.23, 3.25–3.26
  information required 3.19–3.23
  judicial authority of requesting state, issued by 3.19–3.20
  key principles for challenges 3.23–3.38
  other warrants, deficient particulars of 3.23, 3.35
  sentence, deficient particulars of 3.24, 3.36–3.38
  SOCA, checking by 3.19–3.21
video links 2.7, 2.13, 9.33, 11.56
voluntary returns 5.17, 12.6

Wandsworth Prison 2.15, 8.55–8.56
warned list 11.25
wasted costs 9.10
Westminster Magistrates' Court (WMC) *see also* **duty solicitors at Westminster Magistrates' Court**
  administration 1.26
  appropriate judges, production before 4.19, 4.22–4.25, 8.17–8.18
  arrest 4.15–4.19, 4.22–4.25
  as soon as practicable requirement 4.23–4.25
  bail 8.54
  bundles 9.39
  cells, first interaction in 5.1
  counsel, certificate for 9.41
  Court 1 (full hearings) 2.7, 2.13
  Court 2 (remand hearings (custody and bail) and short extradition hearings 2.7, 2.13
  Court 3 (video-link remand hearings, short hearings and initial hearings) 2.7, 2.13
  court rooms 2.7, 2.13
  dedicated courtroom 1.4
  detention to secure attendance 4.15, 4.21
  duty solicitors 1.4, 1.31, 2.7–2.8
  International Jurisdiction Office 1.4, 2.12, 4.16, 9.10
  legal aid 9.41, 12.13–12.37
  number of requests 1.3–1.4
  referral time 2.11, 4.16, 8.18
  security 8.54
  transport, arranging 4.24
withdrawal of representation 11.53–11.67
withdrawal of requests 5.17, 12.6
witnesses
  evidence in chief 10.19
  order of witnesses 10.14
  statements 7.20, 9.27, 9.32, 10.33, 11.48, 11.70

CPS factsheet

- Surrender of persons from one territory to another to sentence, prosecution or to continue serving

- Export Extradition — Requesting State "an outgoing request" to UK

- Import Extradition — UK makes a request to another state

- Is it an extradition offence? See EA'03

- Cat 1 territories — 27 states of EU — EAW
  National Crime Agency — designated authority

- EAW — certify it then arrest person + take to WMC

- **Initial Hearing** — WMC ①
  Judge decides → is this person named on warrant?
  → fixes date for Extradition hearing (21 days of arrest this must be fixed)
  → decide on Bail

- **Extradition Hearing** — WMC ②

  A) Is this an extraditable offence? → more than >3 years in requesting state if offence not in UK? *could lead to prison >12 months*

  B) Any bars to Extradition?

  C) compatible with ECHR?

  D) extradition proportionate to seriousness of conduct + likely sentence?

  E) No statutory grounds to refuse the request

7 days to Appeal from HC